Fodor's InFocus

CALIFORNIA WINE COUNTRY
1st Edition

Where to Stay and Eat
for All Budgets

Must-See Sights
and Local Secrets

Ratings You Can Trust

Fodor's Travel Publications New York, Toronto, London, Sydney, Auckland
www.fodors.com

FODOR'S IN FOCUS CALIFORNIA WINE COUNTRY

Series Editor: Douglas Stallings

Editor: Jennifer Paull

Editorial Production: Evangelos Vasilakis

Author: Sharron Wood

Editorial Contributors: Constance Jones, Cheryl Crabtree

Maps & Illustrations: David Lindroth, *cartographer*; William Wu; Bob Blake and Rebecca Baer, *map editors*

Design: Fabrizio LaRocca, *creative director*; Guido Caroti, Siobhan O'Hare, *art directors*; Tina Malaney, Chie Ushio, Ann McBride, *designers*; Melanie Marin, *senior picture editor*

Cover Photo: Cabernet grapes in the Carmel Valley; Jeff Greenberg/age fotostock

Production/Manufacturing: Matthew Struble

SPECIAL SALES

This book is available for special discounts for bulk purchases for sales promotions or premiums. Special editions, including personalized covers, excerpts of existing books, and corporate imprints, can be created in large quantities for special needs. For more information, write to Special Markets/Premium Sales, 1745 Broadway, MD 6-2, New York, New York, NY 10019, or e-mail specialmarkets@randomhouse.com.

AN IMPORTANT TIP & AN INVITATION

Although all prices, opening times, and other details in this book are based on information supplied to us at press time, changes occur all the time in the travel world, and Fodor's cannot accept responsibility for facts that become outdated or for inadvertent errors or omissions. **So always confirm information when it matters,** especially if you're making a detour to visit a specific place. Your experiences—positive and negative—matter to us. If we have missed or misstated something, **please write to us.** We follow up on all suggestions. Contact the California Wine Country editor at editors@fodors.com or c/o Fodor's at 1745 Broadway, New York, New York 10019.

PRINTED IN THE UNITED STATES OF AMERICA

10 9 8 7 6 5 4 3 2 1

Be a Fodor's Correspondent

Your opinion matters. It matters to us. It matters to your fellow Fodor's travelers, too. And we'd like to hear it. In fact, we *need* to hear it. When you share your experiences and opinions, you become an active member of the Fodor's community. Here's how you can help improve Fodor's for all of us.

Tell us when we're right. We rely on local writers to give you an insider's perspective. But our writers and staff editors also depend on you. Your positive feedback is a vote to renew our recommendations for the next edition.

Tell us when we're wrong. We update most of our guides every year. But things change. If any of our descriptions are inaccurate or inadequate, we'll incorporate your changes in the next edition and will correct factual errors at fodors.com *immediately*.

Tell us what to include. You probably have had fantastic travel experiences that aren't yet in Fodor's. Why not share them with a community of like-minded travelers? Share your discoveries and experiences with everyone directly at fodors.com. Your input may lead us to add a new listing or a higher recommendation.

Give us your opinion instantly at our feedback center at www.fodors.com/feedback. You may also e-mail editors@fodors.com with the subject line "California Wine Country Editor." Or send your nominations, comments, and complaints by mail to California Wine Country Editor, Fodor's, 1745 Broadway, New York, NY 10019.

Happy Traveling!

Tim Jarrell, Publisher

CONTENTS

CLOSE UPS

MAPS

ABOUT THIS BOOK

Our Ratings

We wouldn't recommend a place that wasn't worth your time, but sometimes a place is so experiential that superlatives don't do it justice: you just have to be there to know. These sights, properties, and experiences get our highest rating, **Fodor's Choice** indicated by orange stars throughout this book. Black stars highlight sights and properties we deem **Highly Recommended** places that our writers, editors, and readers praise again and again.

Credit Cards

Want to pay with plastic? **AE, D, DC, MC, V** following restaurant and hotel listings indicate whether American Express, Discover, Diners Club, MasterCard, and Visa are accepted.

Restaurants

Unless we state otherwise, restaurants serve both lunch and dinner daily. We mention dress only when there's a specific requirement and reservations only when they're essential or not accepted—it's always best to book ahead.

Hotels

Unless we tell you otherwise, you can assume that the hotels have private bath, phone, TV, and air-conditioning. We always list facilities but not whether you'll be charged an extra fee to use them, so when pricing accommodations, find out what's included.

Many Listings

★	Fodor's Choice
★	Highly recommended
⊠	Physical address
♦	Directions
⬧	Mailing address
☎	Telephone
🖶	Fax
⊕	On the Web
✉	E-mail
✆	Admission fee
☉	Open/closed times
Ⓜ	Metro stations
▭	Credit cards

Hotels & Restaurants

☒	Hotel
➡	Number of rooms
♦	Facilities
ⅩⅠ	Meal plans
✕	Restaurant
⌂	Reservations
⌇	Smoking
♙	BYOB
✕☒	Hotel with restaurant that warrants a visit

Outdoors

🏌	Golf
⛺	Camping

Other

♺	Family-friendly
⇨	See also
⊠	Branch address
☞	Take note

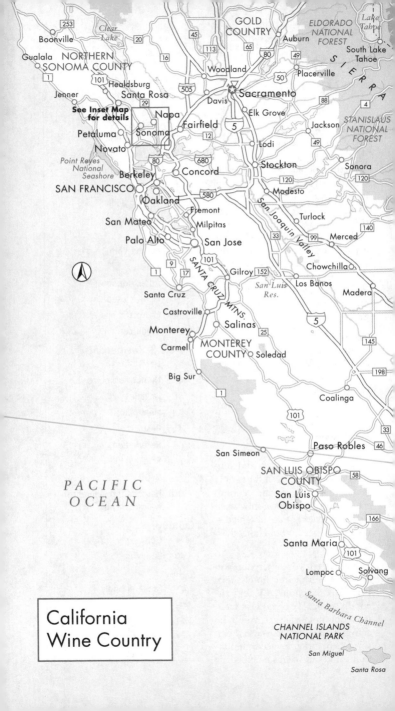

California
Wine Country

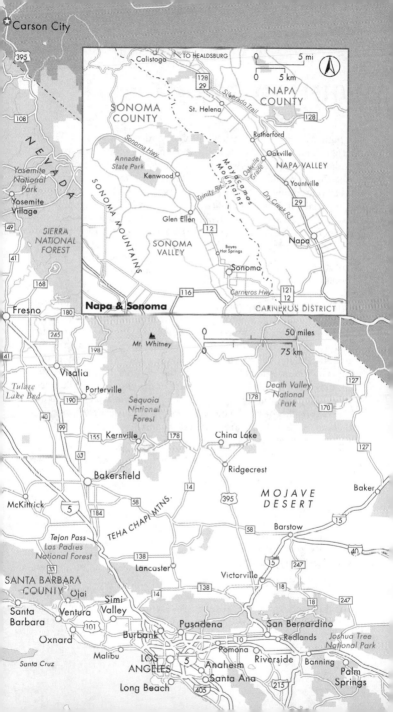

WHEN TO GO

In high season (April through October), and on weekends and holidays during much of the year, Wine Country roads can be busy and tasting rooms can be crowded, especially in Napa, but much less so on the Central Coast. If you prefer less hustle and bustle, tour on a weekday.

Winter

Though many visitors avoid traveling from December to March, in part because they are the wettest months in California, winter is still a good time to visit California's wineries. In December and January, naked, spindly grapevines huddle in rows. The hills turn green with velvety grass in February, and the first wildflowers spread beneath the oaks. While the vineyards lie dormant you're more likely to meet winemakers in their tasting rooms, for they have some time to discuss their work with visitors. The tasting rooms, wineries, and inns tend to be slightly less busy in winter than at other times of the year, although the pace picks up a bit between Christmas and New Year's Day.

Spring

Spring is another great time to visit the wine regions because it brings even more wildflowers: golden poppies, buttercups, blue and cream irises, and red, white, blue, and yellow lupines. Winemakers stick close to their work, because this is not only the season when they are bottling last year's vintages, but also a time of dubious weather, when late frosts can descend on the vineyards and kill the tender leaf buds. The crowds of visitors start to grow in late April, but you can still enjoy quiet moments.

Summer

If you travel between July and September, expect the days to be hot and dry. The wineries get mobbed with visitors, and so do the hotel swimming pools. If the weather is favorable, the first of the grapes, those destined for crisp white wines and sparklers, will be harvested as early as August.

Fall

Fall is both the busiest and most exciting season to watch the wineries at work. This is the time when field hands and machinery comb the vineyards for ripe clusters, trucks groan with loaded fruit bins as they lumber along the roads, and winery workers dash about seeing to massive vats of fermenting juice. The air is heavy with the aroma of grapes. As October wears into November, the vineyards turn flaming red and burnished gold.

Visiting
Wineries

WORD OF MOUTH

"I don't necessarily agree with the notion that larger wineries should be skipped. For a well-rounded wine country experience, you want a good mixture of different kinds of wineries, both large and small."

—TravelDiva

LIFE IS LIVED WELL in the California Wine Country, where eating and, above all, drinking are cultivated as high arts. And if all those magazines, epicurean memoirs, and gorgeously shot movies saturated with lush, romantic images of the area have made you pine for a visit, the good news is that you likely won't be disappointed when you get here. The meandering back roads, vineyard-blanketed hills, and ivy-draped wineries—not to mention the luxurious restaurants, hotels, and spas—really *are* that beautiful.

Whether you're a serious wine collector making your annual pilgrimage to the Napa Valley, or you're a wine newbie who doesn't know the difference between a merlot and mourvèdre but is eager to learn, you can have a great time touring California. Your gateway to the wine world is the tasting room, where the staff (and occasionally even the actual winemaker) are almost always happy to chat with curious guests. Tasting rooms range from the grand to the humble, offering everything from a few sips of wine to in-depth tours of the wine-making facilities and vineyards. The one constant, however, is a deep, shared pleasure in the experience of wine tasting.

WINE TASTING 101

Wine tasting has the reputation of an occult art that's usually practiced by snooty French sommeliers who toss around esoteric adjectives as they swirl their glass. Don't be intimidated. At its core, wine tasting is simply about determining which wines you like best. However, knowing a few basic tasting steps and a few key quality guidelines can make your winery visit much more enjoyable, and help you remember which wines you liked and why long after you return home. ■TIP→ **Above all, however, follow your instincts at the tasting bar: there is no right or wrong way to describe wine.**

If you watch the pros, you'll probably notice that they take time to inspect, swirl, and sniff the wine before they get around to sipping it. Follow their lead and take your time, going through each of the following steps for each wine. Starting with the pop of the cork and the splashing of wine into a glass, all of your senses play a part in wine tasting.

Making the Most of Your Time

1

Many first-time visitors to the Wine Country understandably dash from one spot to another, trying to jam as many wineries as possible into a short vacation. It's a far better strategy, however, to slow down and smell the rosés, so to speak. Still, if you're expected back at work in a couple of days, no one can blame you for wanting to maximize your wine-tasting fun. The following tips will help:

■ Visit on a weekday, especially if you're here during high season (May to November), to avoid traffic-clogged roads and crowded tasting rooms.

■ Call ahead. Some wineries require reservations to visit or tour. If you have your heart set on visiting a specific place, double-check their open hours and tour times to avoid disappointment.

■ Get an early start. Tasting rooms are often deserted before 11 AM or so, when most area visitors are still lingering over a second cup of coffee. If you come early, you'll have the staff's undivided attention.

■ If you only have a few days, limit yourself to Napa, Sonoma, or the Central Coast. Otherwise, you'll spend half your time on the road.

USE YOUR EYES

Before you taste it, take a good look at the wine in your glass. Holding the glass by the stem, raise it to the light. Whether it's white, rosé, or red, your wine should be clear, without cloudiness or sediments, when you drink it. Some unfiltered wines may seem cloudy at first, but they will clear as the sediments settle.

In the natural light, place the glass in front of a white background such as a blank sheet of paper or a tablecloth. **Check the color.** Is it right for the wine? A California white should be golden: straw, medium, or deep, depending on the type. Rich, sweet, dessert wine will have more intense color, but chardonnay and sauvignon blanc will be paler. A rosé should be a clear pink, from pale to deep, without too much red or any orange. Reds may lean toward ruby or garnet coloring; some have a purple tinge. They shouldn't be pale (the exception is pinot noir, which can be quite pale yet still have character). In any color wine, a brownish tinge is a flaw that indicates the wine is too old, has been incorrectly stored, or has gone bad. If you see brown, try another bottle.

BREATHE DEEP

You might notice that experienced wine tasters spend more time sniffing the wine than drinking it. This is because this step is where the magic happens: aroma plays a huge role in wine's flavor. After you have looked at the wine's color, **sniff the wine once or twice** to see if you can identify any aromas. Then gently move your glass in a circular motion to swirl the wine around. Aerating the wine this way releases more of its aromas. (It's called "volatilizing the esters," if you're trying to impress someone.) Stick your nose into the glass and take another long sniff.

Wine should smell good to you. You might pick up the scent of apricots, peaches, ripe melon, honey, and wildflowers in a white wine; black pepper, cherry, violets, and cedar in a red. Rosés (which are made from red wine grapes) smell something like red wine, but in a scaled-back way, with hints of raspberry and sometimes a touch of pomegranate. You might encounter surprising smells, such as tar—which some people actually appreciate in certain (generally expensive, red) wines.

For the most part, though, wine's aroma should be clean and pleasing to you, not "off." If you find a wine's odor odd or unpleasant, there's probably something wrong. Watch out for hints of wet dog or skunk, or for moldy, horsey, mousy, or sweaty smells. Sniff for chemical faults such as sulfur, or excessive vanilla scents (picked up from oak barrels) that overwhelm the other aromas. A vinegar smell indicates that the wine has started to spoil. A rotten wood or soggy cardboard smell usually means the wine is corked and the cork has gone bad, ruining the wine. If the wine in your glass has any of these funky aromas, dump it and ask your server to open another bottle.

JUST A SIP

Once you've checked its appearance and aroma, take a sip—not a swig or a gulp—of the wine. **As you sip wine, gently swish it around in your mouth**—this releases more aromas for your nose to explore. Do the aroma and the flavor complement each other, improve each other? While moving the wine around in your mouth, also think about the way it feels: silky or crisp? Does it coat your tongue or is it thinner? Does it seem to fill your mouth with flavor or is it weak? This combination of weight and intensity is referred to as body: a good wine may be light-, medium-, or full-bodied.

Do you like it? If not, don't drink it. Even if there is nothing actually wrong with a wine, what's the point of drinking it if you don't like it? A wine can be technically perfect but nevertheless taste strange, unpleasant, or just boring to you. It's possible to learn to appreciate wine that doesn't appeal to your tastes, but unless you like a wine right off the bat, it probably won't become a favorite. In the tasting room, dump what you don't like and move on to the next sample.

The more complex a wine is, the more flavors you will detect in the course of tasting. You might taste different things when you first take a sip ("up front"), when you swish ("in the middle" or "at mid-palate"), and just before you swallow ("at the end" or "on the back-palate"). A good table wine should be neither too sweet nor too tart, and never bitter. Fruitiness, a subtle near-sweetness, should be balanced by acidity, but not to the point that the wine tastes sour or makes your mouth pucker. An astringent or drying quality is the mark of tannins, a somewhat mysterious wine element that comes from grape skins and oak barrels. In young reds this can taste almost bitter—but not quite. All these qualities, together with the wine's aroma, blend to evoke the flavors not only of fruit but of unlikely things such as leather, tobacco, or almonds.

SPIT OR SWALLOW?

You may choose to spit out the wine (into the dump bucket or a plastic cup) or swallow it. The pros typically spit, since they want to preserve their palate (and sobriety!) for the wines to come, but you'll find that swallowers far outnumber the spitters in the winery tasting rooms. Either way, **pay attention to what happens after the wine leaves your mouth**—this is the finish, and it can be spectacular. What flavors stay behind or appear? Does the flavor fade away quickly or linger pleasantly? A long finish is a sign of quality; wine with no perceptible finish is inferior.

Vino Vocabulary

If you've ever read a wine review in *Wine Spectator*, you've probably seen a confounding array of adjectives used to describe wines' aroma and flavor, from "citrus rind," "passion fruit," and "toast" to nose-wrinkling words like "horsey" and "sweaty." Wine tasters use hundreds of common terms, and even more of their own devising, to try to capture a wine's elusive qualities. You don't need to memorize a laundry list of terms, but becoming familiar with a few of the most common words used by wine tasters will help you to talk wine with the best of them. The following are some of the major categories of aromas you might detect.

■ Chemical: You might be surprised to discover that a subtle odor of diesel or tar is not necessarily considered a bad thing, depending on the varietal and wine's overall balance of flavors. The smell of skunk, rotten eggs, or fingernail polish remover, though, is a sign that something has gone wrong in the wine-making process.

■ Earthy: Pinot noir is likely to be described as smelling like wet earth or mushrooms. White wines with a high acidity might be called "stoney" or "flinty" or said to have a mineral quality (think of what it

might taste like to lick a clean pebble).

■ Floral: White wines might give off a whiff of roses, violets, orange blossoms, or other flowers.

■ Fruity: The number of fruits used to describe wines is almost endless, but those you'll hear most often are citrus (usually lemons or grapefruit), stone fruits (peaches and apricots), tropical fruit (pineapple or lychee), and berries of all sorts.

■ Spicy: The flavor of pepper is commonly detected in gewürztraminer and syrah. Cloves and anise are other spicy flavors often tasted in red wines.

■ Vegetal or herbaceous: White wines, especially sauvignon blanc, are often described as "grassy" if they have a whiff a new-mown lawn, while reds are more likely to be described as reminiscent of tea or pipe tobacco. Good cabernet sauvignons often have an aroma of eucalyptus. But wines that have more than a hint of vegetal characteristics, especially of green pepper or asparagus, are usually frowned upon.

■ Woody: Since many wines are aged in charred wooden barrels, it's not surprising that some have hints of oak, cedar, smoke, or vanilla.

TASTING ROOMS & WINERY TOURS

Wineries in Napa, Sonoma, and the Central Coast range from opulent faux châteaus with vast gift shops to rough converted barns where you might have to step over the vintner's dog in the doorway. But it doesn't matter if you're visiting an elaborate tasting room complete with art gallery and upscale restaurant, or you're squeezed into the corner of a cinder-block warehouse amid stacked boxes and idle equipment: either way, tasting rooms are designed to introduce newcomers to the pleasures of wine and to inform visitors about the wines made at that winery. So don't worry if you're new to tasting. Relax, grab a glass, and join in for a good time.

Unfortunately, at most California wineries these days you'll have to pay for the privilege of tasting. Though free tastings were the norm 20 years ago, now it's more common to have to pay $5 to $20, and fees of even $25 to $40 aren't unheard of at some top-notch spots.

In general, you'll find the highest fees in Napa, slightly lower fees in Sonoma, and even lower prices in the Central Coast, though there are plenty of exceptions to this rule. And no matter which region you're in, you'll still find the occasional freebie—though it's likely to be at a spot that's off the major tourist thoroughfares and on some little-traveled back road. For some tips on keeping a day of wine-tasting from breaking the bank, see the box on money-saving tips on the next page.

TIP TO SIP? In tasting rooms, tipping is very much the exception rather than the rule. Most frequent visitors to the Wine Country never tip those pouring the wines in the tasting rooms, though if a server has gone out of his or her way to be helpful—by pouring special wines not on the list, for example—leaving $5 or so would be a nice gesture.

Many wineries are regularly open to the public, usually daily from around 10 AM to 5 PM, though many close as early as 4 or 4:30, especially in winter, so it's best to get a reasonably early start if you want to fit in more than a few spots. Many wineries require advance reservations to visit, and still others are closed to the public entirely. When in doubt, call in advance.

CLOSE UP

Money-Saving Tips

Those $20 tasting fees can add up awfully quickly if you're not careful, so consider the following tips for whittling down your wine-tasting budget.

■ Many hotels distribute coupons for free or discounted tastings to their guests—don't forget to ask.

■ If you and your travel partner don't mind sharing a glass, servers are happy to let you split a tasting. (This is also a good way to pace yourself and make sure you're not tipsy before lunchtime.)

■ Get off the beaten track.

Wineries along heavily traveled routes in Napa and Sonoma typically charge the most. Smaller spots along the back roads and wineries in the Central Coast often charge less—or sometimes nothing at all.

■ Some wineries will refund all or part of the tasting fee if you buy a bottle. Of course, this can easily lead to spending *more* than you had originally budgeted, but if you're planning on buying some bottles anyway, you can at least get some free tastings out of it.

Though you might have the tasting room all to yourself if you visit midweek in winter, in summer, during crush, and on weekends you might find yourself bumping elbows with other tasters and vying for the attention of the server behind the bar. If you prefer smaller crowds, look for wineries off the main drags of Highway 29 in Napa and Highway 12 in Sonoma. Also look for wineries that are open by appointment only; they tend to schedule visitors carefully to avoid a big crush at any one time. Wineries tend to be least crowded earliest in the morning, so consider getting an early start.

Finally, remember, those little sips add up, so pace yourself. If you plan to visit several wineries, try just a few wines at each so you don't hit sensory overload, when your mouth can no longer distinguish subtleties. (This is called palate fatigue.) ⚠ **Choose a designated driver for the day: Wine Country roads are often narrow and curvy, and you may be sharing the road with bicyclists and wildlife as well as other wine tourists.** Although wineries rarely advertise it, many will provide a free nonalcoholic drink for the designated driver; it never hurts to ask.

IN THE TASTING ROOM

In most tasting rooms, you'll find on the bar a list of the wines available that day, or you'll receive one from the server. The wines will be listed in a suggested tasting order, starting with the lightest-bodied whites and progressing to the most intense reds. Dessert wines will come at the end.

Most often you'll find an assortment of different wines from the winery's most recently released vintages. There might also be a list of reserve vintages (special wines aged somewhat longer) that you can taste for a separate fee. To create a more cohesive tasting experience, tasting rooms sometimes offer "flights" consisting of three or four particular wines selected to complement or contrast with each other. These might be vertical (several vintages of one wine), horizontal (several wines from one vintage), or more intuitively assembled.

Decide which of the wines you'd like to taste. Don't feel the need to tackle them all. In fact, many wineries will indicate at the bottom of the list that you are limited to four or five tastes (although, in fact, servers will rarely hold you to this limit if the tasting room isn't too crowded). If you can't decide which wines to choose, tell the server what types of wines you usually like and ask for a recommendation.

The server will pour you an ounce or so of each wine you select. As you taste it, feel free to take notes or ask questions. ■TIP→ **If you use your list of the wines available for your note taking, you'll have a handy record of your impressions at the end of your vacation, which might help next time you go shopping for wine.** There might be a plate of crackers on the bar; nibble them when you want to clear your palate of one wine's flavor before tasting the next.

Don't be shy—the staff are there to educate you about their wine. If you don't like a wine, or you've simply tasted enough, feel free to pour the rest into one of the dump buckets usually kept on the bar (if you don't see one, just ask).

TAKING A TOUR

Even if you're not a devoted wine drinker, a winery can be fascinating, as you'll see how wine is made. Tours tend to be the most exciting (and the most crowded) in September and October, when the harvest and crushing are underway.

Buying & Shipping Wine

Don't feel obliged to buy a bottle of wine just because the winery has given you a taste, especially if you paid a tasting fee. You should never feel pressured to make a purchase. Still, many visitors like to buy a bottle or two from small wineries as a courtesy, especially when they have taken more than a few minutes of the staff's time.

If you discover a bottle you particularly like, ask about where it's available. Although some wines, especially those made by the bigger operations, are widely distributed, many are available only at the wineries themselves, and perhaps served at a handful of restaurants or sold at wine shops in the San Francisco area. You might want to stock up if you won't be able to get it at home.

If you like several of a winery's bottles, and would like the convenience of having their wines delivered to you, consider joining their wine club, which will periodically send wine to you (except in some states), offer members-only releases, and give you a discount on all of your purchases.

If you're buying wine, ask about the winery's direct-shipment program. Most wineries are happy to ship the wine you buy, as long as you live in a state that lets consumers receive California wine directly from the winery. The rules apply whether you make your purchase in the tasting room, join the wine club, or order online.

Sending wine home is getting easier, especially since the U.S. Supreme Court set a new precedent in 2005. The court found unconstitutional the discriminatory bans on interstate, direct-to-consumer wine shipments in New York and Michigan. More states are opening their borders to such shipments from California, but laws vary greatly from state to state. The penalties for noncompliance in some states can be severe, so if you're going to ship wine home, it is wise to do so either through the winery or a professional shipper. (Wineries will also sell you Styrofoam chests you can use to check bottles of wine on your flight home.) ■TIP→ **For up-to-date information, check www.wineinstitute.org/programs/shipwine.**

In harvest season you'll likely see workers picking in the vineyards and hauling fruit bins and barrels around with forklifts. At other times of the year, winery work consists of monitoring the wine, "racking" it (eliminating sediment by transferring it from one tank or barrel to another), and bottling the finished wine.

Depending on the size of the winery, a tour might consist of a few visitors or a large group, following the staff guide from vineyard to processing area and from barrel room to tasting room. The guide explains what happens at each stage of the wine-making process, usually emphasizing the winery's particular approach to growing and wine making. You'll find out the uses for all that complex machinery, stainless steel equipment, and red-wine-stained oak barrels; feel free to ask questions at any point in the tour. If it's harvest or bottling time, you might see and hear the facility at work. Otherwise, the scene is likely to be quiet, with a few workers tending the tanks and barrels.

THE LOUD & THE RESTLESS Tasting rooms are for just that—tasting wines, rather than overindulging—and most visitors are on pretty good behavior. If you go to enough wineries, however, you'll eventually run into a loud, rowdy, or tipsy group. Wineries try to avoid these disruptions, often by prohibiting limousines or requiring advance reservations for groups of more than eight. But once in a while, partiers get in anyway. All that's left to do is wait them out or return to the winery for a quieter visit after they're gone. This is a rare issue, even on Saturdays, but you can almost guarantee you won't have a run-in if you visit wineries on a weekday.

Some winery tours, which typically last 30 minutes to an hour, are free, in which case you're usually required to pay a separate fee if you want to taste the wine. If you've paid a fee for the tour—often $10 to $20—your wine tasting is usually included in that price. ■TIP→If you plan to take any tours, wear comfortable shoes, since you might be walking on wet floors or stepping over hoses or other equipment.

At many of the larger wineries, the basic, introductory tours, typically offered several times daily, are complemented by less frequent specialized tours and seminars focusing on subjects such as viticultural techniques, wine making history, and food-and-wine pairing. Prices for these events typically range from $20 to $50, sometimes a bit more if lunch is included. Check the wineries' Web sites for more information.

HOW WINE IS MADE

THE CRUSH

The process of turning grapes into wine generally starts at the **crush pad,** where the grapes are brought in from the vineyards (some mass operations with sophisticated machinery actually start crushing in the field). Good winemakers carefully monitor their vineyards throughout the year. Their presence is especially critical at harvest, when regular checks of the grapes' ripeness determines the proper day for picking. Once that day arrives, the crush begins.

Wineries pick their grapes by machine or by hand, depending on the terrain and on the type of grape. Some delicate white varieties such as chardonnay are harvested at night with the help of powerful floodlights. Why at night? Because the fruit-acid content in the pulp and juice of the grapes peaks in the cool night air. The acids—an essential component during fermentation and aging, and an important part of wine's flavor—plummet in the heat of the day. Red wine grapes, which carry their acid in their skins, don't have to be picked at night, because the heat doesn't have the same effect on them.

Grapes must be handled with care so none of the juice is lost. They arrive at the crush pad in large containers called gondolas and drop gently onto a conveyor belt that deposits the grapes into a **stemmer-crusher.** A drum equipped with steel fingers knocks the grapes off their stems and pierces their skins, so the juice can flow off freely. The grapes and juice fall through a grate and are carried via stainless steel pipes to a press or vat. The stems and leaves drop out of the stemmer-crusher and are recycled to the vineyards as natural fertilizer. After this general first step, the production process goes one of four ways to make a white, red, rosé, or sparkling wine.

MAKING WHITE WINES

The juice of white wine grapes goes first to **settling tanks,** where the skins and grape solids sink to the bottom, separating from the clear free-run juice on top. The material in the settling tanks still contains a lot of juice, so after the free-run juice is pumped off, the remains go into a **press.** A modern press consists of a perforated drum containing a

1

Teflon-coated bag. As this bag is inflated like a balloon, it slowly pushes the grapes against the outside wall and the liquids are squeezed from the solids and flow off. Like the free-run juice, the press juice is pumped into a **fermenter,** which is either a stainless steel tank (which may be insulated to keep the fermenting juice cool) or an oak barrel.

Press juice and free-run juice are fermented separately, but a little of the press juice may be added to the free-run juice for complexity. Because press juice tends to be strongly flavored and may contain undesirable flavor components, winemakers are careful not to add too much of it. White press juice is always fermented in stainless-steel tanks; free-run juice may be handled differently. Most white wines are fermented at 59°F to 68°F (15°C to 20°C). Cooler temperatures develop delicacy and fruit aromas and are especially important in fermentation of sauvignon blanc and riesling.

During fermentation, yeast feeds on the sugar in grape juice and converts it to alcohol and carbon dioxide. Wine yeast dies and fermentation naturally stops in two to four weeks, when the alcohol level reaches 15 percent. If there's not enough sugar in the grapes to reach the desired alcohol level, the winemaker can add extra sugar before or during fermentation, in a process called **chaptalization.**

To prevent oxidation, which damages wine's color and flavor, and to kill wild yeast and bacteria, which can produce off flavors, winemakers almost always add sulfur dioxide, in the form of sulfites, before fermenting. A winemaker may also choose to encourage **malolactic fermentation** ("malo") to soften a wine's acidity or deepen its flavor and complexity. This is done by inoculating the wine with lactic bacteria soon after alcoholic fermentation begins or right after it ends, or by transferring the new wine to wooden vats that harbor the bacteria. Malo, which can also happen by accident, is undesirable in lighter-bodied wines meant to be drunk young.

For richer results, free-run juice from chardonnay, and some from sauvignon blanc, might be fermented in oak barrels, in individual batches, with each vineyard and lot kept separate. **Barrel fermentation** creates more depth and complexity, as the wine picks up vanilla flavors and other harmonious traits from the wood. The barrels used by California winemakers may be imported from France or Eastern Europe, or made domestically of American oak. They are very expensive and can be used for only a few years.

When the wine has finished fermenting, whether in a tank or barrel, it is generally **racked**—moved into a clean tank or barrel to separate it from the lees, the spent yeast and any grape solids that have dropped out of suspension. Sometimes chardonnay and special batches of sauvignon blanc are left on the lees for extended periods of time before being racked—at the winemaker's discretion—to pick up extra complexity. Wine may be racked several times as sediment continues to settle out.

After the first racking, especially if it is white, the wine may be **filtered** to take out solid particles that can cloud the wine and any stray yeast or bacteria that can spoil it. Wine may be filtered several times before bottling to help control a wine's development during maturation. This is a common practice among commercial producers, but many fine-wine makers resist filtering, as they believe it leads to less complex wines that don't age as well.

White wine may also be **fined** to clarify it and stabilize its color. In fining, agents such as a fine clay called bentonite or albumen from egg whites are mixed into the wine. As they settle out, they absorb undesirable substances that can cloud the wine. As with filtering, the process is more common with ordinary table wines than with fine wines.

Typically, winemakers blend several batches of new wine together to balance flavor. Careful **blending** gives the winemaker an extra chance to create a perfect single-varietal wine, or to combine several varietals that complement each other in a blend. Premium vintners also make unblended vineyard-designated wines that highlight the attributes of grapes from a single vineyard.

New wine is stored in stainless steel or oak casks or barrels to rest and develop before bottling. This stage, called **maturation or aging,** may last anywhere from a few months to over a year for white wine. Barrel rooms are kept dark to protect the wine both from light and from heat, either of which can be damaging. Some wineries keep their wines in air-conditioned rooms or warehouses, others have bored long, tunnel-like **caves** into hillsides, where the wine remains at a constant temperature.

If wine is matured or aged for any length of time before bottling, it will be racked and perhaps filtered several times.

It's All on the Label

CLOSE UP

1

If you look beyond the photograph of a weathered château or the quirky drawing of a cartoon creature on a bottle of wine, it will tell you a lot about what's inside. If you want to decode the details of what's inside, look for the following information:

■ Alcohol content: In most cases, U.S. law requires bottles to list the alcohol content, which typically hovers around 13 or 14 percent, but big red wines from California can soar to 16 percent or more.

■ Appellation: At least 85 percent of the grapes must have come from the AVA listed on the bottle. A bottle that says MT. VEEDER, for example, contains mostly grapes that are grown in the compact Mt. Veeder appellation, but if the label simply says CALIFORNIA, the grapes could have come from anywhere in the state.

■ Estate or Estate Grown: Wines with this label must be made entirely of grapes grown on land owned or operated by the winery.

■ Reserve: An inexact term meaning "special," this can refer to how or where the grapes were grown or how the wine was made.

■ Varietal: If a grape variety is listed on the label, it means that at least 75 percent of the grapes in this wine are of that varietal. If there's no varietal listed, it's probably a blend a various types of grapes.

■ Vineyard name: If the label lists a vineyard, then at least 95 percent of the grapes used must have been harvested there. A vineyard name is more commonly, though not exclusively, found on higher-end bottles of wine.

■ Vintage: If a year appears on the label, it means that at least 95 percent of the grapes in the wine were harvested in that year. If no vintage is listed, it's likely that the grapes came from more than one year's harvest.

■ Wine name: Many wineries will give their wines a catchy name, to help consumers pick it out in a crowd.

Once it is bottled, the wine is stored for **bottle aging**. This is done in a cool, dark space to prevent the corks from drying out; a shrunken cork allows oxygen to enter the bottle and spoil the wine. In a few months, most white wines will be ready for release.

MAKING RED WINES

Red wine production differs slightly from that of white wine. Red wine grapes are crushed the same way white wine grapes are, but the juice is not separated from the grape skins and pulp before fermentation. This is what gives red wine its color. After crushing, the red wine **must**— the thick slurry of juice, pulp, and skins—is fermented in vats. The juice is "left on the skins" for varying periods of time, from a few days to two weeks, depending on the grape variety and on how much color the winemaker wants to extract.

Fermentation also extracts flavors and chemical compounds such as **tannins** from the skins and seeds, making red wines more robust than whites. In a red designed for drinking soon after bottling, tannin levels are kept down; they should have a greater presence in wine meant for aging. In a young red not ready for drinking, tannins feel dry or coarse in your mouth, but they soften with age. Over time, a wine with well-balanced tannin will maintain its fruitiness and backbone as its flavor develops. Without adequate tannin, a wine will not age well.

Creating the **oak barrels** that age the wine is a craft in its own right. At Demptos Napa Cooperage, a French-owned company that employs French barrel-making techniques, the process involves several elaborate production phases. The staves of oak are formed into the shape of a barrel using metal bands, and then the rough edges of the bound are smoothed. Finally, the barrels are literally toasted to give the oak its characteristic flavor, which will in turn be imparted to the wine.

Red wine fermentation occurs at a higher temperature than that for whites—reds ferment at about 70°F to 90°F (21°C to 32°C). As the grape sugars are converted into alcohol, great amounts of carbon dioxide are generated. Carbon dioxide is lighter than wine but heavier than air, and it forms an **"aerobic cover"** that protects the wine from oxidation. As the wine ferments, grape skins rise to the top and are periodically mixed back in so the wine can extract the maximum amount of color and flavor. This is done either in the traditional fashion by punching them down with a large handheld tool, or by pumping the wine from the bottom of the vat and pouring it back in at the top.

At the end of fermentation, the free-run wine is drained off. The grape skins and pulp are sent to a press where the remaining wine is extracted. As with the whites, the winemaker may choose to add a little of the press wine to the free-run wine—if he feels it will add complexity to the finished wine. Otherwise the press juice goes into bulk wine—the lower quality, less expensive stuff. The better wine is racked and maybe fined; some reds are left unfined for extra depth.

Next up is **oak-barrel aging,** which takes a year or longer. Unlike many of the barrels used for aging and fermenting chardonnay, the barrels used for aging red wine are not always new. They may already have been used to age char donnay, which has extracted most of the wood's flavors. Oak, like grapes, contains natural tannins, and the wine extracts these tannins from the barrels. Oak also has countless tiny pores through which water in the wine slowly evaporates, making the wine more concentrated. To make sure the aging wine does not oxidize, the barrels have to be regularly **topped off** with wine from the same vintage.

The only way even the best winemaker can tell if a wine is finished is by tasting it. A winemaker constantly tastes wines during fermentation, while they are aging in barrels, and regularly, though less often, while they age in bottles. The wine is released for sale when the winemaker's palate and nose say it's ready.

MAKING SPARKLING WINES

Sparkling wines are, despite the mystique surrounding them, nothing more or less than wines in which carbon dioxide is suspended, making them bubbly. Good sparkling wine will always be fairly expensive, because a great deal of work goes into making it.

White sparkling wines can be made from either white or black grapes. In France, Champagne is traditionally made from pinot noir or chardonnay grapes, while in California, pinot blanc, riesling, or sometimes other white grapes might also be used as well. If black grapes are used, they must be picked very carefully to avoid crushing them. The goal is to minimize contact between the inner fruit (which is usually white) and the skins, where the purply-red color pigments reside. The grapes are rushed to the winery, crushed very gently, and the juice is strained off the skins right away, again, to prevent the juice from coming in contact with pigments and turning red. Even so, some sparklers have more of a pink tinge to them than the winemaker intends.

The freshly pressed juice and pulp, or must, is **fermented with special yeasts** that preserve the wine's fruit, the characteristic fruit flavor of the grape variety used. Before bottling, this finished "still" wine (wine without bubbles) is mixed with a *liqueur de tirage,* a blend of wine, sugar, and yeast. This mixture causes the wine to ferment again—in the bottle, where it stays for six to 12 weeks. **Carbon dioxide,** a by-product of fermentation, is produced and trapped in the bottle, where it dissolves in the wine (instead of escaping into the air, as happens during fermentation in barrel, vat, or tank). This captive carbon dioxide transforms the still wine into a sparkling wine.

Bottles of new sparkling wine are stored on their sides in deep cellars. The wine now ages *sur lie,* or **"on the lees"** (the dead yeast cells and other deposits trapped in the bottle). This aging process enriches the wine's texture and increases the complexity of its bouquet. The amount of time a sparkling wine ages *sur lie* bears a direct relation to its quality: the longer the aging, the more complex the wine.

The lees must be removed from the bottle before a sparkling wine can be enjoyed. This is achieved in a process whose first step is called **riddling.** In the past, each bottle, head tilted slightly downward, was placed in a riddling rack, an A-frame with many holes of bottleneck size. Riddlers gave each bottle a slight shake and a downward turn, every day if possible. This continued for six weeks, until each bottle rested upside down in the hole and the sediment had collected in the neck, next to the cork. Simple as this sounds, it is actually very difficult to do. Hand-riddling is a fine art perfected after much training. Today, most sparkling wines are riddled in ingeniously designed machines called gyro palettes, which riddle up to 500 or more bottles at one time, though at a few wineries, such as Schramsberg, the work is still done by hand, by a "master riddler" who has been with the winery for more than 30 years.

After riddling, the bottles are **disgorged.** The upside-down bottles are placed in a very cold solution, which freezes the sediments in a block that attaches itself to the crown cap sealing the bottle. The cap and frozen plug are removed, the bottle is topped off with a wine-and-sugar mixture called **dosage** and recorked with the traditional Champagne cork. The dosage determines the final sweetness of a sparkling wine.

Sparkling wines with 1.5 percent sugar or less are labeled **"brut"**; those with 1.2 to 2 percent sugar are called **"extra dry"**; those with 1.7 to 3.5 percent are called **"sec"** (the French for "dry"); and those with 3.5 to 5 percent, **"demi-sec"** (half-dry). **"Doux"** (sweet) sparkling wine has more than 5 percent sugar. Most sparkling-wine drinkers refuse to admit that they like their bubbly on the sweet side, and this labeling convention allows them to drink sweet while pretending to drink dry. It's a marketing ploy invented in Champagne at least a century ago. A sparkling wine to which no dosage has been added will be bone dry (and taste sour to some) and may be called **"extra-brut"** or "natural."

Most sparkling wines are not vintage dated but are "assembled" (the term sparkling-wine makers use instead of "blended") to create a **cuvée,** a mix of different wines and sometimes different vintages consistent with the house style. However, sparkling wines may be vintage dated in very great years.

Sparkling wine may also be made by time- and cost-saving bulk methods. In the bulk **Charmat process,** invented by Eugene Charmat early in the 20th century, the secondary fermentation takes place in large tanks rather than individual bottles. Each tank is basically treated as one huge bottle. After the bubbles have developed, the sediments are filtered from the wine and the wine is bottled. But at a price: while the sparkling wine may be ready in as little as a month, it has neither the complexity nor the bubble quality of the more slowly made sparklers. In the United States, sparkling wine made in this way must be labeled BULK PROCESS or CHARMAT PROCESS. Sparkling wines made in the traditional, time-consuming fashion may be labeled MÉTHODE CHAMPENOISE or WINE FERMENTED IN THIS BOTTLE.

THE FRENCH CONNECTION Sparkling wines were perfected in Champagne, France's northernmost wine district, where wines tend to be a bit acidic because grapes do not always fully ripen. That's why sparkling wines have traditionally been naturally tart, even austere. Because of their progenitor's birthplace, many sparkling wines are often called Champagne. However, this term designates a region of origin, so it really shouldn't be used for American sparkling wines. That's not to say that Napa and Sonoma County sparkling wines are in any way inferior to French ones. The French Champagne houses are fully aware of the excellence of the California product and have been quick to cash in on the laurels gathered by such pioneers as Hanns Kornell, Schramsberg, and Iron Horse by establishing sparkling-wine cellars in Sonoma and Napa with American partners.

MAKING ROSÉ WINES

Rosé or blush wines are also made from red wine grapes, but the juicy pulp is left on the skins for a matter of hours—12 to 36—not days. When the winemaker decides that the juice has reached the desired color, it is drained off and filtered. Yeast is added, and the juice is left to ferment. Because the must stays on the skins for a shorter time than the must of red wines, fewer tannins are leached from the skins, and the resulting wine is not as full-flavored as a red. You might say that rosé is a lighter, fruitier version of red wine, not a pink version of white.

A ROSÉ BY ANY OTHER NAME Rosé has gotten a bad rap in recent years, mostly because it's sometimes confused with inexpensive, sickly-sweet white zinfandels that are a similar hue, but the French have been making excellent dry rosés for decades. Many California vintners have jumped on the rosé bandwagon of late, and it seems like almost every tasting room features at least one of these refreshing wines.

THE SWEET SCIENCE OF VITICULTURE

It's no accident that California is renowned as one of the best wine-making regions in the world. If the weather is too hot, some grapes can produce too much sugar and not enough acid, resulting in overly alcoholic wines. Too cool and grapes won't ripen properly, and some will develop an unpleasant vegetal taste. And rain at the wrong time of year can wreak havoc on vineyards, causing grapes to rot on the vine. What's more, the wrong type of soil can leave with vines with "wet feet," which can seriously hamper their growth. These and many other conditions must be just right to coax the best out of persnickety wine grapes, and the Central Coast, Napa, and Sonoma have that magical combination of sun, rain, fog, slope, and soil that allow many varieties of wine grape to thrive.

1

LOCATION, LOCATION, LOCATION

Many California growers and winemakers generally agree that that no matter what high-tech wine-making techniques might be used at the winery, in fact the wine is really made in the vineyard. This emphasis on *terroir* (a French term that encompasses the soil, the microclimate, and overall growing conditions of a region) suggests that the quality of a wine is determined by what happens before the grapes are crushed. Even a small winery can produce spectacular wines from small vineyards if it has the right location and grows the grapes best suited to its soil and microclimate. (For a rundown on California's main grape varieties, see the Winespeak chapter at the end of this book.)

When a region's terroir is unique in the U.S., the Alcohol and Tobacco Tax and Trade Bureau can designate it an American Viticultural Area (AVA), more commonly called an **appellation.** What makes things a little confusing is that appellations often overlap. California is an appellation, for example, but so is the Napa Valley. Napa and Sonoma counties are each county appellations, but they, too, are divided into even smaller regions, usually called subappellations. Different appellations—there are almost 100 AVAs in California, with 16 in the county of Napa alone—are renowned for different wines.

Appellation always refers to the source of a wine's grapes, not to the place where the wine was made. Wineries can indicate the appellation on a bottle's label only if 85 percent of the grapes used in the wine were grown in that appellation. Many wineries buy grapes from outside their AVA (some do not even have vineyards of their own), so it is quite possible that they will label different wines with the names of different regions.

Grapes grown in particular areas diverge widely in quality, and when it is to their advantage winemakers make sure to mention prestigious appellations, and even specific vineyards, on their labels. If the grapes have come from multiple AVAs within a given region—say, the Sierra Foothills—the wine can be labeled with the name of the region. Wines simply labeled CALIFORNIA, then, are usually made of grapes from more than one region.

Best Wine Country Picnics

There's no shortage of swanky restaurants in the Wine Country—but how about the pleasures of eating a simple, hands-on meal outdoors? Many wineries have designated picnic areas, and it's easy to find portable treats at local markets and specialty food purveyors in every Wine Country town. Check out picnic policies in advance, though, before you go out of your way: a majority of wineries either don't have the facilities necessary or lack the permit that allows them to host picnickers. Also, don't be surprised if you find a winery that allows picnicking but not drinking wine: again, this is the result of quixotic permit policies. If alcohol *is* allowed, etiquette dictates that you buy a bottle from the winery whose grounds you are using.

■ **Napa Valley:** Stock up on high-falutin' staples like pâté and imported cheeses at the Dean & Deluca store on Route 29, 1½ mi south of downtown St. Helena, before driving up to Rutherford Hill Winery to eat under their olive trees with a view of the valley.

■ **Dry Creek Valley:** On your way to Preston Vineyards, stop at the Dry Creek General Store for sandwiches and other picnic fixings. At Preston, if you're lucky, you'll find some housemade bread for sale to add to your stash. Buy a bottle of refreshing sauvignon blanc to enjoy in the grassy yard.

■ **Sonoma:** In the town of Sonoma, stock up on almost everything you need at the Sonoma Cheese Factory on the north side of the plaza, then swing by The Cheesemaker's Daughter for an artisanal cheese or two and some sweet treats. Take your haul to Gundlach-Bundschu Winery, where the views from up the slopes are unbeatable.

■ **Russian River:** On the east side of Healdsburg's plaza, buy all the fixings for a picnic at the Oakville Grocery. Then drive on Westside Road to picnic at Rochioli Vineyards with a bottle of sauvignon blanc or pinot noir.

GEOLOGY 101

Wherever grapes are grown, geology matters. Grapevines are among the few plants that give their best fruit when they grow in poor, rocky soil. On the other hand, grapes just don't like wet feet. The ideal vineyard soil is easily permeable by water; this characteristic is even more crucial than its mineral content. Until the 1990s, California growers paid far more attention to climate than geology when deciding where to plant vineyards and how to manage them. As demand for premium wine has exploded, though, winemakers are paying much more attention to the soil part of the terroir equation. Geologists now do a brisk business advising growers on vineyard soil.

Different grape varieties thrive in different types of soil. For instance, cabernet sauvignon does best on well-drained, gravelly soils; soil that's too wet or contains too much heavy clay or organic matter will give the wine an obnoxious vegetative quality that even the best wine-making techniques cannot remove. Merlot grapes, however, can grow in soil with more clay and still be made into a delicious, rich wine. Sauvignon blanc grapes do quite well in heavy clay soils, but the winegrower has to limit irrigation and use some viticultural muscle to keep the grapes from developing unacceptable flavors. Chardonnay likes well-drained vineyards but will also take heavy soil.

The soils below Napa Valley's crags and in the wine-growing valleys of Sonoma County are dizzyingly diverse. Some of the soils are composed of dense, heavy sedimentary clays washed from the mountains; others are very rocky clays, loams, or silts of alluvial fans. These fertile, well-drained soils cover much of the valleys' floors. Other areas have soil based on serpentine, a rock that rarely appears aboveground. In all, there are about 60 soil types in the Napa and Sonoma valleys, allowing a wide variety of grapes to be grown in a relatively small area.

The geology of the Central Coast is less complex: calcareous (calcium-rich) shale predominates at higher elevations, while loamy alluvial soils with fewer nutrients make up flatter land. Good rainfall, soaked up by rocky clay, makes the higher elevation areas prime spots for dry farming without irrigation. The sandier, drier flatlands require more irrigation but are much easier to cultivate because of their topography.

In Wine Country you'll hear a lot about limestone, a nutrient-rich rock in which grapevines thrive. Some California winemakers claim to be growing in limestone when in fact they are not. In fact, only small patches of California's Wine Country have significant amounts of limestone. The term is often used to describe the streak of light-colored, almost white soil that runs across the Napa Valley from the Palisades to St. Helena and through Sonoma County from the western flanks of the Mayacamas Mountains to

Windsor. The band is actually comprised of volcanic material that has no limestone content. The error is easily made on the Central Coast, where seashells from a prehistoric ocean floor turned into calcareous shale. Limestone forms in much the same way.

DOWN ON THE FARM

Much like a fruit or nut orchard, a vineyard can produce excellent grapes for decades—even a century—if it's given the proper attention. The growing cycle starts in winter, when the vines are bare and dormant. While the plants rest, the grower works to enrich the soil and repair the trellising system (if there is one) that holds up the vines. This is when **pruning** takes place to regulate the vine's growth and upcoming season's crop size.

In spring, the soil is aerated by plowing, and new vines go in. The grower trains established vines so they grow, with or without trellising, in the shape most beneficial for the grapes. **Bud break** occurs when the first new bits of green emerge from the vines, and a pale green veil appears over the winter's gray-black vineyards. A late frost can be devastating at this time of year. Summer brings the flowering of the vines, when clusters of tiny green blossoms appear, and **fruit set,** when the grapes form from the blossoms. As the vineyards turn luxuriant and leafy, more pruning, along with leaf-pulling, keeps foliage in check so the vine directs nutrients to the grapes, and so the sun can reach the fruit. As summer advances the grower will **thin the fruit,** cutting off (or "dropping") some bunches so the remaining grapes intensify in flavor. A look at the vineyards reveals heavy clusters of green or purple grapes, some pea-size, others marble-size, depending on the variety.

Fall is the busiest season in the vineyard. Growers and winemakers carefully monitor the ripeness of the grapes, sometimes with equipment that tests sugar and acid levels and sometimes simply by tasting them. As soon as the grapes are ripe **harvest** begins amid the lush foliage. In California, this generally happens in September and October, but sometimes a bit earlier or later depending on the type of grape and the climatic conditions. Picking must be done as quickly as possible, within just a day or two, to keep the grapes from passing their peak. Most California grapes are harvested mechanically, but some are picked by

Vintage Variables

Oenophiles make much of wine's vintage—the year in which the grapes were harvested—because the climate in the vineyard has a big impact on a wine's character. From one year to the next, depending on the weather, a single vine can yield very different wines.

It's impossible to generalize about which vintages are best and worst because growing conditions vary so much from region to region, and sorting out the many elements that influence a wine can be as confusing as untangling a string of last year's Christmas lights. Vines that grow just around the bend from each other can have completely different weather years.

In very general terms, grapes grown in cool, wet regions tend to do better in warmer years, while hotter regions tend to get better results in cooler years. A cool growing season can suppress crop yield, and lower crop yield boosts quality. Grapes ripen more slowly in cool years, gaining more intense flavors and higher acid; the potential of wines meant for aging improves. Cold spring weather, however, can prevent fruit from forming in the first place. Rain can have the same effect. Too much rain any time during the growing season, or any rain at all in late summer

worries growers because it can bring mildew, bunch rot, and off flavors.

All of this comes with caveats. Weather affects different varietals differently: for example, cabernet sauvignon does well in most conditions, but zinfandel and chenin blanc are especially susceptible to bunch rot from late-season rain. The notoriously finicky pinot noir grape suffers in hot weather and can get sunburned, but it is also sensitive to a too-cool growing season. From region to region, a given varietal might respond to similar conditions differently. Frequent fog, for instance, to some extent hardens Central Coast grapes against mildew, while a drizzly day at the wrong time of year can spell doom for a Sonoma crop.

Federal law requires that at least 95 percent of the wine in a bottle labeled with a vintage year must be grown that year. If you see no vintage on the bottle, as is common with jug wines, what's inside is a blend of wines from different years. If you do know the vintage, however, you can glean some information about the wine by looking at the conditions when and where it was grown. Knowing the age of the wine can also help you decide when to open it.

hand (⇨ *The Crush, above*). After harvest, the vines start to regenerate for next year.

Sometimes by preference and sometimes by necessity, winemakers don't grow all the grapes they need. Small wineries with only a few acres of grapes are limited in the varietals and quantities they can grow. (The smallest producers don't even have their own wineries, so they pay to use the equipment and storage space at a custom crush facility.) Midsize wineries may aim to get bigger. If it doesn't buy more acreage, a winery that wants to diversify or expand production has to buy grapes from an independent grower.

Many winemakers purchase at least some of their grapes. Some wineries have negotiated long-term contracts with top growers, buying grapes from the same supplier year after year. This way, the winemaker can control the consistency and quality of the fruit just as if it came from the winery's own vineyard. Other wineries buy from several growers, and many growers sell to more than one winery.

Winemakers who buy from growers face a paradoxical problem: it's possible to make a wine that's too good and too popular. As the demand for a wine—and its price—rises, so will the price of the grapes used to make it. Other wineries sometimes bid up the price of the grapes, with the result that a winemaker can no longer afford the grapes that made a wine famous. This competitiveness among winemakers for specific batches of grapes underscores the importance of terroir and of growers.

Napa Valley

WORD OF MOUTH

"If your touring is limited to Highway 29 in Napa, everything will seem very busy and crowded, [but] if you take the time and trouble to research some alternatives and get off the beaten path, you will have some amazing experiences in Napa."

—napamalt

NAPA VALLEY RULES the roost of American wine production. With more than 275 wineries and many of the biggest brands in the business, there are more splashy wineries and big-name vintners here than anywhere else in the state. Vastly diverse soils and microclimates give Napa winemakers the chance to make a tremendous variety of wines. But what's the area like beyond the glossy advertising and bold-face names?

For every blockbuster winery whose name you'll recognize from the pages of *Wine Spectator*—Robert Mondavi, Charles Krug, Beringer, and Stag's Leap Wine Cellars, to name a very few—you'll also find a low-frills winery that will warmly welcome you into its modest tasting room. On the other end of the spectrum are Napa's "cult" cabernet producers—Screaming Eagle, Harlan Estate, Araujo Estate, Dalla Valle, and Dominus Estate among them—whose doors are closed tight to visitors.

Several small, quirky towns strung along Highway 29 house the wine industry workers and the visitors who come to appreciate their efforts. The up-and-coming town of Napa—the valley's largest town—lures with its cultural attractions and reasonably priced accommodations (relatively speaking). A few miles farther north, compact Yountville is a culinary boomtown, densely packed with top-notch restaurants. Continuing north, St. Helena teems with elegant boutiques and restaurants; mellow Calistoga, chock-full of spas and hot springs, feels a bit like an Old West frontier town and has a more casual attitude than many Wine Country towns.

Because the Napa Valley attracts everyone from hard-core wine collectors to bachelorette partiers, it is not necessarily the best place to get away from it all. But there's a reason it's the number-one California Wine Country destination. The local viticulture has inspired a robust passion for food, and several outstanding chefs have taken root here, sealing Napa's reputation as one of the best restaurant destinations in the country. And here visitors will get a glimpse of California's history, from the wine cellars dating back to the late 1800s to the flurry of Steamboat Gothic architecture dressing up Calistoga. Binding all these temptations together is the sheer scenic beauty of the place. Much of Napa Valley's landscape unspools in orderly, densely planted rows of vines. Even the climate cooperates, as the warm summer days and refreshingly cool evenings that are so favorable for grape growing make perfect weather for traveling, too.

GETTING AROUND NAPA

Highway 29, the Napa Valley Highway, heads north from Vallejo first as a busy four-lane highway, then narrows to a two-lane road at Yountville. Beyond Yountville, expect Highway 29 to be congested, especially on summer weekends. Traveling through St. Helena can be particularly slow during morning and afternoon rush hours. You'll probably find slightly less traffic on the Silverado Trail, which roughly parallels Highway 29 all the way from the town of Napa to Calistoga. Cross streets connect the two like rungs on a ladder every few miles, making it easy to cross over from one to the other.

NAPA VALLEY APPELLATIONS

Although almost all of Napa County, which stretches from the Mayacamas Mountains in the west to Lake Berryessa in the east, comprises the Napa Valley AVA, this large viticultural region is divided into many smaller AVAs, or sub-appellations, each with its own unique characteristics.

Four of these—Oak Knoll, Oakville, Rutherford, and St. Helena—stretch clear across the valley floor. The **Oak Knoll AVA**, formally recognized in 2004, is one of the coolest appellations in Napa, chilled by coastal fog. The **Oakville AVA**, just north of Yountville, is studded by both big-name wineries (like Robert Mondavi and Opus One) and awe-inspiring upstarts (like the super-private Screaming Eagle). Oakville's gravelly, well-drained soil is especially good to cabernet sauvignon.

A sunny climate and well-drained soil make **Rutherford AVA** one of the best locations for cabernet sauvignon in California, if not the world. North of Rutherford, the **St. Helena AVA** is one of Napa's toastiest, as the slopes surrounding the narrow valley reflect the sun's heat. Bordeaux varietals are the most popular grapes grown here —particularly cabernet sauvignon but also merlot.

Stags Leap District AVA, a small district on the east side of the valley marked by dramatic volcanic palisades. Cabernet sauvignon and merlot are by far the favored grapes. Cool evening breezes encourage a long growing season and

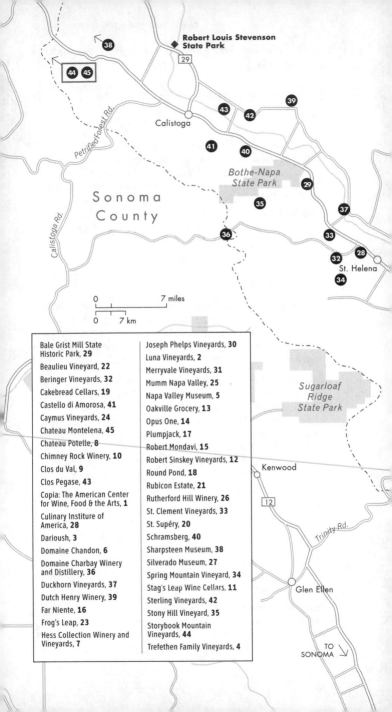

Robert Louis Stevenson State Park

Sonoma County

Calistoga

Bothe-Napa State Park

St. Helena

Sugarloaf Ridge State Park

Kenwood

Glen Ellen

TO SONOMA

0   7 miles
0   7 km

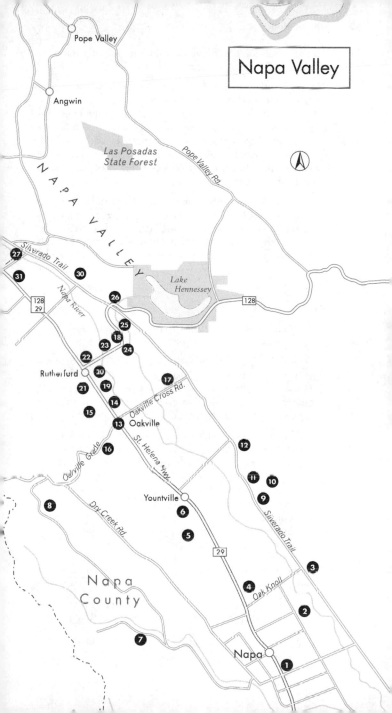

intense fruit flavors. Some describe the resulting wines as "rock soft" or an "iron fist in a velvet glove."

Mount Veeder and **Spring Mountain AVAs** each encompass parts of the mountains from which they take their names. And both demonstrate how stressing out grape vines can yield outstanding results; the big winner is cabernet. Growing grapes on these slopes takes a certain temerity—or fool-hardiness, depending on your point of view, especially since many of the vineyards are so steep that they have to be tilled and harvested by hand.

There are plenty of other notable appellations, like up-and-comer Howell Mountain. The climate zones are nearly as much of a crazy quilt as the appellations. The great variability in the climate, as well as the soils, explains why valley vintners can make so many different wines, and make them so well.

TOWN OF NAPA

46 mi northeast of San Francisco via I–80 east and north, Rte. 37 west, and Rte. 29 north.

The town of Napa is the valley's largest, and visitors who get a glimpse of the strip malls and big-box stores from Highway 29 often speed right past on the way to the smaller and more seductive Yountville or St. Helena. But Napa no longer entirely merits its dowdy reputation.

After many years as a blue-collar town with its back to the Wine Country scene, Napa may be on the verge of becoming a popular—even hip—destination. In part because of the recent expansion of the nearby Carneros vineyards, Napa has been busily sprucing up its historic downtown area. Many of the once-empty storefronts have morphed into wine bars, restaurants, bookstores, and Internet cafés. Exciting restaurants have popped up along the banks of the Napa River, especially in the Historic Napa Mill, a complex of late-19th-century brick buildings, and plans are afoot to break ground on a Ritz-Carlton on the river's banks in 2008.

The oldest town in the Napa Valley, Napa was founded in 1848 in a strategic location on the Napa River, where the Sonoma-Benicia Road (Highways 12 and 29) crossed at a ford. The first wood-frame building built that year was a saloon, and the downtown area still preserves an old river-town atmosphere. Many Victorian residences have survived, and in the original business district a few older buildings have been preserved, including the turn-of-the-20th-century courthouse and several riverfront warehouses.

Although there are still some empty storefronts downtown, and Napa definitely has the air of a work in progress, the town is attracting more and more visitors every year, many of them looking for a slightly more reasonably priced place to lay their head after a day of wine tasting than farther up the valley. If you set up your home base here, you'll undoubtedly want to spend some time getting out of town and into the beautiful countryside, but don't neglect attractions in town, which could easily fill a full day.

★ ❶ The brainchild of Robert Mondavi and his wife, Margrit, **Copia: The American Center for Wine, Food & the Arts** is a shrine to American food and wine. The modern complex hosts a frenetic lineup of lectures, wine tastings, cookbook signings, and gardening demos. The entry fee includes the permanent exhibit, "Forks in the Road"—exploring the American relationship with food and wine, from TV dinners to haute cuisine—and the rotating exhibits and excellent tours of the garden.

One popular feature allows you to purchase a card that can be used at 10 different wine stations, where you can taste the favorite wines of Copia staffers, compare the same varietal grown in different parts of the world, or find out what a "corked" wine smells like. ■ TIP → **Call in advance or check the Web site for information on winemaker dinners, luncheon seminars, wine-and-cheese pairings, and other events.** The Oxbow Public Market, a collection of artisanal food producers, opened just outside Copia in winter 2007. ✉ *500 1st St.* ☎ *707/259–1600* ⊕ *www.copia.org* 💲 *$5* ⊘ *Wed.–Mon. 10–5.*

VINEYARDS AROUND NAPA

❷ **Luna Vineyards,** the southernmost winery on the Silverado Trail, was established in 1995 by veterans of the Napa wine industry intent on making less-conventional wines, particularly Italian varieties. (Their whites are styled after those from Friuli, the reds after those from Tuscany.) A spacious tasting room with high ceilings, warmed by an enormous fireplace in cool weather, is a lovely spot for tasting their

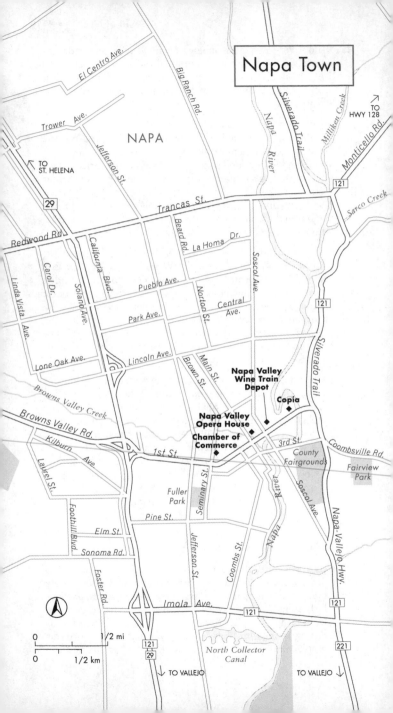

pinot grigio, merlot, sangiovese, and a late-harvest dessert wine of semillon and sauvignon blanc called Mille Baci ("a thousand kisses" in Italian). ✉ *2921 Silverado Trail* ☎ *707/255-2474* ⊕ *www.lunavineyards.com* 🍷 *Tasting $5–$15, tour $5–$15* ⊙ *Daily 10–5; tour by appointment.*

2

❸ **Darioush** is not quite like any other winery in the valley: you'll know that as soon as you turn into the driveway and see the 16 freestanding, sand-colored columns looming in front of a palatial travertine building that looks like a cross between the Parthenon and a sultan's palace. That grand visitors center, opened in 2004, was designed to evoke Persepolis, the capital of ancient Persia. The Persian heritage of owner Darioush Khaledi surfaces in more subtle ways, too, from the Middle Eastern–inflected music playing in the tasting room to the Persian pistachios served with the wines. The estate's 95 acres are planted with chardonnay, viognier, petit verdot, malbec, merlot, shiraz, and the cabernet sauvignon for which Oakville is so well known. The only way to fully tour the property, though, is to sign up for the $50 fine-wine tasting, which is given at 2 PM daily. ✉ *4240 Silverado Trail* ☎ *707/257-2345* ⊕ *www.darioush.com* 🍷 *Current release tasting $20* ⊙ *Daily 10:30–5; tour by appointment.*

❹ The big terra-cotta-colored building at **Trefethen Family Vineyards** is a remnant of the old Eshcol Winery, built in 1886. It's the only three-story gravity-flow winery built from wood remaining in Napa (other remaining gravity-flow wineries are made from stone, which has weathered the last century much better). Trefethen makes superb chardonnay, cabernet sauvignon, and pinot noir, as well as an excellent dry riesling. If you'd like to find out for yourself how well their wines age, pay for the reserve tasting, which gets you a seat in the clubby library behind the main tasting and pours of some of their older vintages (known as library wines). There's a cork tree planted in the garden outside the tasting room—so *that's* what the stuff looks like before it ends up on the sharp end of your corkscrew. ✉ *1160 Oak Knoll Ave.* ☎ *707/255-7700* ⊕ *www.trefethenfamilyvineyards.com* 🍷 *Tasting $10–$20, tour free* ⊙ *Daily 10–4:30; tour daily by appointment at 10:30 and 2.*

WHERE TO STAY & EAT

$$–$$$$ ✕**Angèle.** The Napa Valley's Rouas family (of Auberge du Soleil fame) is behind this French bistro in an 1890s Napa River boathouse. Although the main dining room is plenty romantic, with vaulted wood-beam ceilings and candles on every table, in good weather ask for one of the tables outside. Classic dishes such as French onion soup and filet mignon with a red wine sauce are well executed by chef Tripp Mauldin and then served with Gallic charm by an attentive staff. The short dessert list is very French: crème brûlée, chocolate terrine, and apple tart. ⊠*540 Main St.* ☎*707/252–8115* ⊟*AE, D, DC, MC, V.*

$$–$$$$ ✕**Julia's Kitchen.** You can watch the chefs in the open kitchen concoct subtle French-Cal cuisine such as olive-oil-poached halibut, crispy veal sweetbreads, and salads assembled from freshly picked greens from the organic gardens out front. Classic French dishes such as beef bourguignon are an homage to the restaurant's namesake, and unusual desserts, such as the strawberry mascarpone meringue, show off the talents of the inventive pastry chef. Although the surroundings are modest for a restaurant at this level—it looks something like a nicely appointed hotel dining room—service is usually spot-on. ⊠*500 1st St.* ☎*707/265–5700* ⊟*AE, D, DC, MC, V* ⊘*Closed Tues. No dinner Mon.*

$$–$$$ ✕**Pilar.** Husband-and-wife team Didier Lenders and Maria del Pilar Sanchez forged this tiny, unpretentious foodie favorite. A minimalist interior with a slate-blue concrete floor could be considered austere, but when you're enjoying the inventive French and Latin flavors coming out of the kitchen, it somehow seems urbane and stylish. Serrano ham with fennel salad and Manchego cheese hints at Sanchez's Spanish and Mexican heritage, while a pear financier for dessert could come from a Parisian pâtisserie (Lenders was born in France). Otherwise, expect California favorites with a twist, like wild striped bass served with a green lentil ragout. An unusual wine list pairs California wines with their "soul-mate wines" from around the globe. ⊠*807 Main St.* ☎*707/252–4474* ⊟*AE, D, MC, V* ⊘*Closed Sun.–Mon. No lunch Tues.–Thurs.*

★ $–$$$ ✕**Bistro Don Giovanni.** Dramatic flower arrangements brighten this lively bistro, a longtime favorite of both locals and critics. The Cal-Italian food is simultaneously inventive and comforting: risotto with squab and radicchio, pizza with pear and prosciutto, and rabbit braised in cabernet. Whole, wood-oven-roasted fish is an unusual specialty. Seats on the covered patio are coveted in fair weather, but a fireplace and an impressive bar indoors make the restaurant a good choice at any time of year. ✉*4110 Howard La./Rte. 29* ☎*707/224-3300* ⊟*AE, D, DC, MC, V.*

★ **$-$$$** ✕**Bounty Hunter.** A triple threat, Bounty Hunter is a wine store, wine bar, and restaurant in one. You can stop by for just a glass of wine from their impressive list—40 available by the glass in both 2- and 5-ounce pours, 400 by the bottle—but it's best to come with an appetite. There's a small selection of delicious salads and sandwiches, while meltingly tender barbecue comes from the smoker and grill out back. For something lighter, try the artichoke dip or charcuterie plate. The space is casually chic, with pressed-tin ceilings and marble-topped café tables. ■TIP→**It's open until midnight on Friday and Saturday, making it a popular spot among locals for a late-night bite.** ✉*975 1st St.* ☎*707/255-0622* ⌲*Reservations not accepted* ⊟*AE, MC, V.*

$-$$$ ✕**ZuZu.** Ochre-colored walls and a weathered wood bar set the scene for a menu composed almost entirely of tapas. These little dishes, so perfect for sharing, and Latin jazz on the stereo help make this place a popular spot for festive get-togethers. Diners down *cava* (Spanish sparkling wine) or sangria with dishes such as white anchovies with endive, ratatouille, and salt cod with garlic croutons. Expect a wait on weekend nights, when local twentysomethings are out in force. ✉*829 Main St.* ☎*707/224-8555* ⊟*AE, MC, V* ⌲*Reservations not accepted* ⊘*No lunch weekends.*

MAKING TRACKS Turn the driving over to someone else—a train conductor. The **Napa Valley Wine Train** (☎707/253-2111 or 800/427-4124 ⊕www.winetrain.com) slowly chugs from Napa to St. Helena with several restored 1915-17 Pullman railroad cars. The trip, which follows part of an 1847 rail route, often includes a meal, such as brunch or dinner. While it's no bargain (starting around $90) and can seem a bit hokey, the train gives you a chance to enjoy the vineyard views without any driving worries. For the most lavish experience, book a romantic late-evening dinner in the circa-1950 railcar with a glass dome that lets in the moonlight. Otherwise, consider dining during the daylight hours, the better to see the scenery passing by your window.

$$–$$$$ ✕⚏**Silverado Resort.** On a summer day this property buzzes with activity, from golfers dropping off their bags to a gaggle of spa-goers capping off their treatments with a cocktail in the lobby lounge. The sprawling resort complex has it all, including two 18-hole golf courses, 17 tennis courts, and 10 swimming pools. The Mansion, overlooking Milliken Creek, is the hub of the property, with a lounge and restaurant inside and conference facilities nearby. Guest condos, spread out over the 1,200-acre property, are nothing special—some look like they are stuck in a 1980s time warp—but all except the smallest come equipped with a fireplace, a patio or deck, and a kitchen. The Royal Oak restaurant serves an excellent menu of updated surf-and-turf classics, while The Grill, a more casual restaurant, serves California cuisine with an Asian flair, with a focus on sustainable seafood. **Pros:** Great for groups with different interests, Robert Trent Jones Jr.–designed golf courses, efficient staffers. **Cons:** Fee for Wi-Fi access, some rooms have dated interiors, the Mansion can be bustling with groups. ✉*1600 Atlas Peak Rd., 94558* ☎*707/257–0200* ⊕*www.silveradoresort.com* ⤷*280 suites* &*In-room: kitchen (some), refrigerator, Wi-Fi. In-hotel: 2 restaurants, room service, bar, golf courses, tennis courts, pools, gym, spa, bicycles, no elevator, laundry facilities, laundry service, concierge* ⊟*AE, D, DC, MC, V.*

★ $$$$ ⚏**Milliken Creek Inn.** Though it dates back to 1857, this onetime stagecoach inn purrs with modern luxury. Soft jazz and complimentary port set a romantic mood in the intimate lobby, and the chic rooms take a page from the style book of British-colonial Asia, with a khaki-and-cream color scheme and palm-frond ceiling fans. You can enjoy the views over the tree-lined banks of the Napa River from almost everywhere: your room's balcony over breakfast, an Adirondack chair on the lawn, or the treatment rooms of the intimate spa. **Pros:** Cloudlike beds, serene spa open to hotel guests only, breakfast delivered to anywhere on the grounds. **Cons:** Expensive, high-tech hydrotherapy spa tubs take some figuring out, tiny bathrooms in some rooms. ✉*1815 Silverado Trail, 94558* ☎*707/255–1197* ⊕*www. millikencreekinn.com* ⤷*12 rooms* &*In-room: refrigerator, DVD, Wi-Fi. In-hotel: room service, spa, no elevator, laundry service, concierge, no kids under 16, no-smoking rooms.* ⊟*AE, D, DC, MC, V* ��*CP.*

★ Fodor'sChoice ⚏**Blackbird Inn.** Arts-and-crafts style infuses $$–$$$$ this 1905 building, from the lobby's enormous fieldstone fireplace to the lamps that cast a warm glow over the impressive wooden staircase. The style is continued in the attractive guest rooms, which balance sturdy, turn-of-the-20th-century oak beds and matching night tables with spacious, modern bathrooms—most with spa bathtubs. The inn is within walking distance of Napa's restaurant-rich downtown area. **Pros:** Gorgeous architecture and period furnishings, convenient to downtown Napa, free DVD library. **Cons:** Must book well in advance, some traffic noise, some rooms are small. ✉*1755 First St., 94559* ☎*707/226–2450 or 888/567–9811* ⊕*www.blackbird-innnapa.com* ⥄*8 rooms* ⚄*In-room: DVD, Wi-Fi. In-hotel: no elevator, no-smoking rooms.* ☐*AE, D, MC, V* ⦿*CP.*

$$–$$$$ ⚏**Napa River Inn.** Part of a complex of restaurants, shops, and a spa, this waterfront inn is within easy walking distance of downtown Napa. Accommodations spread through three neighboring buildings: rooms in the 1884 Hatt Building have original architectural details, including maple hardwood floors. Some rooms have canopy beds, fireplaces, and old-fashioned slipper tubs. Brighter colors dominate in the adjacent Plaza and Embarcadero buildings. Some Embarcadero rooms have small balconies and an understated nautical theme. **Pros:** Convenient to many restaurants and shops, accommodating staff, a wide range of room sizes and prices. **Cons:** Ongoing construction in the area causes some noise and hampers some views, allergic guests may not appreciate pet-friendly policy. ✉*500 Main St., 94559* ☎*707/251–8500 or 877/251–8500* ⊕*www.napariverinn.com* ⥄*65 rooms, 1 suite* ⚄*In-room: refrigerator, Wi-Fi. In-hotel: 2 restaurants, bar, spa, bicycles, laundry service, concierge, no-smoking rooms, some pets allowed (fee)* ☐*AE, D, MC, V* ⦿*CP.*

$–$$ ⚏**Chateau Hotel.** Despite a name that evokes a French castle, this is actually just a basic motel. Clean rooms, a location at the entrance to the Napa Valley, a neighboring restaurant, and free stays for children under age 12 are conveniences that make up for the rooms' lack of charm. Spacious conference facilities mean it's a popular place for business travelers on a budget. **Pros:** Inexpensive for the area, pool keeps kids entertained, fairly spacious rooms. **Cons:** Dimly lit lobby and hallways, carpets and furnishings are a bit threadbare, bathrooms could use updating. ✉*4195 Solano Ave., west of Rte. 29, exit at Trower Ave.,*

94558 ☎*707/253–9300, 800/253–6272 in* CA ⊕*www.*
napavalleychateauhotel.com ⬗*109 rooms, 6 suites* ⬗*In-*
room: refrigerator (some), Wi-Fi. In-hotel: pool, no eleva-
tor, no-smoking rooms. ▤*AE, D, DC, MC, V* |○|*CP.*

NIGHTLIFE & THE ARTS

Napa nightlife tends toward the sleepy side, but locals
sip wine and listen to live blues, folk, or open mic performances at cozy **Caffe Cicero,** open until midnight Thursday
to Saturday. ⊠*1234 First St.* ☎*707/257–1802* ⊕*www.caf-*
fecicero.com.

The interior of the 1879 Italianate Victorian **Napa Valley
Opera House,** which had its grand reopening in 2003, isn't
quite as majestic as the facade, but the intimate 500-seat
venue is still an excellent place to see all sorts of performances, from Pat Metheny and Mandy Patinkin to dance
companies and the occasional opera. ⊠*1030 Main St.*
☎*707/226–7372* ⊕*www.napavalleyoperahouse.org.*

SHOPPING

Although Napa doesn't have a slew of cute boutiques like
St. Helena, if you wander around the downtown area,
you're sure to find an interesting bookstore, clothing boutique, or wine shop. Just around the corner from the opera
house, **Bounty Hunter Rare Wine and Provisions** (⊠*975 First
St.* ☎*707/255–0622*) stocks Napa cult cabernets and other
hard-to-find wines. The store shares space with a charming
wine bar with exposed-brick walls and a stamped tin ceiling. Inside the Napa Town Center (bounded by First, Pearl,
Main, and Franklin streets), a pedestrian-friendly complex
of shops connected by brick-lined walkways, **Wineries of
Napa Valley** (⊠*1285 Napa Town Center* ☎*707/253–9450*)
is one of several downtown tasting rooms, where the
knowledgeable staff pour samples from five different small
wineries, such as Goosecross Cellars and Burgess Cellars.
Shackford's Kitchen Store (⊠*1350 Main St.* ☎*707/226–2132*)
looks something like a hardware store, with its bare-bones
concrete floors, but there's no better place in town for all
your cooking needs, whether it's ceramic serving pieces or
a chef's jacket.

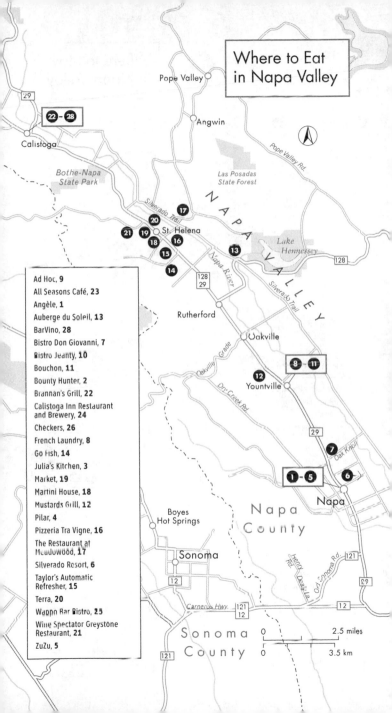

Where to Eat in Napa Valley

Ad Hoc, **9**

All Seasons Café, **23**

Angèle, **1**

Auberge du Soleil, **13**

BarVino, **28**

Bistro Don Giovanni, **7**

Bistro Jeanty, **10**

Bouchon, **11**

Bounty Hunter, **2**

Brannan's Grill, **22**

Calistoga Inn Restaurant and Brewery, **24**

Checkers, **26**

French Laundry, **8**

Go Fish, **14**

Julia's Kitchen, **3**

Market, **19**

Martini House, **18**

Mustards Grill, **12**

Pilar, **4**

Pizzeria Tra Vigne, **16**

The Restaurant at Meadowood, **17**

Silverado Resort, **6**

Taylor's Automatic Refresher, **15**

Terra, **20**

Wappo Bar Bistro, **25**

Wine Spectator Greystone Restaurant, **21**

ZuZu, **5**

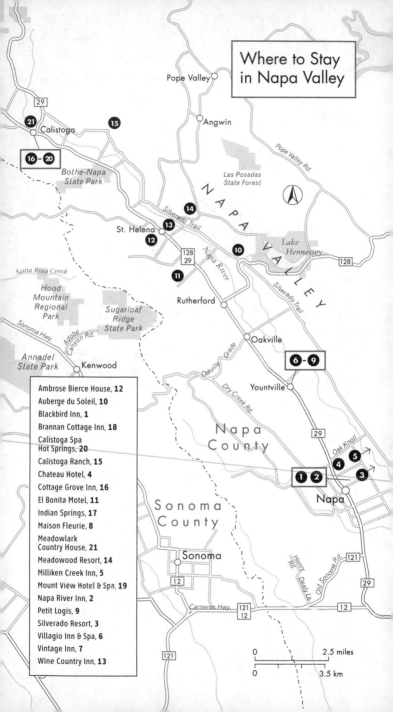

Where to Stay in Napa Valley

Ambrose Bierce House, **12**
Auberge du Soleil, **10**
Blackbird Inn, **1**
Brannan Cottage Inn, **18**
Calistoga Spa
Hot Springs, **20**
Calistoga Ranch, **15**
Chateau Hotel, **4**
Cottage Grove Inn, **16**
El Bonita Motel, **11**
Indian Springs, **17**
Maison Fleurie, **8**
Meadowlark
Country House, **21**
Meadowood Resort, **14**
Milliken Creek Inn, **5**
Mount View Hotel & Spa, **19**
Napa River Inn, **2**
Petit Logis, **9**
Silverado Resort, **3**
Villagio Inn & Spa, **6**
Vintage Inn, **7**
Wine Country Inn, **13**

Up, Up, and Away

Thought those vineyards were beautiful from the highway? Try viewing them from an altitude of about a thousand feet, serenely drifting along with the wind, the only sound the occasional roar of the burners overhead.

Many companies organize hot-air ballooning trips over Napa and Sonoma, offering rides that usually cost between $200 and $250 per person for a one-hour flight, including brunch or lunch afterward. If you were hoping for the ultimate in romance—a flight with no one but your sweetie (and an FAA-approved pilot) on board—be prepared to shell out two to four times as much.

Flights typically take off at the crack of dawn, when the winds are the lightest, so be pre-pared to make an early start and dress in layers. Flights are dependent on weather, and if there's rain or too much fog, expect to be grounded.

The following are a few of the many outfits offering rides. Many hotels can also hook you up with companies in their vicinity, some of whom can pick you up from your lodgings.

■ **Balloons Above the Valley** (☎707/253-2222, 800/464-6824 in CA ⊕www.balloonrides.com).

■ **Bonaventura Balloon Company** (☎707/944-2822 or 800/359-6272 ⊕www.bonaventuraballoons.com).

■ **Napa Valley Balloons** (☎707/944-0228, 800/253-2224 in CA ⊕www.napavalleyballoons.com).

SPORTS & THE OUTDOORS

GOLF

The 27 holes at the **Chardonnay Golf Club** (⊠2555 Jameson Canyon Rd. ☎707/257-1900), which meander through vineyards, can be golfed in three different 18-hole combinations. The greens fee, $59 weekdays and $79 weekends in high season, includes a cart. Serious golfers, however, should consider staying at the **Silverado Resort** (⇨ Where to Stay & Eat, above) to take advantage of their two courses covering 360 acres.

YOUNTVILLE

13 mi north of the town of Napa on Rte. 29.

Numbers in the margin correspond to numbers on the Napa Valley map.

These days Yountville is something like Disneyland for the foodie set. It all started with Thomas Keller's French Laundry, long regarded as one of the best restaurants in the United States, and the only spot in all of Northern California to wrest a coveted three-star ranking from Michelin when they published their first guide to the San Francisco area in 2006. Now Keller is also behind two more casual restaurants just a few blocks away from his mother ship—and that's only the tip of the iceberg. You could stay here for a week and not exhaust all the options in this tiny town with a big culinary reputation.

Yountville is full of small inns and luxurious hotels that cater to those who prefer to be able to stagger a short distance home after a decadent dinner. But it's also well located for excursions to many big-name Napa wineries. Near Yountville, along the Silverado Trail, the Stags Leap District helped put Napa on the wine-making map with its big, bold cabernet sauvignons. Volcanic soil predominates on the eastern slopes of Stags Leap, apparent from the towering volcanic palisades and crags hovering over the vineyards here.

On the other side of Highway 29 from Yountville rises the Mayacamas Range. Unlike on the valley floor, where wineries stand cheek by jowl along Highway 29 and the Silverado Trail, here wineries are fewer and farther between, hidden among the stands of oak, madrone, and redwood trees. Growing grapes in the Mount Veeder AVA takes a certain temerity—or foolhardiness, depending on your point of view. Even though this region gets more rain than the Napa Valley (as witnessed by those redwoods), soils are poor and rocky and the water runs off quickly, forcing grapevines planted here to grow deep roots. Vines thus stressed produce grapes with a high ratio of grape surface to liquid volume, resulting in intensely flavored wines, but the vines on the steep slopes of the 2,677-foot volcanic peak of Mount Veeder must be laboriously picked by hand. Merlot and syrah thrive in these conditions, but the big winner is cabernet.

Though many visitors use Yountville as a home base, touring wineries by day and returning to town for dinner, you could easily while away a few hours in town, picking up picnic fixings at a bakery. While strolling through town, you'll spot the **Pioneer Cemetery and Indian Burial Ground** (⊠*Lincoln and Jackson Sts.*), which were established in

1848. George Yount is buried here, and the cemetery is still used by the remaining members of the local Wappo tribe.

Between bouts of eating and drinking, you might stop by **Vintage 1870** (✉6525 *Washington St.* ☎707/944–2451), a complex of about 26 specialty stores and art galleries that fills a lovely building dating back to 1870. Though most of the stores themselves are nothing special—just a smattering of clothing boutiques and housewares stores—the vine-covered brick structure, which once housed a winery, livery stable, and distillery, is worth a look.

❺ Just across Highway 29 from downtown Yountville is the worthwhile **Napa Valley Museum** (✉*55 Presidents Circle* ☎707/944–0500), on the grounds of the Veterans Home, established in 1881 for disabled veterans of the Mexican War and the Grand Army of the Republic. Its permanent exhibit, *California Wine: The Science of an Art,* explains how science and creativity combine to create a memorable bottle of wine. The displays are unusually engaging; interactive computer quizzes, for example, test your knowledge of wine terms and food-and-wine pairings. Upstairs exhibits on Napa Valley's history and rotating fine-arts shows are also worth a look.

VINEYARDS NEAR YOUNTVILLE

NEAR DOWNTOWN YOUNTVILLE

❻ Domaine Chandon claims one of Yountville's prime pieces of real estate, built into a hillside and surrounded by ancient oaks. Tours of the sleek, modern facilities are available, but the highlight is a tasting. Sparklers here are made only by the labor-intensive—and costly—*méthode champenoise,* which means, among many other things, that the bottles are riddled, or laboriously turned by hand over a period of weeks to collect the sediment. To complete the decadent experience, you can order hors d'oeuvres to accompany wines in the tasting room. ■TIP➔**If you buy a bottle to drink at the winery you'll be charged $5 more than if you take the bottle home.** Save some time to wander around the property and appreciate the fountains and the occasional whimsical artwork, like a field of sculpted stone mushrooms sprouting out of the lawn. ✉*1 California Dr., west of Rte. 29* ☎707/944–2280 ⊕*www.chandon.com* ⊜*Tasting $10–$20, tour $7* ☉*May–Dec., daily 10–6; Jan.–Apr., weekdays 10–5, weekends 10–6; call for tour times.*

The Wine Country on Two Wheels

Thanks to the scenic country roads that wind through the region, bicycling is a practically perfect way to get around the Wine Country (lack of designated bike lanes notwithstanding). And whether you're interested in an easy spin to a few wineries or a strenuous haul up a mountainside, there's a way to make it happen.

Bike shops in most towns will rent you a bike and helmet by the day. In addition to doling out maps and advice on the least-trafficked roads, bikeshop staffers can typically recommend a route based on your interests and fitness level.

If you're at all concerned about the logistics of your trip, consider springing for a one-day or multiday bike tour, which usually includes lunch, a guide, and a "sag wagon" in case you poop out before you reach your destination.

Some of your best bets for bike rentals:

Calistoga Bikeshop (⊠ *1318 Lincoln Ave., Calistoga* ☎ *866/942–2453*) offers the self-guided Calistoga Cool Wine Tour package ($79),

which includes free tastings at a number of small wineries. Best of all, they'll pick up any wine you purchase along the way if you've bought more than will fit in the handy bottle carrier on your bike.

Napa Valley Bike Tours (⊠ *6488 Washington St., Yountville* ☎ *707/944–2953*) has the largest fleet of rental bikes in Napa Valley. They will deliver the bikes, which go for $30 to $65 a day, to many hotels in the Napa Valley if you're renting at least two bikes for a full day. One-day guided winery tours are $125.

St. Helena Cyclery (⊠ *1156 Main St., St. Helena* ☎ *707/963–7736*) rents bikes by the hour, as well as by the day (hybrids $30, street bikes $60).

Wine Country Bikes (⊠ *61 Front St., Healdsburg* ☎ *707/473–0610*), in downtown Healdsburg, is perfectly located for treks out into the Dry Creek and Russian River Valleys, two of the better destinations for those on two wheels. Bikes, including tandems, go for $30 to $95 a day. One-day tours are $129.

MT. VEEDER

❼ ★ Fodors Choice When the Swiss brewer and soda merchant Donald Hess arrived in the Napa Valley in 1986, he planted vineyards on the slopes of Mt. Veeder, some on sites so steep the grapes have to be picked by hand. This care definitely shows in the quality of the wines at the **Hess Collection**

Winery and Vineyards. But as tasty as the wines are, you'll probably best remember Hess's personal art collection, on display in the simple, rustic limestone structure: it's hard to forget Leopold Maler's striking *Hommage 1974*, a flaming typewriter created as a protest piece against the repression of artistic freedom, or the large-scale works by contemporary European and American artists such as Robert Motherwell and Frank Stella. The self-guided tour of the art collection is free. ⊠*4411 Redwood Rd., west of Rte. 29* ☎*707/255–1144* ⊕*www.hesscollection.com* ⊠*Tasting $10–$25* ⊙*Daily 10–5 (tasting until 4).*

8 The road to tiny **Chateau Potelle** is steep and winding, but the wines and the views over the vineyards are worth the drive to reach this secluded spot almost 2,000 feet about sea level. Owners Jean-Noël and Marketta Fourmeaux de Sartel used to be official tasters for the French government before striking out on their own in California. A dry rosé of syrah and zinfandel recalls those made in the south of France, but the excellent estate cabernet, blended with a bit of merlot, is pure Mount Veeder, with its mountain intensity. The beautiful location, with 360-degree views of the surrounding vineyards, make it worth the drive from Highway 29. ⊠*3875 Mt. Veeder Rd., 4 mi west of Rte. 29 off Oakville Grade* ☎*707/255–9440* ⊕*www.chateaupotelle. com* ⊠*Tasting $5–$10* ⊙*Daily 11–5.*

STAGS LEAP

9 Architectural understatement seems to be the rule in the Stags Leap District. Austere **Clos du Val** doesn't seduce you with dramatic architecture, but it doesn't have to: the wines, crafted by Frenchman Bernard Portet, have a wide following, especially among those who are patient enough to cellar the wines for a number of years. Though Portet's team makes great zinfandel, pinot noir, and chardonnay, the real claim to fame is the reserve cabernet. If you don't mind spending a bit more, try to visit on a weekend, when they pour reserve and library wines. Anyone is welcome to try a hand at the boccie-style game of pétanque. ⊠*5330 Silverado Trail* ☎*707/259–2200* ⊕*www.closduval. com* ⊠*Tasting $10–$20; tour free* ⊙*Daily 10–5; tour by appointment.*

10 **Chimney Rock Winery** is usually easily spotted from the road—unless the poplar trees surrounding it are in full leaf, hiding it from view. In the somewhat ornate Cape (as in Cape of Good Hope) Dutch style of the 17th century, it seems a bit out of place amid the austere Stags Leap landscape. But you have to love a winery that gradually took over a golf course, putting the land to a much nobler use. The cabernet is more elegant than wines of its caliber tend to be hereabouts, and there's also a very fine fumé blanc and dry rosé of cabernet franc. The comfortable tasting room mirrors the Cape Dutch style of the exterior, with high, wood-beamed ceilings and a fireplace that warms it in winter. ⊠*5350 Silverado Trail* ☏*707/257–2641* ⊕*www. chimneyrock.com* ⬚*Tasting $15–$25, tour $35* ⊙*Daily 10–5; tour Thurs.–Mon. at 11.*

⓫ The modest earth-colored buildings of **Stag's Leap Wine Cellars** give little hint that this is one of the most esteemed wineries in all of Napa. The winery established by Warren and Barbara Winiarski is the home of the 1973 cabernet that won the red wine section of the famous 1976 Paris tasting. Not bad for the first wine produced at their winery! The tasting room is a no-frills affair; visitors here are clearly serious about tasting wine and aren't interested in distractions like a gift shop. It costs a hefty $40 to taste the top-of-the-line wines, including their limited-production, estate-grown cabernets and Bordeaux blends. If you're interested in more modestly priced wines, try the $15 tasting, which usually includes a sauvignon blanc, chardonnay, merlot, and a cabernet. In 2007, Warren Winiarski sold the winery to a corporate partnership, but he will continue to run the place for the next few years. ⊠*5766 Silverado Trail* ☏*707/265–2441* ⊕*www.cask23.com* ⬚*Tasting $15–$40, tour $40* ⊙*Daily 10–4:30; tour by appointment.*

⓬ The tasting room at **Robert Sinskey Vineyards** resembles an oversized horse barn—fitting, since the grapes here grow on old pastureland. Inside, however, the high-ceilinged tasting room is dramatic, and an open kitchen in the back—the site of occasional cooking classes and demos— shows the influence of Robert's wife, Maria Helm Sinskey, a well-known chef and cookbook author. At first sniff and sip, you know you are onto something good in Sinskey's intense, brambly pinot noir, made from grapes grown in the Carneros region. The merlot is just as good. Tours of the cave and cellar wind up with a flight of wines, but for the best sense of how Sinskey wines pair with food, reserve a spot on the culinary tour, which includes a wine and cheese pairing after a stroll through their garden. ⊠*6320 Silverado Trail* ☏*707/944–9090* ⊕*www.robertsinskey.com*

⊠*Tasting $15–$20, tours $25–$40* ☉*Daily 10–4:30; tours by appointment.*

WHERE TO STAY & EAT

$$$$ ✕**Ad Hoc.** When superstar chef Thomas Keller opened this relatively casual spot in 2006, he meant to run it for only six months until he opened a burger joint in the same space, but locals were so charmed by the homey food that they clamored for the stopgap to stay. Now a single, seasonal fixed-price menu ($45) is served nightly. The selection might include a juicy pork loin and buttery polenta, or a delicate *panna cotta* (egg custard) with a citrus glaze. The dining room is warmly low-key, with zinc-topped tables and wine served in tumblers. You can call a day in advance for the menu. ⊠*6476 Washington St.* ☎*707/944–2487* ⊟*AE, MC, V* ☉*Closed Tues. and Wed.*

$$$$ ★ **Fodor'sChoice** ✕**French Laundry.** It's the most coveted reservation in all of California, and probably the United States: chef-owner Thomas Keller serves nine courses of exquisite French-inflected food to his pilgrims in search of a once-in-a-lifetime culinary experience. Yes, it costs a pretty penny to eat here—the menu is $240, not including wine—but that doesn't deter the diners who speed-dial the restaurant two months to the day in advance of the day they are hoping to secure a table. Keller's signature "oysters and pearls," a silky sabayon of pearl tapioca with oysters and sevruga caviar, starts the meal and sets the tone for the feast to come. The setting—an old stone house that was once actually used as a laundry—is beautifully rustic rather than opulent, and the service is impeccable. ■TIP→**Didn't make a reservation? Call on the day you'd like to dine here to be considered in the event of a cancellation.** ⊠*6640 Washington St.* ☎*707/944–2380* ⟝*Reservations essential* Jackets required ⊟*AE, MC, V* ☉*Closed 1st 2 wks in Jan. No lunch Mon.–Thurs.*

$$–$$$ ✕**Bistro Jeanty.** Philippe Jeanty's menu draws its inspiration from the cooking of his French childhood. His traditional cassoulet will warm the cockles of any Francophile's heart, and you'd be hard pressed to find a better *steak frites* in France. The service is professional and friendly, and the wine list has a good percentage of French bottlings in addition to the mandatory local ones. ■TIP→**If you're feeling romantic, ask for a seat in the back room near the fireplace.** ⊠*6510 Washington St.* ☎*707/944–0103* ⊟*AE, MC, V.*

$$–$$$ ✕ **Bouchon.** The team that brought French Laundry to its
★ current pinnacle is behind this place, where everything
from the snazzy zinc bar to the elbow-to-elbow seating to
the traditional French onion soup could have come straight
from a Parisian bistro. *Boudin noir* (blood sausage) with
potato puree and leg of lamb with white beans and *piquillo*
peppers are among the hearty dishes served in the high-ceil-
ing room. The noise level booms during peak hours, so ask
for one of the (very few) outside tables if you prefer peace
and quiet. ■TIP➔ **Late-night meals from a limited menu are
served from 10:30 PM until 12:30 AM—a rarity in the Wine Country, where it's often difficult to find a place to eat after 10 PM.**
✉*6534 Washington St.* ☎*707/944–8037* ▭*AE, MC, V.*

$$–$$$ ✕ **Mustards Grill.** There's not an ounce of pretension at Cindy
Pawlcyn's longtime Napa favorite, despite the fact that it's
booked solid almost nightly with fans of her hearty American comfort with a local twist. The menu mixes updated
renditions of traditional fare such as grilled fish, steak,
and lemon meringue pie with innovative choices such as
seared ahi tuna on homemade sesame crackers with wasabi
crème fraîche. A black-and-white marble tile floor, dark-
wood wainscoting, and upbeat artwork set a scene that's
casual but refined. Service is fast and efficient, and though
the staff seems always to be dashing about, no one ever
rushes you. Make a reservation or you may have a long
wait. ✉*7399 St. Helena Hwy./Rte. 29, 1 mi north of town*
☎*707/944–2424* ▭*AE, D, DC, MC, V.*

★ $$$$ 🛏 **Villagio Inn & Spa.** Luxury here is about calm, not bling.
Stroll past the fountains and clusters of low buildings to
reach the pool, where automated misters cool the sunbath-
ers. Streamlined furnishings, subdued color schemes, and
high ceilings enhance a sense of spaciousness in the guest
rooms. Each room also has a fireplace and, beyond lou-
vered doors, a balcony or patio. In addition to 16 treatment
rooms, a new 13,000-square-foot spa has five spa suites,
perfect for couples who want to spend the day being pam-
pered side-by-side. Rates include afternoon tea, a bottle of
wine, and a generous buffet breakfast. **Pros:** Comfortable
poolside cabanas, bountiful breakfast buffet, steps away
from many of Yountville's best restaurants. **Cons:** Prices
for interior courtyard rooms are steep, spa-construction
noise affects some rooms. ✉*6481 Washington St., 94599*
☎*707/944–8877 or 800/351–1133* ⊕*www.villagio.com*
⤳*86 rooms, 26 suites* ◊*In-room: safe, DVD, Wi-Fi. In-
hotel: room service, bar, tennis courts, pool, spa, bicycles,*

no elevator, laundry service, concierge no-smoking rooms ☐AE, D, DC, MC, V ⦿CP.

$$$$ 🖹 **Vintage Inn**. Rooms in this luxurious inn are housed in two-story villas scattered around a lush, landscaped 3½-acre property. French fabrics and plump upholstered chairs outfit spacious, airy guest rooms with vaulted beamed ceilings, all of which have a private patio or balcony, and a fireplace. All the rooms have the same luxurious bathrooms, with double sinks and whirlpool tubs large enough to share. You're treated to a bottle of wine and afternoon tea and scones. **Pros:** Spacious bathrooms, lavish breakfast buffet, luscious bedding. **Cons:** Prices for interior courtyard rooms are steep, exterior rooms get a little street noise, pool area smaller than at sister property Villagio Inn & Spa. ⊠*6541 Washington St., 94599* ☎*707/944–1112 or 800/351–1133* ⊕*www.vintageinn.com* ➡*68 rooms, 12 suites* ⚿*In-room: safe, refrigerator, DVD, Wi-Fi. In-hotel: restaurant, room service, bar, tennis courts, pool, spa, bicycles, no elevator, laundry service, concierge, no-smoking rooms, some pets allowed (fee)* ☐*AE, D, DC, MC, V* ⦿*CP.*

$$$–$$$$ 🖹 **Petit Logis**. Surrounded by Yountville's best restaurants—you could practically roll out of bed and land in Bouchon—this one-story, five-room inn used to be a row of shops. Though it doesn't look like much from the outside, inside, murals and 11-foot-high ceilings give the rooms a rakish European charm. Though the individually decorated rooms generally recall the 19th century, bathrooms have modern luxuries such as whirlpool baths big enough for two, a treat not usually found at this price in Napa. Breakfast is served at a nearby restaurant, or you can fend for yourself at the fabulous Bouchon Bakery next door. **Pros:** Good price for Yountville, huge whirlpool tubs. **Cons:** Bedding needs upgrade, office often closed, staff could be friendlier. ⊠*6527 Yount St., 94599* ☎*707/944–2332* ⊕*www.petitlogis.com* ➡*5 rooms* ⚿*In-room: refrigerator; In-hotel: no elevator, no-smoking rooms* ☐*AE, MC, V* ⦿*BP.*

★ $–$$$ 🖹 **Maison Fleurie**. If you'd like to be within easy walking distance of most of Yountville's best restaurants, and possibly score a great bargain, look into this casual, comfortable inn. Rooms share a French country style (think floral bedspreads and blooming trompe l'oeil paintings) but vary dramatically in size and amenities. The largest have a private entrance, deck, fireplace, and spa bathtub. But for a much lower rate you can get a tiny but well-kept room—

and save for a French Laundry meal instead. **Pros:** Tiniest rooms are some of the least expensive in town, free bike rental, refrigerator stocked with free sodas. **Cons:** Breakfast room crowded at peak times, some rooms look dated. ✉*6529 Yount St., 94599* ☎*800/788–0369* 🌐*www.maisonfleurienapa.com* *13 rooms* *In-room: Refrigerator (some), DVD (some), no TV (some), Wi-Fi. In-hotel: pool, bicycles, no elevator, no-smoking rooms* *AE, DC, MC, V* *CP.*

OAKVILLE

2 mi northwest of Yountville on Rte. 29.

Numbers in the margin correspond to numbers on the Napa Valley map.

Barely a blip on the landscape as you drive north on Route 29, Oakville is marked only by its eponymous store.

13 The ultimate picnic-packers stop, the small **Oakville Grocery** (✉*7856 St. Helena Hwy./Rte. 29* ☎*707/944–8802*), built in 1881 as a general store, carries a surprisingly large selection of unusual and chichi groceries and prepared foods. Despite maddening crowds that pack the narrow aisles on weekends, it's still a fine place to sit on a bench out front and sip an espresso between winery visits.

Oakville's small size belies the big mark it makes in the wine-making world. Slightly warmer than Yountville and Carneros to the south, but a few degrees cooler than Rutherford and St. Helena to the north, the Oakville area benefits from gravelly, well-drained soil in most locations. This allows roots to go deep—sometimes more than 100 feet deep—so that the vines produce intensely flavored grapes.

The winemakers who have staked their claim here are an intriguing blend of the old and the new. Big-name wineries like Far Niente, Robert Mondavi, and Opus One have been producing well-regarded wines—mostly notably cabernet sauvignon—for decades. But upstarts such as Plumpjack are getting just as much press these days. Tiny **Screaming Eagle Winery** (closed to the public) is hotter than hot these days. Founded in 1992, and with new owners and a new winemaker installed in 2006, the winery makes only about 600 cases annually of their "cult" cabernet, which sells for hundreds of dollars per bottle...*if* you're lucky enough to get your hands on one.

Across the highway from the Oakville Grocery the **Oakville Grade** (✉ *West of Rte. 29*) is a roadway snaking through the mountain range that divides Napa and Sonoma, offering breathtaking views of both valleys. Although the road surface along this twisting half-hour route is good, it can be difficult to negotiate at night, and the continual curves mean that it's not ideal for those who suffer from motion sickness.

OAKVILLE VINEYARDS

⑭ The combined venture of California winemaker Robert Mondavi and the late French baron Philippe de Rothschild, **Opus One** produces only one wine: a big, inky Bordeaux blend that was the first of Napa's ultra-premium wines, fetching unheard-of prices before it was overtaken by cult wines like Screaming Eagle. The winery's futuristic limestone-clad structure, built into the hillside, seems to be pushing itself out of the earth. Although the tour, which focuses on why it costs so much to produce this exceptional wine, comes off as a bit snooty, the facilities are undoubtedly impressive, with gilded mirrors, exotic orchids, and a large semicircular cellar modeled on the Château Mouton Rothschild winery in France. You can also taste without the tour, if you've called ahead for a reservation. ✉ *7900 St. Helena Hwy./Rte. 29* ☎ *707/944– 9442* ⊕ *www.opusonewinery.com* ✑ *Tasting $25, tour $30* ☉ *Daily 10–4; tasting and tour by appointment.*

⑮ If your only experience of **Robert Mondavi** wines is the $5 or $10 stuff you've seen in the grocery store, you might be surprised to learn that Mondavi's top wines are revered, and that perhaps no other winery has done more to promote the excellence of Napa Valley wines throughout the world. If you've never been on a winery tour before, their comprehensive introductory tour, followed by a seated tasting, is a good way to learn about oenology, as well as Robert Mondavi's role in California wine-making. If you skip the tour, head through arch at the center of the sprawling Mission-style building, and take a stroll under the arcades to the tasting rooms. Definitely consider springing for the $30 reserve room tasting, where you can enjoy four generous tastes of Mondavi's top-of-the-line wines, including their famed reserve cabernet Concerts, mostly jazz and R&B, take place in the summer on the lawn; call ahead for tickets. ✉ *7801 St. Helena Hwy./Rte. 29* ☎ *888/766–6328*

⊕*www.robertmondaviwinery.com* ⌑*Tasting* $10–$30, *tour* $25 ⊙*Daily 10–5; tour daily on the hr 10–4.*

16 ★ **Fodor'sChoice** Although the fee for the combined tour and tasting is one of the highest in the valley, **Far Niente** is worth visiting if you're tired of elbowing your way through crowded tasting rooms and are looking for a more personal experience. Here you're welcomed by name and treated to a glimpse of one of the most beautiful Napa properties. Small groups are shepherded through the 1885 tri-level stone winery for a lesson on the labor-intensive method for making Far Niente's wines, a highly touted chardonnay and cabernet sauvignon. The next stop is the Carriage House, where you'll see the founder's gleaming collection of classic race cars, which includes a 1961 Corvette roadster, a curvaceous 1954 Jaguar, and a rare, bright yellow 1951 Ferrari 340 America. The tour ends with a seated tasting of wines and cheeses, capped by a sip of the spectacular Dolce, a late-harvest dessert wine made by Far Niente's sister winery. ⊠*1 Acacia Dr.* ☎*707/944–2861* ⊕*www.farniente.com* ⌑$50 ⊙*Tasting and tour by appointment.*

17 If Opus One is the Rolls-Royce of the Oakville District— expensive, refined, and a little snooty—then **Plumpjack** is the Mini Cooper: fun, casual, and sporty. With its metal chandelier and wall hangings, the tasting room looks like it could be the stage set for a modern Shakespeare production. (The name "Plumpjack" nods to the Bard's character, Sir John Falstaff.) Dave Matthews, rather than Mozart, plays on the sound system. A St. Helena chardonnay has a good balance of baked fruit and fresh citrus flavors, while a merlot is blended with a bit of cabernet sauvignon, giving the wine enough tannins to ensure it can be aged for another five years or so. ⊠*620 Oakville Cross Rd.* ☎*707/945–1220* ⊕*www.plumpjack.com* ⌑*Tasting* $10 ⊙*Daily 10–4.*

RUTHERFORD

2 mi northwest of Oakville on Rte. 29.

You could easily drive through the tiny community of Rutherford, at the intersection of Highway 29 and Rutherford Cross Road, in the blink of an eye, but this may well be one of the most important wine-related intersections in the United States. With its singular microclimate and soil, Rutherford is an important viticultural center, with more big-name wineries than you can shake a corkscrew at, including Beaulieu, Caymus Vineyards, and Rubicon Estate.

Cabernet sauvignon is king here. The well-drained, loamy soil is ideal for those vines, and since this part of the valley gets plenty of sun, the grapes develop exceptionally intense flavors. Legendary winemaker André Tchelistcheff's famous claim that "it takes Rutherford dust to grow great cabernet" is now quoted by just about every winery in the area that produces the stuff. That "Rutherford dust" varies from one part of the region to another, but the soils here are primarily gravel, sand, and loam, a well-drained home for cabernet grapes that don't like to get their feet wet.

18 Although there are more blockbuster wineries here than you could possibly visit in a day, or even two, you might want to switch your taste buds to olive oil for an hour or two. Olive oil tasters quaff the stuff almost as you would wine, analyzing it for various characteristics and determining how different varieties might be blended together. **Round Pond** grows five varieties of Italian olives and three types of Spanish olives. Within an hour of being handpicked (sometime between October and February), the olives are crushed in the mill on the property to produce pungent, peppery oils that are later blended and sold. Call a few days in advance to arrange a tour of the mill followed by an informative tasting, during which you can sample several types of oil, both alone and with Round Pond's own red wine vinegars and other tasty foods. ✉ *877 Rutherford Rd.* ☎ *877/963-9364* ⊕ *www.roundpond.com* 🏷 *Tour $20* ☉ *Tour by appointment.*

RUTHERFORD VINEYARDS

19 Jack and Dolores Cakebread snapped up the property at **Cakebread Cellars** in 1973, after Jack fell in love with the area while visiting on a photography assignment. Since then, they've been making luscious chardonnays, as well as merlot, a pinot-syrah-zinfandel blend, a great sauvignon blanc, and a beautifully complex cabernet sauvignon. You must make an appointment for a tasting, a seated event that takes place in a wing of the winery added in 2007—look for the elevator crafted out of a stainless-steel fermentation tank and the ceiling lined with thousands of corks. Tours, also by appointment, get you a glimpse of the winery operations, as well as Dolores's kitchen garden. The

100-year-old farmhouse at the heart of the property has been turned into a culinary center, where you can sometimes attend cooking classes and demos. ⊠*8300 St. Helena Hwy.* ☏*707/963–5221* ⊕*www.cakebread.com* ⊠*Tasting $10, tour $10* ⊙*Daily 10–4:30; tasting and tour by appointment.*

❷⓪ Though you might be tempted to enter the beautifully restored 1882 farmhouse at **St. Supéry** to look for the tasting room, in fact the wines are poured in the building behind it, a bland structure that looks like it belongs in a suburban office park. You'll likely forgive the aesthetic lapse once you taste their fine wines and wander through their thoughtful exhibits. An excellent, free self-guided tour allows you a peek at the barrel and fermentation rooms, as well as a gallery of rotating art exhibits. At the ingenious "sniffing station" you can test your ability to identify different smells that might be present in wine. If you're interested in seeing the interior of the farmhouse, sign up for a guided tour. ⊠*8440 St. Helena Hwy. S/Rte. 29* ☏*707/963–4507* ⊕*www.stsupery.com* ⊠*Tasting $15–$20, tour $20* ⊙*Daily 10–5; guided tour daily at 1 and 3.*

❷① This is the house *The Godfather* built: Starting in 1975, filmmaker Francis Ford Coppola started snapping up Napa property, including both vineyards and an ivy-covered 19th-century château. In 2006, he renamed the property **Rubicon Estate**, intending to focus on his premium wines. (His less expensive wines are showcased at another winery in Geyserville.) It costs $25 to even set foot on the property, but once you're in, you're given the white-glove treatment. After a valet takes your car, a greeter hands you a "passport" that will be stamped with the names of the wines you taste. And those wines available for tasting include some of Coppola's best, including the flagship Estate Rubicon, a deep-red, cabernet-sauvignon-based blend. The entry fee also includes a spot on the Legacy Tour, which focuses on the history of the estate and is a great way to appreciate some of the architectural details of the Inglenook chateau. ⊠*1991 St. Helena Hwy./Rte. 29* ☏*707/963–9099* ⊕*www.rubiconestate.com* ⊠*$25* ⊙*Daily 10–5; tour daily at 10:30, 11:30, 12:30, 1:30, 2:30, and 3:30.*

❷② Founded in 1900 by Georges de Latour, **Beaulieu Vineyard** managed to stay open during Prohibition, making "wines for sacramental and governmental purposes." However, it wasn't until André Tchelistcheff, the man who helped define the California style of wine-making, worked his magic here from 1938 until his death in 1973, that the winery gained its international reputation. Beaulieu continues to make top-quality wines, from some reasonably priced chardonnays, merlots, and zinfandel to the higher-end reserve pinot noir and Dulcet Reserve, a cabernet-and-syrah blend. It's worth the few extra dollars to visit the reserve tasting room—more intimate and usually less crowded than the main tasting room—to try their flagship wine, the outstanding Georges de Latour Private Reserve Cabernet Sauvignon, which Beaulieu has been making since 1936. ⊠ *1960 St. Helena Hwy./Rte. 29* ☎ *707/967–5200* ⊕ *www.bvwines.com* ⛨ *Tasting $5–$25* ☉ *Daily 10–5.*

㉓ ★ Fodor's Choice **Frog's Leap** is the perfect place for wine novices to begin their education. The owners maintain a goofy sense of humor about wine that translates into an entertaining yet informative experience. What else would you expect from a place that calls one of its wines Leapfrögmilch? On the tour you'll pass through their big red barn and walk to the edge of the vineyard, where you'll learn about their organic growing techniques and see some of the solar panels that power the facilities. Their commitment to the environment is evident everywhere, from the gardens where visitors can sometimes pick the produce, to the guides' enthusiasm for the beneficial insects. During a tasting in the eco-conscious visitors center, guides pour Frog's Leap's latest zinfandel, cabernet sauvignon, merlot, and sauvignon blanc. ⊠ *8815 Conn Creek Rd.* ☎ *707/963–4704* ⊕ *www.frogsleap.com* ⛨ *Tasting and tour free* ☉ *Mon.–Sat. 10–4; tasting and tour by appointment.*

㉔ Caymus Vineyards is run by wine master Chuck Wagner, who started making wine on the property in 1972. His family, however, had been farming in the valley since 1906, when it grew prunes as well as grapes. The concentration is solely on cabernet sauvignon these days, and their flagship Special Reserve Cabernet maintains a consistently luscious quality year after year. Though you have to reserve to taste, it's worth planning ahead to visit: it's unusual to be able to taste this kind of outstanding wine for free, and the small, low-key seated tasting is a great way to learn about the valley's cabernet artistry. No tours are given, but you can see old photos of the property on the walls of the tasting room. ⊠ *8700 Conn Creek Rd.* ☎ *707/963–4204* ⊕ *www.caymus.com* ⛨ *Tasting free* ☉ *Daily 10–4; tasting by appointment.*

★ ㉕ Built in 1986, long after other French winemakers had become entrenched in the Napa Valley, **Mumm Napa Valley** made up for lost time with its excellent sparkling wines. The sparklers, served in a glass-enclosed tasting salon or on a terrace, both with a view of the vineyards, vary greatly in style. Once you've found one you like, take your glass and wander next door to the art gallery, where you'll find a permanent exhibit of Ansel Adams photographs as well as a rotating photo exhibit. Free hourly tours sketch out the traditional méthode champenoise and give you a look at a demonstration vineyard. ✉8445 Silverado Trail ☎707/967–7700 ⊕www.mummnapavalley.com ☞Tasting $5–$20, tour free ⊙Daily 10–5; tour daily on the hr 10–3.

㉖ Perched on a hill overlooking the valley, **Rutherford Hill Winery** is a merlot-lover's paradise in a cabernet sauvignon world. When the winery's founders were deciding which grapes to plant, they discovered that the climate and soil conditions of their vineyards resembled those of Pomerol, a region of Bordeaux where merlot is king. The wine caves here are some of the most extensive of any California winery—nearly a mile of tunnels and passageways. You can get a glimpse of the tunnels and the 8,000 barrels inside on the tours, then cap your visit with a picnic in their oak, olive, or madrone orchards. ✉200 Rutherford Hill Rd., east of Silverado Trail ☎707/963–7194 ⊕www.rutherfordhill.com ☞Tasting $10, tour $15 ⊙Daily 10–5; tour daily at 11:30, 1:30, and 3:30.

WHERE TO STAY & EAT

★ $$$$ ✕🖼 **Auberge du Soleil.** Taking a cue from the olive-tree-studded landscape, this renowned hotel cultivates a Mediterranean look. It's luxury as simplicity: earth-tone tile floors, heavy wood furniture, and terra-cotta colors. The spare style is backed with lavish amenities, such as plasma TVs and grand bathrooms, many with whirlpool tubs and extra-large showers with multiple showerheads. The Auberge du Soleil restaurant has an impressive wine list and serves a Mediterranean-inflected menu that relies largely on local produce. The bar serves less expensive fare until 11 PM nightly, and its terrace is the finest spot in the valley to enjoy a cocktail at sunset. **Pros:** Stunning views down the hillside, spectacular spa and pool areas, suites fit for a superstar. **Cons:** Stratospheric prices, lowest-priced rooms are small, rooms in the main house get noise from the restaurant and bar. ✉*180 Rutherford Hill Rd., off Silverado Trail north of Rte. 128, 94573* ☎*707/963–1211 or 800/348–5406* ⊕*www.aubergedusoleil.com* ⇆*18 rooms, 32 suites* ⌂*In-room: kitchen (some), refrigerator, DVD, Ethernet. In-hotel: 2 restaurants, room service, bar, tennis court, pool, gym, spa, no elevator, concierge, no-smoking rooms.* ▤*AE, D, DC, MC, V.*

2

ST. HELENA

5 mi northwest of Oakville on Rte. 29.

Numbers in the margin correspond to numbers on the Napa Valley map.

Downtown St. Helena is a symbol of how well life is lived in the Wine Country. Sycamore trees arch over Main Street (Route 29), where chic-looking visitors flit between boutiques, cafés, and storefront tasting rooms housed in sun-faded red-brick buildings. Genteel St. Helena pulls in rafts of Wine Country tourists during the day, though like most Wine Country towns it fairly rolls up the sidewalks after dark.

Many visitors never get away from the Main Street magnets—dozens of great restaurants and boutiques selling women's clothing, food and wine, and upscale housewares—but you should explore a bit farther, to stroll through quiet residential neighborhoods. A few blocks west of Main Street you'll be surrounded by vineyards, merging into the ragged wilderness edge of the Mayacamas Mountains. Several blocks east of Main Street, off Pope Street, is the Napa River, which separates St. Helena from the Silverado Trail and Howell Mountain.

Around St. Helena the valley floor narrows between the Mayacamas and Vaca mountains. These slopes reflect heat onto the 9,000 or so acres below, and since there's less fog and wind, things get pretty toasty. In fact, this is one of the hottest AVAs in Napa Valley, with midsummer temperatures often reaching the mid-90s. Bordeaux varietals are the most popular grapes grown here—especially cabernet sauvignon but also merlot. You'll also find chardonnay, petite sirah, and pinot noir in the vineyards.

Unlike many other parts of the Napa Valley, where milling grain was the primary industry until the late 1800s, St. Helena took to vines almost instantly. The town got its start in 1854 when Henry Still built a store. Still wanted company and donated lots on his town site to anyone who wanted to erect a business here. Soon his store was joined by a wagon shop, a shoe shop, hotels, and churches. Dr. George Crane planted a vineyard in 1858 and was the first to produce wine in commercially viable quantities. A German winemaker named Charles Krug followed suit a couple of years later, and other wineries soon followed.

In the late 1800s, phylloxera had begun to destroy France's vineyards and Napa Valley wines caught the world's attention. The increased demand for Napa wines spawned a building frenzy in St. Helena. Many of the mansions still gracing the town's residential neighborhoods were built around this time. Also in the late 1800s, some entrepreneurs attempted to turn St. Helena into an industrial center to supply specialized machinery to local viticulturists. Several stone warehouses were built near the railroad tracks downtown. Other weathered stone buildings on Main Street, mostly between Adams and Spring streets, and along Railroad Avenue, date from the same era. Modern facades sometimes camouflage these old-timers, but you can study the old structures by strolling the back alleys.

27 If you have a soft spot for author Robert Louis Stevenson, you could also hit the **Silverado Museum,** which displays one of the best collections of Stevenson memorabilia in the world. Early editions of his books in barrister bookcases and paintings and photographs covering the walls makes the room look something like a private library. Display cases exhibit everything from manuscripts to a lock of his hair. Stevenson's book *Silverado Squatters* was inspired by his months spent in an abandoned mining town on the slopes of nearby Mount St. Helena. ✉ *1490 Library La.* ☎ *707/963–3757* ◉ *www.silveradomuseum.org* ✉ *Donations accepted* ◷ *Tues.–Sun. noon–4.*

28 At the north end of town looms the hulking stone building of the West Coast headquarters of the **Culinary Institute of America,** the country's leading school for chefs. Housed in the imposing **Greystone Winery,** a national historic landmark, the campus consists of 30 acres of herb and vegetable gardens, a 15-acre merlot vineyard, and a Mediterranean-inspired restaurant, which is open to the public. Also on the property are a quirky corkscrew display, a culinary library, and a well-stocked culinary store that tempts aspiring chefs with its gleaming displays of stand mixers and copper cookware. ■TIP→ **One-hour cooking demonstrations (usually Friday through Monday) allow visitors a small taste of the education that students here get. The schedule varies, so call ahead.** ⊠ *2555 Main St.* ☎ *707/967–1100* ⊕ *www.ciachef.edu* ⊞ *Free, demonstrations $15* ⊙ *Restaurant Sun.–Thurs. 11:30–9, Fri. and Sat. 11:30–10; store and museum daily 10–6.*

㉙ If you're looking for a break from swirling, sniffing, and spitting, drive 3 miles north of town, off Highway 29, to visit the **Bale Grist Mill State Historic Park,** whose water-powered mill was built in 1846 and partially restored in 1925. A short trail from the parking lot leads to the mill and granary, where exhibits explain the milling process. Try to schedule a visit on the weekend, when a docent occasionally offers milling demonstrations. A trail leads from the park to Bothe–Napa Valley State Park, where you can pick up a number of hiking trails or linger for a picnic. ⊠ *Hwy. 29, 3 mi north of St. Helena* ☎ *707/942–4575* ⊞ *Park free, mill buildings $3* ⊙ *Daily 10–5.*

VINEYARDS AROUND ST. HELENA

㉚ ★ **Fodor'sChoice** Although an appointment is required to taste at **Joseph Phelps Vineyards,** it's worth the trouble. In fair weather wine tastings are held on the terrace of a huge, modern barnlike building with views down the slopes over oak trees and orderly vines. Though the sauvignon blanc and chardonnay are good, the blockbuster wines are reds, like the intense, jammy Le Mistral, a blend made primarily of syrah and grenache. The 2002 vintage of their superb Bordeaux-style blend called Insignia was selected as *Wine Spectator*'s wine of the year, immediately pushing up prices and demand. Luckily, you'll get a taste of the current vintage of Insignia (it's fairly rare that tasting rooms will pour such highly coveted wines, in this case one that goes for more than $150 a bottle). ⊠ *200 Taplin Rd.* ☎ *707/963–2745* ⊕ *www.jpvwines.com* ⊞ *Tasting $20* ⊙ *Weekdays 9–5, weekends 9–4; tasting by appointment.*

㉛ Right next door to the ivy-covered fieldstone buildings of the Tra Vigne restaurant complex sits **Merryvale Vineyards,** a good place to save for the end of a day, since the winery stays open until 6:30 PM, considerably later than most others. Among the wines, a red Meritage blend called Profile is worth trying, as are a few of the chardonnays. For the full

Merryvale experience, reserve a spot in the weekend Wine Component Tasting seminar ($20). A walk through the winery winds up in the enchanting Cask Room, where the guides focus on wine's essential components—sugar, alcohol, acid, and tannins—and discuss how these elements are balanced by the vintner. ⊠ *1000 Main St.* ☎ *707/963–2225* ⊕ *www.merryvale.com* 🍷 *$5–$20* ⊙ *Daily 10–6; weekend seminars at 10:30.*

❸❷ Arguably the most beautiful winery in Napa Valley, the 1876 **Beringer Vineyards** is also the oldest continuously operating property. The meticulously landscaped grounds, historic mansions, and Beringer's big-name recognition make this one of the most-visited wineries in Napa. ■**TIP→ If you're looking for an undiscovered gem, keep on driving, but if you're a newbie who's interested in learning more about the history of the Napa Valley or about the pairing of wine with food, Beringer makes a great first stop.** The introductory tour gives you a glimpse of the tunnels dug by Chinese laborers in the 19th century. For an additional fee, longer tours and seminars focus on more in-depth topics, such as the property's history, the wine-making process, and wine-and-food pairings. ⊠ *2000 Main St./Rte. 29* ☎ *707/963–4812* ⊕ *www.beringer.com* 🍷 *Tasting $5–$20, tour $10* ⊙ *Late May–late Oct., daily 10–6; late Oct.–late May, daily 10–5; tour daily at 10:45, 1:30, and 2.*

❸❸ At **St. Clement Vineyards,** the Rosenbaum House, a beautifully restored 1878 home, houses a tiny tasting room. Originally built as a family home, the Victorian mansion is now notable for its splendid views from the swing and café tables on the front porch. Tours of the property reveal details about the mansion's history, as well as the workings of the winery in back. Only about 10 percent of the fruit for their wines is grown on the estate; instead, they purchase wine from about a dozen different vineyards to produce their sauvignon blanc, chardonnay, merlot, and cabernet sauvignon. Their most impressive offering is a full-bodied Bordeaux-style blend called Oroppas, a holdover from the days when the winery was owned by Sapporo (read it backwards). ⊠ *2867 St. Helena Hwy.* ☎ *707/963–7221* ⊕ *www.stclement.com* 🍷 *Tasting $10–$25, tour $20* ⊙ *Daily 10–5; tour daily at 10:30 and 2:30.*

★ ❸❹ **Spring Mountain Vineyard** was once the best-known winery in the Napa Valley, not because its chardonnay came in fourth in the famous 1976 Paris tasting but because it

2

served as a setting for the 1980s television soap opera *Falcon Crest*. Luckily, the association with big hair and big shoulder pads has been erased by the development of big cabernets. Still, semi-obscure Spring Mountain, hidden off a winding road behind a security gate, has the feeling of a private estate. Though a small amount of sauvignon blanc is produced, the calling card here is cabernet—big, chewy wines that demand some time in the bottle but promise great things. Tours meander through the beautiful property, from the cellars, a portion of which were dug by Chinese immigrants in the 1880s, to a 120-year-old-barn, to the beautifully preserved 1885 mansion, where tastings take place in the dining room. ✉ *2805 Spring Mountain Rd.* ☎ *707/967–4188* ⊕ *www.springmtn.com* ⌂ *Tour and tasting $25* ☉ *Tour and tasting by appointment.*

🟢 ★ **Fodor'sChoice** When visiting **Stony Hill Vineyard**, it's easy to imagine that this is what the Napa Valley was like 20 years ago, before many of the wineries started building glitzy visitors centers and charging tasting fees. From its secluded perch north of St. Helena, where you see nothing but rolling hills between stands of oak and cypress trees, there's no trace of the busloads of tourists zipping along Highway 29 just a few miles away. ■TIP➔ **The tour is about as low-key as they come, and the guide is apt to simply answer visitors' questions rather than launching into a canned spiel.** The tour ends up on the terrace of the winery owners' home (or in their great room in bad weather), reinforcing the welcoming, rustic feel of the property. Here you'll try their excellent unoaked chardonnay, which skips the usual malolactic fermentation of California chards to emphasize the pure flavor of the chardonnay grapes. ✉ *3331 St. Helena Hwy. N/Rte. 29* ☎ *707/963 2636* ⊕ *www.stonyhillvineyard.com* ⌂ *Tasting and tour free* ☉ *Tasting and tour by appointment.*

🟢 Most people who have heard of **Domaine Charbay Winery and Distillery** know of their flavored vodkas, infused with ingredients like blood oranges, Meyer lemons, and green tea, but there's much more going on at this rustic property 5 mi uphill from St. Helena. On the casual one-hour tour you'll learn about their other passions, like crafting small batches of rum, whiskey, grappa, and pastis. You're likely to meet one or more members of the Karakasevic family, the owners, who have been in the distilling business for thirteen generations. Though most of the distilling is actually done in Mendocino County, here you can see an alembic

CLOSE UP

Napa's Back Roads

It's not hard to escape the maddening crowds on Highway 29, despite Napa Valley being the most touristed Wine Country destination. East of Calistoga and St. Helena, over a ridge from the Napa Valley floor, the Chiles Valley and Howell Mountain AVAs seem a universe away from the rest of Napa County. Instead of being stuck in traffic behind a BMW convertible, you're more likely to have to slow down for lumbering farm machinery or a deer darting across the road.

The rugged heights of the Howell Mountain AVA are spread out over 14,000 acres, but a mere 600 or so are planted with vines. However, this will surely change in the next several years, as vintners vie for coveted permits to clear the dense forests of the high, rolling plateau, and plant vines. Though visitors are still few and far between here—in part because many of the wineries are not open to the public— Howell Mountain seems poised to become the next big thing.

Grapes were first planted in Chiles Valley and neighboring Pope Valley in 1854. Today, the forest has reclaimed formerly cultivated land, but you can still tell the course of the old road by the moss-covered stone walls along its margins. Here and there in the woods you'll discover the ruins of an abandoned winery, and you may stumble over an ancient vine hanging in among the oaks, laurels, and pines.

The region's one quirky tourist attraction is **Litto's Hubcap Ranch** (Pope Valley Road, near Pope Valley Winery), a private home where every fence, tree, and building is plastered with hubcaps. The creator of this odd folk art project, Emanuele "Litto" Dimonte, died in 1985, but his family has kept the thousands of hubcaps he spent years collecting. Though the property is strictly off limits to visitors, you can appreciate Litto's handiwork glinting in the sun as you drive by.

The following are some of the wineries in the area that are open to the public:

Ladera Vineyards. *Ladera* means "hillside" in Spanish, and that alone tells you a lot about this winery, which harvests its grapes from two vineyards on far sides of the Napa Valley: one on rugged and steep Mt. Veeder, on the west side of the valley, and the other on Howell Mountain to the east. Though full-bodied cabernets are Ladera's claim to fame, it also produces a bit of malbec and sauvignon blanc. Tours of the property, which include a glimpse of the underground caves, are available by appointment every day but

Sunday. ✉ *150 White College Rd. South* ☎ *707/965–2445* ⊕ *www.laderavineyards.com.*

Langtry Estate & Vineyards. A gravel driveway leads to this hilltop winery, built to resemble the old Langtry barn that still stands about 2 mi south of the winery, but with a difference—the newer facility is the size of a football field. Langtry owns a whopping 22,000 acres and produces about 150,000 cases a year. Still, it feels like a much smaller operation, and the few visitors in the tasting room are likely to be friends and neighbors of the staff. ✉ *21000 Butts Canyon Rd.* ☎ *707/987–2385* ⊕ *www. langtryestate.com.*

Pope Valley Winery. You may have to peek into the barrel room to find someone to pour wines for you in this simple tasting room with a corrugated tin roof. That's because this rustic little winery producing about 4,000 cases a year doesn't get that many visitors. You'll be warmly welcomed with free tasting of their wines. Tours are not regularly scheduled, but you can ask whether anyone has time to show you around. ✉ *6613 Pope Valley Rd.* ☎ *707/965–1246* ⊕ *www. popevalleywinery.com.*

RustRidge Winery. Though it's only a 15-minute drive from the Napa that most visi-

tors know, secluded RustRidge seems more like Oklahoma or Montana than the California Wine Country. Signs on Lower Chiles Valley Road point you toward their property, where you'll wind your way past barns, horse paddocks, and rusting farm equipment before finding the tasting room. The property was purchased by the Meyer family in 1972 as a thoroughbred horse ranch, and one of the owners continues to breed and train horses here. The family also runs a five-room bed-and-breakfast on site. ✉ *2910 Lower Chiles Valley Rd.* ☎ *707/965–9353* ⊕ *www.popevalleywinery.com.*

copper pot and learn the basics of distillation. They make a small quantity of wine—mostly cabernet sauvignon and port—as well as an excellent, not-too-sweet aperitif wine made from chardonnay and brandy liqueur. By law they're not allowed to offer tastings of their distilled spirits, but a tour concludes with wine tasting. ⊠ *4001 Spring Mountain Rd.* ☎ *707/963–9327* ⊕ *www.charbay.com* ⊠ *Tour and tasting $20* ☉ *Tour and tasting by appointment.*

❸ Although the reputation of merlot has taken a hit, thanks largely to movie *Sideways,* many agree that the merlots at **Duckhorn Vineyards** are some of the finest made anywhere. In fact, Duckhorn fans tend to be so dedicated to their merlots that they sometimes forget there is some fine cabernet sauvignon and sauvignon blanc produced here as well. The airy, high-ceilinged tasting room in the modern arts-and-crafts-style building looks more like a sleek restaurant than your typical tasting room, and you'll be seated at a table and served by staffers who make the rounds to pour. Reservations are required for tours and tastings, although walk-ins are often accommodated on weekdays. ⊠ *1000 Lodi La.* ☎ *707/963–7108* ⊕ *www.duckhorn.com* ⊠ *Tasting $20, tour free* ☉ *Daily 10–4; tour daily at 1* PM.

WHERE TO STAY & EAT

$$$$ ✕ **Martini House.** Beautiful and boisterous, St. Helena's most stylish restaurant occupies a converted 1923 Craftsman-style home, where earthy colors are made even warmer by the glow of three fireplaces. Woodsy ingredients such as chanterelles or juniper berries might accompany sweetbreads or a hearty grilled loin of venison. Inventive salads and delicate desserts such as the blood-orange sorbet demonstrate chef-owner Todd Humphries' range; rare bottlings on the knockout wine list include several Napa Valley cult wines. In warm weather, angle for a table on the patio, where lights sparkle in the trees. ⊠ *1245 Spring St.* ☎ *707/963–2233* ▭ *AE, D, DC, MC, V* ☉ *No lunch Mon.–Thurs.*

★ Fodor's Choice ✕ **Terra.** The look may be old-school romance,
$$$–$$$$ with candlelit tables in an 1884 fieldstone building, but the cooking is deliciously of the moment. The eclectic food dreamt up by chef Hiro Sone is inventive but not outré; it draws mostly from French and Italian cuisines, but with unexpected Asian twists that make Sone's dishes truly delightful. He shows just the right touch with quail,

which may be served with eggplant and goat cheese, and the grilled duck with duck-liver wontons manages an East-West harmony that other chefs vainly strive to achieve. Complex desserts, courtesy of Sone's wife, Lissa Doumani, might include a maple sugar crème brûlée served in a baked apple. Servers gracefully and unobtrusively attend to every dropped fork or half-full water glass. ☒ *1345 Railroad Ave.* ☎ *707/963–8931* ◈ *Reservations essential* ▭ *DC, MC, V* ☾ *Closed Tues. and 1st 2 wks in Jan. No lunch.*

$$–$$$$ ✕**Wine Spectator Greystone Restaurant.** Though this bustling restaurant housed in the cavernous old Christian Brothers Winery is on the campus of the Culinary Institute of America, rest assured that there are professional chefs rather than students behind the stoves. And, in fact, you can see those chefs hard at work at several cooking stations in full view of the dining room. (Romantics who want to ensure their dinner companions pay more attention to them than to the chefs might want to opt for one of the seats on the patio with vineyard views.) The frequently changing Mediterranean-influenced menu emphasizes local ingredients: the grilled hanger steak might be served with a Point Reyes blue-cheese tart, and in summer you might find a Sonoma organic chicken with a salad of arugula and grilled corn. ☒ *2555 Main St.* ☎ *707/967–1010* ▭ *AE, D, DC, MC, V.*

$–$$$ ✕**Go Fish.** Prolific restaurateur Cindy Pawlcyn and superstar chef Victor Scargle are the familiar names behind one of the few big-name restaurants in the Wine Country to specialize in seafood. You can either sit at the long marble bar and watch the chefs whip up inventive sushi rolls and other raw-bar bites, or head into the dining room to study the long, mouthwatering menu. The large, lively space works an industrial-chic look, with stainless steel lamps and comfortable banquettes. You might try miso-marinated black cod, clam chowder, or a rich crab-cake sandwich served on a brioche bun. Or have your choice of fish prepared in one of three ways with one of five sauces. ☒ *641 Main St.* ☎ *707/963–0700* ▭ *AE, D, DC, MC, V.*

$–$$$ ✕**Market.** All-American favorites like meat loaf with mashed potatoes and macaroni and cheese are equal parts familiar and refined at this unusually welcoming spot in downtown St. Helena. Locally farmed produce, California farmstead cheeses, and other choice ingredients elevate the homey dishes. Waiters and bartenders greet the regulars by name, and visitors are received just as warmly. Native fieldstone walls and a bar from the late 1800s that reportedly came from San Francisco's Palace Hotel make an attractive backdrop. The entrées tend to be so substantial that it's a challenge to save room for a root-beer float or one of the delicious fruit crisps. ⊠*1347 Main St.* ☎*707/963–3799* ⊟*AE, MC, V.*

$–$$ ✕**Pizzeria Tra Vigne.** Early in the evening families with kids flock to the outdoor tables at this casual pizzeria. Later on, young couples gather around the pool table or watch the game on the plasma TV. At any time of day you'll find fabulous, crisp, thin-crust pizzas, like the unusual Positano, with sautéed shrimp and crescenza cheese. Salads and pasta round out the menu. Service is friendly, if not particularly speedy. ⊠*1016 Main St.* ☎*707/967–9999* ⊟*D, MC, V.*

★ ¢–$ ✕**Taylor's Automatic Refresher.** A slick 1950s-style outdoor hamburger stand goes upscale at this hugely popular spot, where locals are willing to brave lines 20-people deep to order juicy burgers and garlic fries. But in an only-in-the-Wine-Country twist, almost many people order a bottle of wine as a root-beer float, and rare ahi burgers come off the grill quicker than patty melts. Arrive early or late for lunch, or prepare to wait for a spot at one of the shaded picnic tables on the lawn. ⊠*933 Main St.* ☎*707/963–3486* ⊟*AE, MC, V.*

$$$$ ★ Fodor'sChoice ✕⊡**Meadowood Resort.** Everything at Meadowood seems to run seamlessly, starting with the gatehouse staff who alert the front desk to arrivals, so that a receptionist is ready for each guest. Rooms, spread out in various cottages and lodges, have expansive windows that look out over the sprawling wooded grounds, making you feel like a guest at a very rich friend's New England country estate. The supremely comfortable beds defy you to get up in time to take advantage of the many activities—there's even a professional croquet course. The concierge is a whiz at getting reservations at booked-up restaurants, but you should eat at least once in the hotel's elegant-but-unstuffy dining room. Overhauled in 2006, The Restaurant at Meadowood is becoming a dining destination for its luxe dishes (think lobster with black truffles) and expert service. **Pros:** Has one of Napa's best restaurants, lovely onsite hiking trail, serene atmosphere. **Cons:** Very expensive, Wi-Fi can be dodgy in spots. ⊠*900 Meadowood La., 94574* ☎*707/963–3646 or 800/458–8080* ⊕*www.meadowood. com* ⇨*40 rooms, 45 suites* ⌂*In-room: refrigerator, DVD,*

Wi-Fi. In-hotel: 2 restaurants, room service, bar, golf course, tennis courts, pools, gym, no elevator, concierge, no-smoking rooms =AE, D, DC, MC, V.

$$$$ ⊤**Wine Country Inn.** A pastoral landscape of hills surrounds this peaceful New England–style retreat. Rooms are comfortably done with homey furniture like four-poster beds topped with quilts, and many have a wood-burning fireplace, a private hot tub, or a patio or balcony overlooking the vineyards. A hearty breakfast is served buffet-style in the sun-splashed common room, and wine and appetizers are available in the afternoon. The thoughtful staff and vineyard views from many rooms encourage many people to return year after year. **Pros:** Free shuttle to selected restaurants (if reserved early), staff treat you like family. **Cons:** Some rooms suffer from noise from neighbors. ✉*1152 Lodi La., east of Rte. 29, 94574* ☎*707/963-7077* ⊕*www.winecountryinn.com* ➳*24 rooms, 5 suites* △*In-room: refrigerator, no TV, Wi-Fi. In-hotel: pool, no elevator, no-smoking rooms* =*MC, V* ⊚*BP.*

$$$ ⊤**Ambrose Bierce House.** America's favorite literary curmudgeon, Ambrose Bierce, lived here until 1913, when he became bored with the peaceful wine valley and vanished into Pancho Villa's Mexico, never to be seen or heard from again. The vibe at his namesake inn is blast-from-the-past Victorian—buttery yellow tones and a generally lacey feel—but the amenities in the four rooms and suites are strictly up to date. If you're interested in Bierce's writings, you can browse the inn's bookshelves for some of his books. **Pros:** Hot tub, enormous bathtubs, within walking distance of many St. Helena restaurants. **Cons:** Breakfast served only at 9 AM, fire-station siren across the street occasionally goes off. ✉*1515 Main St., 94574* ☎*707/963-3003* ⊕*www.ambrosebiercehouse.com* ➳*2 rooms, 2 suites* △*In-room: Wi-Fi. In-hotel: no elevator, no-smoking rooms* =*D, MC, V* ⊚*BP.*

$–$$$ ⊤**El Bonita Motel** Only in ritzy St. Helena would a basic room in a roadside motel cost around $200 a night in high season. Still, for budget-minded travelers the tidy rooms here are pleasant enough, and the landscaped grounds and picnic tables elevate the property over similar places. Family-friendly pluses include roll-away beds and cribs for a modest extra charge. Its location right on Route 29 makes it convenient, but light sleepers should ask for rooms farthest from the road. A few of the rooms have hot tubs. Pros: Cheerful rooms, hot tub, microwaves. Cons: Road noise is problem in some rooms, service is basic at best. ⊠*195 Main St./Rte. 29, 94574* ☎*707/963–3216 or 800/541–3284* ⊕*www.elbonita.com* ⋈*37 rooms, 4 suites* ⬧*In-room: kitchen, refrigerator, Wi-Fi. In-hotel: pool, no elevator, public Internet, no-smoking rooms, some pets allowed (fee)* ⊟*AE, D, DC, MC, V* ⑩*CP.*

NIGHTLIFE & THE ARTS

A nightcap at one of St. Helena's great restaurants serves as all the nightlife most visitors need, but if want to let your hair down, **Ana's Cantina** (⊠*1205 Main St.* ☎*707/963–4921*) serves up Mexican food, margaritas, and Thursday-night karaoke to a raucous crowd of locals. The art-nouveau **Cameo Cinema** (⊠*1340 Main St.* ☎*707/963–9779* ⊕*www.cameocinema.com*) screens first-run and art-house movies, as well as occasional live performances. Beautifully restored under the direction of Charlotte Wagner, one of the owners of Caymus Vineyards, the 140-seat theater has three rows of couches for the romantically inclined.

SHOPPING

Most of St. Helena's stores are clustered along bucolic Main Street, where 19th-century redbrick buildings recall the town's past, making it a particularly pleasant place to while away an afternoon of window shopping. **On the Vine** (⊠*1234 Main St.* ☎*707/963–2209*) sells one-of-a-kind wearable art and unique jewelry made by local artisans. Look for whimsical purses that could easily be mistaken for a bouquet of flowers and lustrous earrings that resemble a cluster of grapes. **Footcandy** (⊠*1239 Main St.* ☎*707/963–2040*) thrills shoe hounds with its provocative displays of precarious stilettos and high-heeled boots. Thousand-dollar handbags by Marc Jacobs are just the thing to go with Christian Louboutin peep-toe slingbacks or Jimmy Choo snakeskin-trim sandals.

The airy **I. Wolk Gallery** (⊠*1354 Main St.* ☎*707/963–8800*) has works by established and emerging American art-ists—everything from abstract and contemporary realist paintings to high-quality works on paper and sculpture. Contemporary American, European, and Latin American paintings and sculptures are illuminated by a skylight in the **Caldwell Snyder** (⊠*1328 Main St.* ☎*707/200–5050*) gallery. Elaborate confections handmade on the premises are displayed like miniature works of art at **Woodhouse Chocolate** (⊠*1367 Main St.* ☎707/963–8413), a lovely shop that resembles an 18th-century Parisian salon.

The **Spice Islands Marketplace** (⊠*Culinary Institute of America, 2555 Main St.* ☎888/424–2433), north of downtown St. Helena, is the place to shop for all things related to preparing food, from cookbooks to corn zippers. You can often find signed copies of cookbooks by local chefs. Just south of downtown, **Dean & Deluca** (⊠*607 St. Helena Hwy. S/Rte. 29* ☎707/967–9980), a branch of the famous Manhattan store, has everything you could need for a decadent—and expensive—picnic, from a charcuterie counter to produce, pastries, wine, and an espresso bar. Hard-to-find luxury items, like truffle-scented salt and imported chocolates, make it a good spot for food-related gifts. In the middle of Main Street's upscale boutiques, **Jan de Luz** (⊠*1219 Main St.* ☎707/963–1550) sells sumptuous French linens, like dish towels from Provence, along with bath products and gift items in a shop full of reproduction antique furniture.

CALISTOGA

3 mi northwest of St. Helena on Rte. 29.

Numbers in the margin correspond to numbers on the Napa Valley map.

False-fronted shops, 19th-century hotels, and unpretentious cafés lining Lincoln Avenue, the main drag, give Calistoga a slightly rough-and-tumble feel that's unique in the Napa Valley. With Mount St. Helena rising to the north and visible from downtown, it looks a bit like a cattle town tucked into a remote mountain valley. It's easier to find a bargain here than farther down the valley, making Calistoga's quiet, tree-shaded streets and mellow bed-and-breakfasts an affordable home base for exploring the surrounding vineyards and back roads.

Ironically, Calistoga was developed as a ritzy vacation getaway. In 1859, Sam Brannan—Mormon missionary, entrepreneur, and vineyard developer—learned about a place in the upper Napa Valley, called Agua Caliente by the settlers, that was peppered with hot springs and even had an "old faithful" geyser. He snapped up 2,000 acres of prime property and laid out a resort. Planning a place that would rival New York's famous Saratoga Hot Springs, he built an elegant hotel, bathhouses, cottages, stables, an observatory, and a distillery (a questionable choice for a Mormon missionary). Brannan's gamble didn't pay off as he'd hoped, but Californians kept coming to "take the waters," supporting a sprinkling of small hotels and bathhouses built wherever a hot spring bubbled to the surface. These getaways are still going, and you can come for an old-school experience of a mud bath or a dip in a warm spring-fed pool.

38 Founded by Ben Sharpsteen, an animator for Walt Disney who retired to Calistoga, the small **Sharpsteen Museum** has a detailed diorama of the Calistoga Hot Springs Resort in its heyday. Other permanent and rotating exhibits are dedicated to the region's past, from its prehistory to World War II. Next to the museum is the Sam Brannan Cottage, built by the town's founder in the 1860s and one of only three in town to survive from the era. Take a peek at the lavishly furnished period interior. ⊠*1311 Washington St.* ☎*707/942–5911* ⊕*www.sharpsteen-museum.org* ⚏*$3 donation* ⊙*Daily 11–4.*

VINEYARDS AROUND CALISTOGA

39 The tasting room at **Dutch Henry Winery** isn't much more than a nook in the barrel room between towering American and French oak barrels full of their excellent cabernet sauvignon. The winery produces only about 6,000 cases annually—sold mostly on-site and through their wine club—but the wines are truly top-notch. Look for good chardonnay and merlot, and an inky syrah that's grown on the estate. ⊠*4300 Silverado Trail* ☎*707/942–5771* ⊕*www.dutchhenry.com* ⚏*Tasting $10* ⊙*Daily 10–5; tasting by appointment.*

40 ★ **Fodor's**Choice **Schramsberg,** tucked into an idyllic dell on a slope rising from Route 29, is one of Napa's oldest wineries and produces a bunch of bubblies made using the traditional méthode champenoise process. If you want to taste, you must tour first, but what a tour: in addition to seeing the winery's historic architecture (one building was constructed by a ship builder, entirely without metal fastenings), you'll also tour the cellars dug in the late 19th century by Chinese laborers, where a mind-boggling 2 million bottles are stacked in gravity-defying configurations.

Best Wine Country Spas

You don't have to look far to find a spa that will massage, scrub, or soak you into a blissed-out stupor. Spas in Napa and Sonoma have two special angles. First, there are the local mud baths and mineral-water sources, concentrated particularly around Calistoga. Admittedly, not everyone is enamored with dipping into a thick, muddy paste. But once you've had a few minutes to get used to the intense heat and peaty smell, you may never want to leave. Second, there are all those grapes: their seeds, skins, and vines have antioxidant and other healthful properties, claim those who use them in scrubs, lotions, and other spa products.

Below are some of the best spas of the bunch.

Dr. Wilkinson's. Although the oldest spa in Calistoga isn't exactly chic, it's still well loved for its reasonable prices and its friendly, unpretentious vibe. They use a mix of volcanic ash and peat moss in their mud baths. ⊠ *1507 Lincoln Ave., Calistoga* ☎ *707/942–4102* ⊕ *www.drwilkinson.com.*

Fairmont Sonoma Mission Inn & Spa. This is easily the biggest of the Wine Country spas, with several pools and Jacuzzis fed by local thermal mineral springs, steam and dry saunas, and even a dedicated Watsu pool. It's all very well done, but quite crowded on summer weekends. ⊠ *100 Boyes Blvd./Rte. 12, Boyes Hot Springs* ☎ *707/938–9000* ⊕ *www.fairmont.com/sonoma.*

Health Spa Napa Valley. Playing down the fancy products, this spa instead concentrates on healing and rejuvenating the whole body, with private yoga and Pilates classes, personal trainers, and an outdoor pool in addition to the usual spa fare. The grapeseed mud wrap, during which you're slathered with mud while your feet and scalp are massaged, is a more decadent alternative to a mud bath. ⊠ *1030 Main St., St. Helena* ☎ *707/967–8800* ⊕ *www.napavalleyspa.com.*

Kenwood Inn & Spa. "Vinotherapie" treatments— massages, scrubs, and facials based on grape extracts—are a specialty. Though their techniques may be French, the property calls Italy to mind. Persimmon and lemon trees shade several courtyards at the sprawling Tuscan-style villa, where guests of the hotel and spa goers lounge in a number of pools, whirlpools, and saunas. ⊠ *10400 Sonoma Hwy./Rte. 12, Kenwood* ☎ *707/833–1293* ⊕ *www.kenwoodinn.com.*

The tour fee includes generous pours of three very different sparkling wines, as well as one still wine. ⊠*1400 Schramsberg Rd.* ☎*707/942–4558* ⊕*www.schramsberg.com* ⊡*Tasting and tour $25* ⊙*Daily 10–4; tasting and tour by appointment.*

★ ④ Possibly the most astounding sight in all of Napa Valley is your first glimpse of **Castello di Amorosa**, which looks for all the world like a medieval castle, complete with drawbridge and moat, a chapel, stables, and secret passageways. It is the brainchild of Daryl Sattui, whose passion for Italy and for medieval architecture is apparent down to the last obsessive detail. Some of the 107 rooms contain replicas of 13th-century frescos, and the dungeon has an actual "iron maiden" torture device from Nuremberg, Germany. Immediately after opening in 2007, the winery started attracting large crowds lured by the astonishing architecture. The Italian-style wines, available at the winery only, are excellent as well. Reds like cabernet sauvignon and merlot come from grapes grown on the estate, while the whites might have been grown in Mendocino County or the Anderson Valley. ⊠*4045 North St. Helena Hwy.* ☎*707/967–6272* ⊕*www.castellodiamorosa.com* ⊡*Tasting $10–$20; tours $25–$35 weekdays, $30–$40 weekends* ⊙*Daily 9:30–6; tours by appointment.*

☾ ㊷ The approach to **Sterling Vineyards,** about a mile south of Calistoga, is the most spectacular in the valley. Instead of driving up to their tasting room, you board an aerial tramway to reach the pristine, white, Mediterranean-style buildings perched on a hilltop. (The tram is a big hit with kids.) Once up top, you can follow a short self-guided walking tour, with more impressive views over the valley, before taking a seat on the shady terrace for tasting of five different wines. If you're pacing yourself, skip right to the pinot noir and cabernet. The wines, though generally affordable, don't always match up to the vista. ⊠*1111 Dunaweal La., east off Rte. 29* ☎*707/942–3300* ⊕*www.sterlingvineyards. com* ⊡*$15, $20 weekends and holidays, including tramway, self-guided tour, and tasting* ⊙*Daily 10:30–4:30.*

㊸ Outrageously individual, **Clos Pegase** is a refreshing palate cleanser after visiting one too many tasting rooms in the same faux-French or imitation-Italian style. Designed by postmodern architect Michael Graves, the winery is a one-of-a-kind "temple to wine and art" packed with unusual art objects from the collection of owner and publishing entrepreneur Jan Shrem. After tasting the wines, which include a bright sauvignon blanc and mellow pinot noir, merlot, and cabernet, be sure to check out the surrealist paintings near the main tasting room and at the curvaceous Henry Moore sculpture in the courtyard. ✉ *1060 Dunaweal La., east off Rte. 29* ☎ *707/942–4981* ⊕ *www. clospegase.com* ☞ *Tasting $10; tour free* ⊙ *Daily 10:30–5; tour daily at 11 and 2.*

㊹ Tucked into a rock face in the Mayacamas range, **Storybook Mountain Vineyards** is one of the most dramatic wineries in the Wine Country, with vines rising steeply from the winery in theatrical tiers. Zinfandel is king here, and they even make a Zin Gris, an unusual dry rosé of zinfandel grapes. (Traditionally, in Burgundy, *vin gris*—pale rosé—is made from pinot noir grapes.) Storybook's tasting room, in a vaulted cavern connecting two of the tunnels, may well be the most atmospheric in the Napa Valley. Unlike many tunnels and caverns in the area, which are often reinforced with concrete or other modern materials, most of the rough-hewn tunnels here still look as they did when Chinese laborers painstakingly dug them around 1888. ✉ *3835 Highway 128* ☎ *707/942–5310* ⊕ *www.storybookwines.com* ☞ *Free* ⊙ *Tours and tasting by appointment.*

㊺ Quirky **Château Montelena** is the architectural equivalent of a mash-up: the 19th-century, vine-covered building suggests France, but the lake below it is surrounded by Chinese-inspired gardens and dotted with islands topped by Chinese pavilions. For the best view of the odd combination, take the path to the right of the tasting room down to the lake. From here the château, with its little turrets and ornamental crenellations, looks like it's straight out of a fairy tale. In the tasting room, make a beeline for the bright chardonnay, whose bright citrus and green apple flavors shine through, since the wine doesn't undergo malolactic fermentation. Also give the estate-grown cabernet sauvignon a whirl. Reservations are required for the tour. ✉ *1429 Tubbs La.* ☎ *707/942–5105* ⊕ *www.montelena. com* ☞ *Tasting $15–$25, tour $25* ⊙ *Daily 9:30–4. Tour at 2 daily, by appointment.*

OFF THE BEATEN PATH Seven miles north of Calistoga, **Robert Louis Stevenson State Park** encompasses the summit of Mount St. Helena. It was here, in the summer of 1880, in an abandoned bunkhouse of the Silverado Mine, that Stevenson and his bride,

Fanny Osbourne, spent their honeymoon. The stay inspired Stevenson's *The Silverado Squatters,* and Spyglass Hill in *Treasure Island* is thought to be a portrait of Mount St. Helena. The park's approximately 3,600 acres are mostly undeveloped except for a fire trail leading to the site of the bunkhouse—which is marked with a marble tablet—and to the summit beyond. Although the hike to the top of Mount St. Helena isn't exactly a walk in the park—the steep trail tends to get even steeper just when you're wishing it wouldn't—the views are a wonderful payoff. As you near the peak, you'll get a sudden, dramatic look at the Napa Valley stretching south from the foot of the mountains to the salt marshes of San Pablo Bay. The hills of Sonoma County ripple to the west. ■TIP→ If you plan to hike to the top, bring plenty of water and dress appropriately: the trail is steep and lacks shade in spots, but the summit is often cool and breezy. To reach the park, drive up Highway 29 north of Calistoga to the crest of the road, where there are two large dirt parking areas on either side of the highway (a small sign reading ROBERT LOUIS STEVENSON STATE PARK warns you it's coming up). ⊠ *Rte. 29, 7 mi north of Calistoga* ☎ *707/942–4575* ⊕ *www.parks.ca.gov* ⊠ *Free* ⊗ *Daily sunrise–sunset.*

WHERE TO STAY & EAT

$$–$$$$ ✕ **Brannan's Grill.** Arts-and-crafts-style lamps cast a warm glow over the booths and tables at this popular spot. The cooking is hearty but not stuck in tradition; look for a red-wine-braised lamb shank served with a porcini-risotto cake, or sage gnocchi with a rabbit Bolognese sauce. An attractive, well-stocked bar is a congenial spot for cocktails, and live jazz on weekends makes it one of the livelier places in town for a night out. ⊠ *1374 Lincoln Ave.* ☎ *707/942–2233* ▭ *AE, D, MC, V.*

★ $–$$$ ✕ **All Seasons Café.** Bistro cuisine takes a California spin in this sun-filled space, where tables topped with flowers sit upon a black-and-white checkerboard floor. Visitors mingle with winemakers over tasty, impeccably fresh local food at this near-perfect café. The seasonal menu might include roasted monkfish with fennel and carrots. Desserts, such as the crème brûlée and warm chocolate torte, tend toward the homey. You can order reasonably priced wines from their extensive list, or buy a bottle at the attached wineshop and have it poured at your table. Attentive service contributes to the welcoming atmosphere. ✉ *1400 Lincoln Ave.* ☎ *707/942–9111* ☰ *D, MC, V* ⊘ *Call for hours.*

$–$$$ ✕ **Calistoga Inn Restaurant and Brewery.** On pleasant days this riverside restaurant with a sprawling, tree-shaded patio comes into its own. At lunchtime, casual plates like a smoked turkey and Brie sandwich or a Chinese chicken salad are light enough to leave you some energy for an afternoon of wine tasting. At night, when there's often live music played on the patio, you'll find heartier dishes such as flat-iron steak or grilled Sonoma duck breast with a mushroom marsala sauce. Service can be a bit lackadaisical, so order one of the house-made brews and enjoy the atmosphere while you're waiting. ✉ *1250 Lincoln Ave.* ☎ *707/942–4101* ☰ *AE, MC, V.*

$–$$$ ✕ **Wappo Bar Bistro.** Though the setting is homey, with wooden booths inside and an arbor shading the patio, the eclectic food moves beyond the familiar. The menu covers the map, with dishes ranging from *vatapa*, a Brazilian seafood stew thickened with peanuts and coconut milk, to Thai coconut curry with prawns and vegetables. A generous platter of Turkish *meze* (appetizers) makes an excellent dinner, if you're not inclined to share. At times the restaurant can seem understaffed, so be prepared for a wait, which is more enjoyable if you've snagged a table under the vine-covered patio trellis. ✉ *1226 S. Washington St.* ☎ *707/942–4712* ☰ *AE, MC, V* ⊘ *Closed Tues.*

$–$$ ✕ **BarVino.** In 2006 Calistoga got a little more urbane with the addition of this Italian-inflected wine bar in the Mount View Hotel. With red leather seats, stainless steel light fixtures, and a marble bar indoors and café seating out, it's a stylish, modern spot for a glass of wine, with many from small producers you probably haven't heard of. Small plates that could come have straight from Tuscany— olives, mozzarella with an artichoke tapenade, risotto croquettes, a selection of *salumi*—are great for sharing. A handful of well-executed large plates, like pappardelle pasta with wild shrimp and pesto cream, and rosemary-scented chicken breast, round out the menu. ✉ *1457 Lincoln Ave.* ☎ *707/942–9900* ☰ *AE, MC, V* ⊘ *No lunch.*

¢–$$ ✕ **Checkers.** A popular spot with both locals and visitors with children in tow, this restaurant comes across as casual and cheerful with its terra-cotta-colored walls and huge

French advertising posters. The Cal-Italian menu consists mostly of pasta (rigatoni with broccoli, linguini carbonara) and pizzas. One unusual but very popular pick is the Thai pizza with chicken, cilantro, and peanuts. Some of the best dishes are the hearty salads, like the sweet and tangy Napa salad, served with apples, candied walnuts, Gorgonzola, and a poppy-seed dressing. ⊠*1414 Lincoln Ave.* ☎*707/942–9300* ⊟*AE, D, MC, V.*

★ $$$$ ▣**Calistoga Ranch.** Sister to Auberge du Soleil in Rutherford, this property trades in a different sort of luxury. Freestanding shingle cottages in the forested hillside outside town look somewhat rustic from the outside; inside they're anything but. There are cloudlike beds with crisp white bedding, DVD players, and luxe bathrooms with soaking tubs and sybaritic outdoor showers. This indoor-outdoor alignment pervades the ranch: each room has a comfortable outdoor living room, and even the reception area and spa have outdoor seating next to fireplaces. Active types can hit the swimming pool and indoor-outdoor fitness center, and go on guided hikes. Though the young staffers are friendly, they lack the polish of the staff at some similarly priced places. **Pros:** Romantic outdoor shower big enough for two, luxurious country retreat feel, excellent spa. **Cons:** Very expensive, construction is noisy in spots, innovative indoor-outdoor organization works better in fair weather than in rain or cold. ⊠*580 Lommel Rd., 94515* ☎*707/254–2820 or 800/942–4220* ⊕*www.calistogaranch. com* ➬*47 rooms* ⌖*In-room: refrigerator, DVD, Ethernet. In-hotel: restaurant, room service, bar, pool, gym, spa, no elevator, concierge, no-smoking rooms* ⊟*AE, D, MC, V.*

$$$–$$$$ ▣**Cottage Grove Inn.** A long driveway lined with 16 freestanding cottages, each shaded by elm trees, looks a bit like Main Street U.S.A., but inside, the skylit buildings have all the perks you could want for a romantic weekend away. Each has a CD player, a wood-burning fireplace, and an extra-deep two-person whirlpool tub. Each cottage also has its own variation on the overall comfy-rustic look, with telltale names like Fly Fishing Cottage and Provence. Spas and restaurants are within walking distance. Rates include afternoon wine and cheese. **Pros:** Rocking chairs on each shady porch, board games in the lobby, huge bathtubs. **Cons:** No pool, some street noise. ⊠*1711 Lincoln Ave., 94515* ☎*707/942–8400 or 800/799–2284* ⊕*www. cottagegrove.com* ➬*16 rooms* ⌖*In-room: safe, refrigera-*

tor, DVD, Wi-Fi. In-hotel: no elevator, no-smoking rooms ⊟*AE, D, DC, MC, V* ⊙*CP.*

$$$–$$$$ ⊠Indian Springs. Since 1871, this old-time spa has wel-
★ comed clients to mud baths, a mineral pool, and a steam
room, all supplied with mineral water from its four gey-
sers. Rooms in the lodge, though quite small, are beauti-
fully done up in a Zen style, with simple, Asian-inspired
furnishings, Frette linens, and flat-panel televisions. The
cottages dotted around the property have kitchenettes
(ranging from small to fully equipped), encouraging longer
stays; book well in advance for these. If you can be lured
out of the spa or Olympic-sized pool, try out the boccie
court, shuffleboard, or croquet lawn. **Pros:** Lovely grounds
with outdoor seating areas, stylish for price, enormous
mineral pool. **Cons:** Lodge rooms small, oddly uncomfort-
able pillows. ⊠*1/12 Lincoln Ave., 94515* ☎*707/942–4913*
⊕*www.indianspringscalistoga.com* ⟿*24 rooms, 17 suites*
⌂*In-room: no phone, Wi-Fi, kitchen (some), refrigerator
(some). In-hotel: tennis court, pool, spa, no elevator, no
smoking rooms* ⊟*D, MC, V.*

$$$ ★ **Fodor's**Choice ⊠**Meadowlark Country House.** Simultaneously
sophisticated and laid-back, this gay-friendly inn sits on 20
hillside acres just north of Calistoga, amid horse pastures,
gardens, and forest. Each guest room has its own charms:
one has a four-poster bed and opens onto a private garden,
and others have a deck with mountain views. Many rooms
have fireplaces, and most have whirlpool tubs large enough
for two. A spacious two-story guesthouse opens directly
onto the clothing-optional pool and sauna area (open to all
guests), a rarity in these parts. Innkeepers Kurt and Richard are perfectly charming hosts, and the Meadowlark
tends to attract a younger, more relaxed crowd than some
of the frillier B&Bs in the Wine Country. **Pros:** Sauna next
to pool and hot tub, warm and welcoming vibe attracts
diverse guests, some of the most gracious innkeepers in
Napa. **Cons:** Clothing-optional pool policy isn't for everyone. ⊠*601 Petrified Forest Rd., 94515* ☎*707/942–5651
or 800/942–5651* ⊕*www.meadowlarkinn.com* ⟿*5 rooms,
5 suites* ⌂*In-room: kitchen (some), refrigerator (some),
DVD (some), VCR (some), Wi-Fi (some). In-hotel: pool,
no elevator, no-smoking rooms, some pets allowed* ⊟*AE,
MC, V* ⊙*BP.*

$$–$$$ ⊠**Brannan Cottage Inn.** The pristine Victorian cottage with
lacy white fretwork, large windows, and a shady porch is

the only one of Sam Brannan's 1860 resort cottages still standing on its original site. Each room has individual touches such as a four-poster bed, a claw-foot tub, or a velvet settee. Doug and Judy, the very friendly innkeepers, can be counted on for help in planning tasting room itineraries. **Pros:** Innkeepers go the extra mile, most rooms have fireplaces. **Cons:** Owners' dog may be a problem for those with allergies, fee for Wi-Fi access. ✉109 Wapoo Ave., 94515 ☎707/942–4200 ⊕www.brannancottageinn.com ➾6 rooms ⌂In-room: refrigerator, no TV (some), Wi-Fi. In-hotel: no elevator, some pets allowed (fee), no-smoking rooms ⊟AE, MC, V ⊙BP.

$$–$$$ ⊡**Mount View Hotel & Spa.** A National Historic Landmark, the Mount View conjures up Calistoga's 19th-century heyday with its late-Victorian decor. A full-service spa provides state-of-the-art pampering, and three cottages are each equipped with a private redwood deck, whirlpool tub, and wet bar. The hotel's location on Calistoga's main drag, plus the excellent wine bar in the same building, mean you won't need to go far if your spa treatment has left you too indolent to drive. **Pros:** Convenient location, excellent spa treatments. **Cons:** Ground-floor rooms dark, mediocre Continental breakfast, small bathrooms. ✉1457 Lincoln Ave., 94515 ☎707/942–6877 or 800/816–6877 ⊕www. mountviewhotel.com ➾20 rooms, 12 suites ⌂In-room: refrigerator (some), DVD (some), Wi-Fi. In-hotel: restaurant, room service, bar, pool, spa, no elevator, concierge, no-smoking rooms ⊟AE, D, MC, V ⊙CP.

$–$$ ⊡**Calistoga Spa Hot Springs.** Though the rooms are standard motel issue, their well-equipped kitchenettes and the four outdoor heated mineral pools make this a popular spot for those who want to enjoy Calistoga's famed waters on a budget. An on-site spa offers mud baths, massage, and other services at reasonable rates. The location on a quiet side street one block from Calistoga's main drag is another plus. Fodors.com users suggest staking out a prime lounging spot next to the pools before the day-trippers are admitted each morning. **Pros:** A rare family-friendly spot in Napa Valley, unpretentious atmosphere. **Cons:** Dated and drab rooms, children at the mineral pools can spoil tranquillity, kitchenettes lack microwaves. ✉1006 Washington St., 94515 ☎707/942–6269 ⊕www.calistogaspa.com ➾51 rooms, 1 suite ⌂In-room: kitchen. In-hotel: pools, gym, spa, no elevator, laundry facilities, no-smoking rooms ⊟MC, V.

NIGHTLIFE & THE ARTS

Brannan's Grill (✉*1374 Lincoln Ave.* ☎*707/942–2233*) has talented mixologists behind the mahogany bar, making it a good stop for an after-dinner cocktail. While you're there, take a look at the vaulted ceiling, redwood beams, and hard-forged iron trestles; the building was constructed in 1903 as a garage. On Friday through Sunday nights a superb jazz vibraphone player provides entertainment. Live music, a laid-back atmosphere, and the garden patio make the **Calistoga Inn Restaurant and Brewery** (✉*1250 Lincoln Ave.* ☎*707/942–4101*) a popular spot for a house-brewed beer on warm summer nights.

SHOPPING

Shops and restaurants along Lincoln Avenue in downtown Calistoga tend to cater to locals rather than visitors, and you'll find few of the high-priced boutiques popular in places like St. Helena. The **Calistoga Depot** (✉*1458 Lincoln Ave.* ☎*No phone*) is a small cluster of gift shops, a café, and a wine shop and tasting room housed in an old train depot and its six restored railway cars. **Enoteca Wine Shop** (✉*1348B Lincoln Ave.* ☎*707/942–1117*), on Calistoga's main drag, conveniently displays almost all of their wines with extensive tasting notes, which makes it easier to choose from among their unusually fine collection, which includes hard-to-find bottles from Napa and Sonoma and many French wines.

Locally handcrafted beeswax candles are for sale at **Hurd Beeswax Candles** (✉*1255 Lincoln Ave.* ☎*707/963–7211*). Unusual tapers twisted into spiral shapes are a specialty. At the edge of downtown Calistoga, the **Wine Garage** (✉*1020 Highway 29* ☎*707/942–5332*) is the stop for bargain hunters, since each of the bottles goes for $25 or less. It's a great way to discover the work of smaller wineries producing undervalued wines.

A Great Napa Drive

Traffic permitting, it would be easy to zip from one end of the valley to the other along Highway 29 in about 45 minutes, passing scores of wineries along the way. Indeed, that's what plenty of visitors do, but a much better strategy is to appreciate the wineries at a more leisurely pace.

From the town of Napa, start around 10 AM and drive north on Highway 29 to the Trancas Street/Redwood Road exit. Take the shady Redwood Road (to the left), and when it narrows down from four lanes to two, stay to your left. Just after a sharp curve, look for the Hess Winery sign. When you see it, turn sharply left to stay on Redwood Road; you'll see the entrance to the winery almost immediately. (The trip from Napa to Hess should take about 15 minutes.) Here you'll want to allow at least an hour or so to browse the excellent modern art collection before you pass through the tasting room on your way out.

After your visit, turn right out of the winery back onto Redwood Road. At the next T, turn left onto Mt. Veeder Road. Next, turn right on Oakville Grade, and you'll be twisting and turning your way downhill to Highway 29. (Take your time, and pack the Dramamine for those prone to car sickness). Turn left on Highway 29 and

you'll see the driveway to Robert Mondavi almost immediately on your left. Their introductory tour is particularly good for wine newbies, but if you've arranged to take an afternoon tour at Schramsberg, you'll have to skip the tour and head straight to one of the two tasting rooms.

After your stop at Mondavi, head north on Highway 29 for about five minutes to Dean & Deluca, where you can find the most decadent picnic items possible: imported cheeses and charcuterie, locally made pastries and chocolates, and more condiments than you might know what to do with. Pop into the Flora Springs tasting room next door, taste what's on offer, and pick up a bottle before heading to the picnic tables on the back patio for a leisurely lunch.

If you've made a reservation for one of the excellent afternoon tours at Schramsberg, head north on Highway 29 to Peterson Road, where you'll turn left and then make a quick right onto narrow, winding Schramsberg Lane. After touring their extensive caves and tasting their sparklers, return to Highway 29 and turn right (south) to return to St. Helena. You'll have an hour or two to browse the shops along Main Street before they close for the evening.

The Carneros District

WORD OF MOUTH

"My most favorite place to sample bubbly is Domaine Carneros . . . . For my taste, their sparkling wines are the best—very much in the French style. You can order a little sampler and sit on the terrace with the most unbelievable view and think that you have died and gone to heaven."

—Sharkmom

THE CARNEROS AVA HAS A BUZZ about it. Also known as Los Carneros, this compact viticultural region stretches across the cool lower reaches of Sonoma and Napa counties. The word *carneros* means "sheep" in Spanish, and the slopes now covered with vines were once thought to be good only as pasture. Today, however, the only sheep you're likely to see are the metal sheep sculptures grazing in front of the di Rosa Preserve, as winemakers have snapped up almost every available acre, sending land values through the roof. Though vintners have clearly wised up to the value of the Carneros region, visitors have been slower to catch on. Most zip right through in their haste to get to big-name spots to the north—but if you check out a few of these places, odds are you'll become a convert.

To understand how different the Carneros is from the other California wine-producing regions, you must approach it from the roads that border the water. From San Francisco, travel north on U.S. 101 to Novato and take the Highway 37 turnoff to the east, which will take you along the northern reaches of San Francisco Bay, at this point called San Pablo Bay. On a gray day, the flat marshes and low hills near the bay look bleak indeed, more like Scottish moor than a California shore. During summer and autumn, strong west winds blow in from the ocean each afternoon, tempering the hot days.

The soils here are shallow and not particularly fertile, which means that the vines struggle to produce fruit. Though it seems that this would be a drawback, it's in fact a plus. Vines that grow slowly and yield less fruit tend to produce very concentrated, high-acid grapes that are ideal for wine making. Grape growers in the mid-19th century recognized this and planted vast tracts here. Because of the low yields, some of the land was allowed to revert to sheep pasture after phylloxera destroyed the vines in the 1890s. But the reputation of the grapes survived, and shortly after the repeal of Prohibition, vines once again began to spread across the hills.

Pinot noir and chardonnay grapes are considered king here, as they thrive in the moderate temperatures of the exposed, windy slopes. These days, however, winemakers are also trying out merlot and syrah, which are also considered well suited to the cool winds, thin soil, and low rainfall. (Carneros generally gets less rain than elsewhere in Napa and Sonoma.) Even warm-climate grapes such as cabernet sauvignon can ripen well in favored Carneros locations. Though many of these grapes are cultivated by small Carneros wineries that use them to make estate wines, many are instead purchased by wineries elsewhere in Napa and Sonoma. High-profile places like Robert Sinskey, Domaine Chandon, and Beaulieu Vineyard have all tapped the Carneros grape supply to make wines of great complexity and depth.

3

GETTING AROUND CARNEROS

The Carneros region is closer to San Francisco than any other part of the Wine Country: on a good day you can be sipping wine here within 45 minutes of crossing the Golden Gate Bridge. The main route through the region is the east-west Carneros Highway, also known as Highway 121, which connects Highway 12, the main north-south route through Sonoma Valley, with Highway 29, the main north-south route through Napa Valley.

WESTERN CARNEROS

37 mi from San Francisco via U.S. 101 north to Rte. 37 east.

Numbers in the margin correspond to numbers on the Carneros District map.

The western stretches of the Carneros District, from the foot of the Sonoma Mountains to the breezy banks of San Pablo Bay, fall in Sonoma County. The cool air and early afternoon fog is perfectly suited to cool-climate varieties like the pinot noir and chardonnay. Here they are often turned into still wines, but about 20 percent of those grapes are transformed into lively sparkling wines, like the crisp and citrusy ones you'll find at Gloria Ferrer Champagne Caves.

The gently rolling hills of western Carneros are still relatively undeveloped, and visitors tend to pass through quickly on their way to destinations farther up Sonoma Valley. And, though Carneros is almost completely devoid of restaurants and lodgings, the town of Sonoma is rarely more than a 15-minute drive away.

★ ❶ If you happen to be driving north along Highway 121 from San Francisco, you might be mystified to see a bizarre

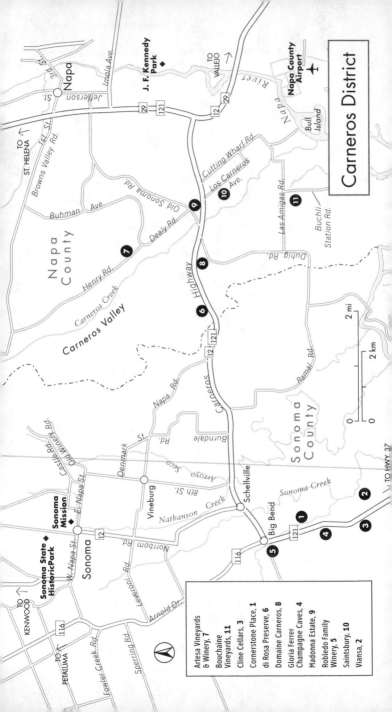

Carneros District

Artesa Vineyards & Winery, **7**
Bouchaine Vineyards, **11**
Cline Cellars, **3**
Cornerstone Place, **1**
di Rosa Preserve, **6**
Domaine Carneros, **8**
Gloria Ferrer Champagne Caves, **4**
Madonna Estate, **9**
Robledo Family Winery, **5**
Saintsbury, **10**
Viansa, **2**

sculpture on the right side of the road, a larger-than-life baby-blue tree fashioned out of thousand of tiny spheres. The "Blue Tree" marks your arrival at **Cornerstone Place**, a 9-acre complex of shops, galleries, a café, tasting rooms, a Sonoma Valley Visitors Bureau office, and many different "architectural gardens." About 20 landscape artists were each given a small plot of land and carte blanche to create a high-concept installation, and it's worth taking the time to explore these sometimes whimsical, sometimes pretentious, but always interesting landscapes. ⊠*23570 Hwy. 121* ☎*707/933–3010* ⊕*www.cornerstonegardens.com* ⊠ *Free.* ☉*Architectural gardens daily 10–5; hours of other attractions vary.*

VINEYARDS

❷ Reminiscent of a Tuscan villa, with its ocher-color buildings surrounded by olive trees, sprawling **Viansa** focuses on Italian varietals such as sangiovese, dolcetto, and tocai friulano. Fodor's readers are generally split when summing up the charms of the winery. Some love the market on the premises that sells sandwiches and deli foods to complement the Italian-style wines, as well as a large selection of dinnerware, cookbooks, and condiments. Others find the cavernous size of the market and the crowds that tend to congregate here off-putting. Regardless, the picnic area that overlooks the wetlands below is a fine place to enjoy a glass of wine while bird-watching. ⊠*25200 Arnold Dr.* ☎*707/935–4700* ⊕*www.viansa.com* ⊠*Tasting $5–$20, tour $5* ☉*Daily 10–5; tour daily at 11, 2:15, and 3.*

❸ If you visit **Cline Cellars** on a summer day, you'll likely get a blast of the wind for which the Carneros region is known. The stiff breeze is the result of the Petaluma Gap, a sort of wind tunnel created by a break in the mountains. Although Cline has planted vineyards here—mostly Rhône varietals such as syrah, roussanne, and viognier rather than the pinot noir and chardonnay grapes more common in the region—most of the grapes it uses come from old vines grown in Contra Costa County, where zinfandel and heat-loving marsanne, mourvèdre, and carignane thrive. Be sure to taste the dark red carignane, but there are also syrah and zinfandel for more traditional palates. The 1850s farmhouse that houses the tasting room has a pleasant wraparound porch for enjoying the weeping willow trees, ponds, and rosebushes on the property. ⊠*24737 Arnold*

Dr. ☎707/940–4030 ⊕*www.clinecellars.com* ☜*Tasting and tour free* ⊙*Daily 10–6; tour daily at 11, 1, and 3.*

❹ The Spanish hacienda–style architecture recalls the native country of the Ferrer family, who make both sparkling and still wines at **Gloria Ferrer Champagne Caves.** The Spanish sparkling-wine maker Freixenet was the first winery to start producing Carneros fizz, establishing this site in 1982. Vintner Bob Iantosca crafts superb sparkling wines from his beloved chardonnay and pinot noir grapes, but still finds the time to make a small quantity of still wines, making him something of a rarity among winemakers. Tours here, which include the *cava*, or cellar, where several feet of earth maintain a constant temperature, and a glimpse of some antique wine-making equipment, are offered daily. Call the day of your visit after 9:45 AM for the tour times. ✉*23555 Carneros Hwy./Rte. 121* ☎707/996–7256 ⊕*www.gloriaferrer.com* ☜*Tasting $2–$10, tour free* ⊙*Daily 10–5.*

★ ❺ The **Robledo Family Winery,** founded by Reynaldo Robledo, Sr., a former migrant worker from Michoacán, Mexico, is truly a family affair. You're likely to encounter one of the charming Robledo sons in the tasting room, where he'll proudly tell you the story of the immigrant family while pouring tastes of their sauvignon blanc, pinot noir, merlot, cabernet sauvignon, and other wines, including a chardonnay that comes from the vineyard right outside the tasting room's door. All seven Robledo sons and two Robledo daughters, as well as matriarch Maria, are involved in the winery operations. If you don't run into them on your visit to the winery, you'll see their names and pictures on the bottles of wine, such as the Dos Hermanas late-harvest dessert wine, or the port dedicated to Maria Robledo. ✉*21901 Bonness Rd.* ☎707/939–6903 ⊕*www.robledo-familywinery.com* ☜*Tasting $5–$10* ⊙*Mon.–Sat. 10–5, Sun. 11–4.*

WHERE TO STAY

$$ ▦**Vineyard Inn.** Built as a roadside motor court in 1941, this inn with red-tile roofs brings a touch of Mediterranean style to an otherwise lackluster and somewhat noisy location at the junction of two main highways. It's across from two vineyards and is the closest lodging to Infineon Raceway, a major car and motorcycle racetrack. Though the standard rooms are rather small, a convenient location and a modest price make it a fine home base for those

Organic Wines

If, as many grape-growers insist, a wine is only as good as the vineyard it comes from, those who have adopted sustainable, biodynamic, or organic viticulture methods may be on to something. These approaches have exploded in popularity since the 1990s.

But what do vintners mean by "organic"? Although organic viticulture is governmentally recognized and regulated (by the State of California as well as by the United States and the European Union), it is vaguely defined and its value is hotly debated—just like the rest of organic farming. It boils down to a rejection of chemical fertilizers, pesticides, and fungicides. Biodynamic farming, meanwhile, is a trademarked term for a similar anti-artificial approach, with a spiritual slant.

Partly because it is difficult and expensive to qualify for official certification, partly because organic vineyards have smaller yields, and partly because it is hard to grow grapes organically except in warm, dry climates, organic viticulture remains the exception rather than the rule in the industry.

Even rarer than wines produced from organically grown grapes are completely organic wines. To make an organic wine, not only do the grapes have to come from organic

vineyards, but processing must use a minimum of chemical additives. Most winemakers argue that it is impossible to make truly fine wine without using at least some additives, such as sulphur dioxide (sulfites), an antioxidant that protects the color, aroma, bright flavors, and longevity of wine. And, of course, organic winemaking is more expensive.

Many wineries that might qualify as partially or entirely organic resist the label, wary of its impact on their reputation. Still, the movement is gaining momentum. Major players such as Mondavi and Beringer are experimenting, and many others—from Hess and Chalk Hill to Frog's Leap and Tablas Creek—grow some or all of their grapes organically. Bonterra Vineyards, Coturri Winery, Organic Wine Works, La Rocca Vineyards, and Coates Vineyards are among the very few producers which make completely organic wines.

As demand for organic products grows, supply will no doubt follow suit. In the meantime, if you want organic wine, read the label carefully. To be labeled organic, a wine must contain 100% certified organic grapes and have no added sulfites. Wines that contain sulfites can indicate that they are made from certified organic grapes.

who'd rather spend their money elsewhere. ■TIP→The inn sometimes closes for a few weeks during slow season, so check the schedule if you're booking a room in December or January. Pros: Attractive courtyard with tables and chairs, friendly innkeepers. Cons: Next to two busy highways, must drive everywhere. ⊠23000 Arnold Dr., at junction of Rtes. 116 and 121, 95476 ☎707/938–2350 or 800/359–4667 ⊕www.sonomavineyardinn.com ⌁19 rooms, 2 suites ♿In-room: refrigerator (some), DVD (some), Wi-Fi. In-hotel: pool, no elevator, no-smoking rooms ☐AE, MC, V ⦿ICP.

EASTERN CARNEROS

42 mi northeast of San Francisco via U.S. 101 north to Rte. 37 east to Rte. 29 north and east.

Numbers in the margin correspond to numbers on the Carneros District map.

Stretching from the Sonoma County line to the Napa River in the town of Napa, the eastern half of the Carneros region generally shares the same wine-growing climate and soils with the western half. Though you'll find the same rustic, relatively undeveloped atmosphere in eastern Carneros, wineries pop up more frequently along Highway 121 here, and the route is lined with vineyards where bits of shiny reflective tape, tied to the vines to keep the birds away, flicker in the sunlight.

To take a break from wine tasting, grab a picnic lunch and take Cuttings Wharf Road south to the Napa River, stop at the public boat ramp, and dangle your feet in the river. Keep a lookout for white egrets, great blue herons, wood ducks, and other waterfowl. But beware, as these waters are tricky and rise and fall with the tide. If the bleak marshes to the south look familiar, there's a reason: Francis Ford Coppola shot some of the Mekong Delta scenes for Apocalypse Now here.

❻ ★ Fodor'sChoice When you're driving along the Carneros Highway on your way to Napa from San Francisco, it would be easy to zip by one of the region's best-kept secrets: the di Rosa Preserve. Metal sculptures of sheep grazing in the grass mark the entrance to this sprawling, art-stuffed property. Thousands of 20th-century artworks by hundreds of Northern California artists crop up everywhere—in galleries, in the former di Rosa residence, on every lawn, in every courtyard, and even on the lake. Some of the works were commissioned especially for the preserve, such as Paul Kos's meditative *Chartres Bleu,* a video installation in a chapel-like setting that replicates a stained-glass window of the cathedral in Chartres, France. If you stop by without a reservation, you'll only gain access to the Gatehouse Gallery, where there's a small collection of riotously colorful figurative and abstract sculpture and painting. ■TIP→ **For the full effect, reserve ahead for a one-hour tour of the grounds, or opt for the two-hour tour, which allows more time to browse the main gallery.** ✉*5200 Carneros Hwy.* ☎*707/226–5991* ⊕*www.dirosapreserve.org* ✇*$3; tours $10–$15* ⊗*Tues.– Fri. 9:30–3; call for tour times.*

VINEYARDS

❼ With its modern, minimalist look in the tasting room, which is dug into a Carneros hilltop, and contemporary sculptures and fountains on the property, **Artesa Vineyards & Winery** is a far cry from the many faux French châteaus and rustic Italian-style villas in the region. Although the Spanish owners once made sparkling wines, now they produce primarily still wines under the talented winemaker Dave Dobson, including some well-regarded cabernet sauvignons, chardonnays, and pinot noirs. Two rooms off the tasting room display exhibits on the Carneros region's history and geography, as well as antique wine-making tools. ✉*1345 Henry Rd., north off Old Sonoma Rd. and Dealy La.* ☎*707/224–1668* ⊕*www.artesawinery.com* ✇*Tasting $10–$15, tour free* ⊗*Daily 10–5; tour daily at 11 and 2.*

★ **❽** The majestic château of **Domaine Carneros** looks for all the world like it belongs in France, and in fact it does: it's modeled after the Château de la Marquetterie, an 18th-century mansion owned by the Taittinger family near Epernay, France. Carved into the hillside beneath the winery, Domaine Carneros's cellars produce dry, delicate sparkling wines reminiscent of those made by Taittinger, and use only grapes grown locally. Instead of offering tastings like most wineries, Domaine Carneros sells full glasses, flights, and bottles of their bubbly treat and serves them with hors d'oeuvres to those seated in the Louis XV–inspired salon or on the terrace overlooking the vineyards. Though this makes a visit here a tad more expensive than most stops on a winery tour, it's also one of the most opulent ways to enjoy the Carneros District. ✉ *1240 Duhig Rd.* ☎ *707/257–0101* ⊕ *www.domainecarneros.com* ✇ *Tasting $6–$15, tour $25* ⊙ *Daily 10–6; tour daily at 11, 1, and 3.*

❾ Winemaker Andrea Bartolucci, whose family has been growing grapes in Napa since 1922, oversees the 160 gently rolling acres of vines at **Madonna Estate**. Here he uses organic and dry farming techniques to grow nearly a dozen kinds of grapes. (Dry farming, which leaves established vines to rely on rainwater, stresses the plants, resulting in a smaller yield but more intensely flavored grapes.) Though the winery's location right on Highway 121 is less scenic than some and the tasting room is modest, it's worth a visit for a taste of their crisp, lean pinot grigio, with a fresh melony aroma; the smoky, creamy chardonnay aged in French oak; and the earthy pinot noir. The muscat canelli, gewürztraminer, and riesling, produced in small quantities, are available only at the winery. ✉ *5400 Old Sonoma Rd.* ☎ *707/255–8864* ⊕ *www.madonnaestate.com* ✇ *Tasting $5–$15* ⊙ *Daily 10–5; reserve room Wed.–Sun. 10–4; tours by appointment.*

❿ Back in 1981, when **Saintsbury** released its first pinot noir, conventional wisdom was that only the French could produce great pinot. No matter that a few cutting-edge winemakers, like Beaulieu's André Tchelistcheff, had been making pinot from Carneros grapes since the late 1930s. But what a difference a few decades make: the Carneros region is now thought to produce some of the best pinots in the world. If you're still in doubt, try Saintsbury's earthy, intense Brown Ranch pinot noir. Their other pinot noirs are lighter in style and more fruit-forward. Named for the English author and critic George Saintsbury (he of *Notes on a Cellar-Book* fame), the winery also makes chardonnay from estate-grown grapes and a substantial, delightful vin gris. The quality of the wine makes Saintsbury well worth a visit, but you must make an appointment to do so. ✉ *1500 Los Carneros Ave.* ☎ *707/252–0592* ⊕ *www.saintsbury. com* ✇ *Free* ⊙ *Weekdays by appointment only.*

★ ⓫ Just a few miles off the Carneros Highway but seeming much further off the beaten path, tranquil **Bouchaine Vineyards** lies between Carneros and Huichica creeks and the tidal sloughs of San Pablo Bay. The alternately breezy and foggy weather works well for the Burgundian varietals pinot noir and chardonnay, which account for most of their vines, but look for a zesty sauvignon blanc and a late-harvest chardonnay called Bouche d'Or as well. In fair weather, leisurely seated tastings take place on the lovely back patio, from which you are likely to see hawks, starlings, or even golden eagles soaring above the vineyards (they have to place netting over the vines to keep the birds away from the fruit). Their commitment to sustainable practices is evident everywhere, from their use of compost from San Francisco restaurants in their vineyards to the construction of the winery's redwood facade, made from their original wine tanks. ⊠*1075 Buchli Station Rd.* ☎*707/252–9065* ⊕*www.bouchaine.com* ⊠*Tasting $5* ⊙*Daily 10–4:30.*

WHERE TO STAY & EAT

$–$$$ ✕**Boon Fly Café.** Part of the Carneros Inn complex, west of downtown Napa, this small spot has a rural charm-meets-industrial-chic theme. Outside, rocking chairs and swings occupy the porch of a modern red barn; inside, things get sleek with high ceilings and galvanized steel tabletops. The small menu of three squares a day updates American classics, with dishes such as braised short ribs with mashed potatoes and roasted *cipollini* (wild) onions, and flatbread topped with bacon, Point Reyes blue cheese, and sautéed mushrooms. If there's a wait for a table, never fear: belly up to the wine bar, where you'll find good selection of reasonably priced glasses. ⊠*4018 Sonoma Hwy.* ☎*707/299–4872* ⚐*Reservations not accepted* ▬*AE, D, MC, V.*

$$$$ ★ **Fodor'sChoice** 🛏**Carneros Inn.** Freestanding board-and-batten cottages with rocking chairs on each porch are simultaneously rustic and chic at this luxurious property. Inside, each cottage is flooded with natural light but still manages to maintain privacy with windows and French doors leading to a private garden. (The suites are actually two-cottage clusters.) Flat-panel TVs, ethereal beds topped with Frette linens and pristine white down comforters, and spacious bathrooms with heated slate floors and large indoor-outdoor showers may make it difficult to summon the will to leave the cottage and enjoy the hilltop infinity swimming pool and hot tub. In addition to two restaurants open to the public, the Hilltop Dining Room, with views of the neighboring vineyards, is open to guests only. **Pros:** Cottages afford lots of privacy, young and hip feel, huge bathrooms. **Cons:** Ongoing construction, long drive from up-valley destinations, small bedrooms with limited stor-

age space. ✉*4048 Sonoma Hwy., 94559* ☎*707/299–4900*
⊕*www.thecarnerosinn.com* ⇆*76 cottages, 10 suites* ⚿*In-room: refrigerator, DVD, Ethernet. In-hotel: 3 restaurants, room service, bar, pool, gym, spa, no elevator, laundry service, concierge, no-smoking rooms* ▭*AE, D, DC, MC, V.*

Sonoma
Valley

WORD OF MOUTH

"In contrast to its more famous neighbor to the east (Napa), you will find the Sonoma wineries more inviting and less hectic—I actually like them better. In the Napa Valley, there are very few wineries where you can take a picnic lunch and spread out on the lawn. In Sonoma, they seem to go out of their way to invite you to use their facilities."

—StuDudley

ALTHOUGH THE SONOMA VALLEY may not have quite the cachet of the neighboring Napa Valley, wineries here entice with their unpretentious attitude and smaller crowds. The glitzy Napa-style tasting rooms with enormous gift shops and $25 tasting fees are the exception here rather than the rule. Sonoma's landscape seduces, too, its roads gently climbing and descending on their way to wineries hidden from the road by trees.

That's not to suggest that Sonoma is exactly undiscovered territory. On the contrary, along the main corridor through the Sonoma Valley—Highway 12 from Sonoma to Santa Rosa—you'll spot sophisticated inns and spas between the ubiquitous wineries. And in high season, the towns of Glen Ellen and Kenwood are filled with well-heeled wine buffs. Still, the pace of life is a bit slower here than in Napa— you'll see as many bicyclists as limos zipping from one winery to the next. And the historic Sonoma Valley towns offer glimpses of the past. The town of Sonoma, with its atmospheric central plaza, is rich with 19th-century buildings. Glen Ellen, meanwhile, has a special connection with author Jack London.

Bounded by the Mayacamas Mountains on the east and Sonoma Mountain on the west, this scenic valley extends north from San Pablo Bay nearly 20 mi to the eastern outskirts of Santa Rosa. The varied terrain, soils, and climate (cooler in the south because of the bay influence and hotter toward the north) allow grape growers to raise cool-weather varietals such as chardonnay and pinot noir as well as merlot, cabernet sauvignon, and other heat-seeking vines.

GETTING AROUND SONOMA VALLEY

Highway 12, also called the Sonoma Highway, is the main thoroughfare through the Sonoma Valley, running north-south through Sonoma, Glen Ellen, and Kenwood. Traffic tends to move fairly smoothly along this route, except on some summer weekends. To get to Napa from the Sonoma Valley, you can drive south of the town of Sonoma and follow Highway 121/Highway 12, also know as the Carneros Highway, east, or you can pick up Trinity Road, which turns into Oakville Grade Road, for a beautiful—but slow and winding—trip over the Mayacamas range.

SONOMA VALLEY APPELLATIONS

Although Sonoma *County* is a large, diverse growing region encompassing several different appellations, the much smaller Sonoma *Valley*, at the southern end of Sonoma County, is comparatively compact and consists mostly of the **Sonoma Valley AVA**, which stretches from southeast of Santa Rosa south toward San Pablo Bay. The weather and soils here are unusually diverse. Pinot and chardonnay are most likely to be found in the southernmost parts of the AVA, which is cooled by fog from the San Pablo Bay, while zinfandel, cabernet, and sauvignon blanc are more popular further north, near Glen Ellen and Kenwood, which tend to be a few degrees warmer.

The **Sonoma Mountain AVA** rises to the west of Glen Ellen on the western border of the Sonoma Valley AVA. Benefiting from a sunny mountain location and poor rocky soil, the vineyards here produce deep-rooted vines and intensely flavored grapes that are made into unique, complex red wines, especially hearty cabernet sauvignons.

With only 650 acres planted with vines, the idyllic **Bennett Valley AVA** is one of the smallest appellations in California. Surrounded by the mountains on three sides but cooled by coastal breezes that sneak through the Crane Canyon wind gap, it's ideal for cooler-weather grapes like pinot noir and chardonnay, but also does well with syrah, cabernet sauvignon, and sauvignon blanc.

TOWN OF SONOMA

14 mi west of Napa on Rte. 12; 45 mi northeast of San Francisco via U.S. 101 to Rte. 37 to Rte. 121/12.

Numbers in the margin correspond to numbers on the Sonoma Town map.

The town of Sonoma, the valley's cultural center, is the oldest town in the Wine Country. Founded in the early 1800s, when California was still part of Mexico, it is built around a large, tree-filled plaza. One of the few towns in the valley with many attractions not related to food and wine, Sonoma has plenty to keep you busy for a couple of hours here before you head out to tour the wineries.

FAIR PLAY Wonder why the stone City Hall, built on Sonoma's plaza in 1906, looks the same from all angles? Its four sides were

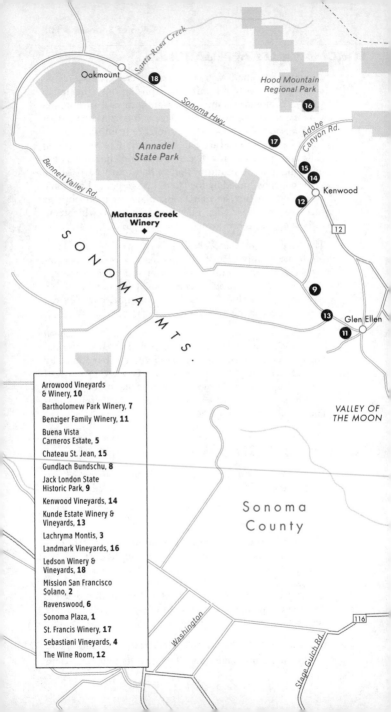

Oakmount

Santa Rosa Creek

18

Sonoma Hwy.

Hood Mountain Regional Park

16

Adobe Canyon Rd.

17

Annadel State Park

15
14 Kenwood

Bennett Valley Rd.

12

S O N O M A

Matanzas Creek Winery ◆

M T S.

9

13 Glen Ellen

11

VALLEY OF THE MOON

S o n o m a
C o u n t y

Washington

116

Stage Gulch Rd.

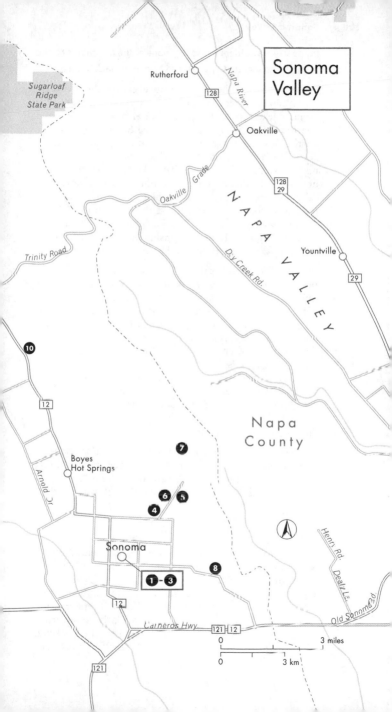

Sonoma Valley

Rutherford

Oakville

Oakville Grade

Trinity Road

Napa River

NAPA VALLEY

Dry Creek Rd.

Yountville

Sugarloaf
Ridge
State Park

Boyes
Hot Springs

Arnold Dr.

Sonoma

Napa
County

Carneros Hwy

Henn Rd.

Dealy Ln.

Old Sonoma Rd.

0   3 miles

0   3 km

purposely made identical so that none of the merchants on the plaza would feel that city hall had turned its back to them.

❶ Sonoma Plaza is where American rebels proclaimed California's independence from Mexico on June 14, 1846, the event marked by a statue on the northeast side. Several historic buildings are clustered along Spain Street, on the north side of the plaza. Notable examples include the now-empty **Blue Wing Inn** (✉ *133 East Spain St.*) which was built by General Mariano Vallejo, the last Mexican governor of California, as a guesthouse. It became a notorious saloon during gold rush days, when the scout Kit Carson, the bandit Joaquin Murietta, and the army officer Ulysses S. Grant were patrons. The **Toscano Hotel** (✉ *20 East Spain St*) dates from the 1850s; step inside the front door to see a musty-smelling re-creation of the hotel's lobby and bar.

Although Sonoma has more than its share of historic adobes from the city's Mexican period, this is not at all a musty museum town. Nor is the plaza a museum piece—it's a place where people hang out on the shady benches, have picnics, and listen to musical performances at the small amphitheater. The plaza is a hive of activity on summer days, with children blowing off steam in the playground while their folks stock up on picnic supplies and browse the shops surrounding the square. Be sure to walk into the courtyards **El Paseo** and the **Mercato** on the west side of the plaza, where cafés and boutiques line the passageways. A visitors center on the east side of the plaza doles out helpful information on the town and region.

❷ On one corner of the Sonoma Plaza, the **Mission San Francisco Solano,** whose chapel and school were used to bring Christianity to the Native Americans, is now a museum with a fine collection of watercolors of California missions painted around 1905. ✉ *114 Spain St. E* ☎ *707/938–9560* 💲*$2, includes Sonoma Barracks on central plaza and Lachryma Montis* ☉ *Daily 10–5.*

❸ An oak tree–lined driveway leads to **Lachryma Montis,** a Victorian Gothic house that General Vallejo built for his large family in 1852. The house, insulated with adobe, represents a blend of Mexican and American cultures. Opulent furnishings, including white-marble fireplaces and a French rosewood piano, are particularly noteworthy. Docents occasionally conduct free tours on the weekend. ✉ *W. Spain St., near 3rd St. E* ☎ *707/938–9559* 💲*$2, tour free* ☉ *Daily 10–5.*

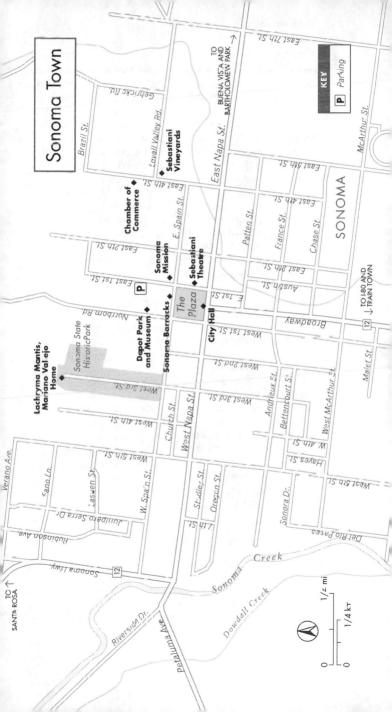

Crush Camp

Are your winery visits making you eager to pitch in and get your hands dirty? Are you starting to look longingly at the pruning shears and rows of vines? Consider signing up for one of the short, hands-on wine-making programs offered by a few wineries, usually in September and October. You'll see the inner workings of harvest and even blend your own bottle. Below are top options for these "crush camps."

■ **Camp Schramsberg.** Three-day sessions at Schramsberg Vineyards focus on making sparkling wines. Campers pick grapes in the vineyards and follow them to the crusher. Winemakers explain and teach traditional methods such as riddling—and as a dramatic finish, the art of opening a bottle of bubbly by slicing its neck with a sabre. An additional camp in spring focuses on the art of assemblage, or blending sparkling wine. ☎707/942–4558 ⊕www.schramsberg.com.

■ **Harvest Adventure.** During this one-day camp hosted by

St. Supéry, there's an overview of the wine-making process; a stint of picking; and a blending tutorial during which you'll prepare your own bottle. If you like, you can go barefoot and do some old-school grape stomping in a barrel. ☎800/231–9116 ⊕www.stsupery.com.

■ **"No Wimpy" Harvest Experience.** Staffers at Ravenswood give guests a tour of the vineyards before they retire to the barrel room to blend their own bottle, combining zinfandel, carignane, and petite sirah, in this three-hour program. ☎707/933–2349 ⊕www.ravenswood-wine.com.

■ **Sonoma Grape Camp.** Stints in the vineyard are broken up by food and wine workshops before you learn about blending wine from Ferrari-Carano's winemaker. Luxe hotel accommodations are included in the pricey package. ☎707/522–5860 ⊕www.sonomagrapecamp.com.

VINEYARDS AROUND SONOMA

❹ Originally planted by Franciscans of the Sonoma Mission in 1825, the **Sebastiani Vineyards** were bought by Samuele Sebastiani in 1904. Although the winery is best known for its red wines, you can also find some unusual whites here, like a white pinot noir. You might think you've stumbled into a housewares store rather than a winery when you walk in the door, the tasting room is so chockablock with porcelain serving pieces, bath products, and even socks with pictures of grapes on them. Press on to the back of the room to find the pours. In addition to the regularly scheduled historical tours of the winery, a trolley tour offers an informative glimpse of the vineyards. ⊠*389 4th St. E* ☎*707/938–5532* ⊕*www.sebastiani.com* ☙*Tour $5, trolley tour $7.50* ☉*Daily 10–5; tour daily at 11, 1, and 3; trolley tour Thurs.–Sat. at 2.*

❺ It was at **Buena Vista Carneros Estate,** the oldest continually operating winery in California, that Count Agoston Haraszthy de Mokcsa laid the basis for modern California wine making in 1857, bucking the conventional wisdom that vines should be planted on well-watered ground by instead planting on well-drained hillsides. Buena Vista's best wines are those produced from the Ramal Vineyard in Carneros, planted with pinot noir, chardonnay, merlot, and syrah. Its facility in the Carneros is closed to the public, but this Sonoma winery has a tasting room inside the atmospheric 1862 Press House, plus a shady courtyard for picnicking. The daily tours are especially good if you're a history buff, as they discuss Haraszthy and the saga of wine making in the valley. ⊠*18000 Old Winery Rd., off Napa Rd., follow signs from plaza* ☎*707/938–1266 or 800/678–8504* ⊕*www.buenavistacarneros.com* ☙*Tasting $5–$20, tour $20* ☉*Daily 10–5, open until 5:30 weekends June–Oct.; call for tour times.*

❻ **Ravenswood** has a punchy three-word mission statement: "no wimpy wines." They generally succeed, especially with their signature big, bold zinfandels, which are sometimes blended with petite sirah, carignane, or other varietals. The grapes come from all over the Wine Country, including the Alexander Valley and Dry Creek AVAs. The winery itself is dug into the mountains like a bunker—you almost get the feeling these Sonomans are digging in to ward off a threatened invasion from Napa, on the other side of the ridge. Tours include barrel tastings of wines in progress in the cellar. Several times each summer, Ravenswood organizes barbecues, serving up the hearty foods that pair with zinfandel so well; call ahead for a schedule. ⊠*18701 Gehricke Rd., off E. Spain St.* ☎*707/938–1960* ⊕*www.ravenswoodwine.com* ☙*Tasting $10–$15, tour $15* ☉*Daily 10–5; tour at 10:30.*

★ ❼ Although **Bartholomew Park Winery** is a newbie, founded only in 1994, grapes were grown in some of its vineyards as early as the 1830s. The emphasis here is on handcrafted, single-varietal wines—cabernet, merlot, zinfandel, and sauvignon blanc. The wines themselves make it worth a stop, but another reason to visit is its small museum, with vivid exhibits about the history of the winery and the Sonoma region. Another plus is the beautiful, slightly off-the-beaten-path location. Though the winery is only 2 mi from downtown Sonoma, the town seems far away when picnicking on the woodsy grounds. ⊠ *1000 Vineyard La.* ☎ *707/935–9511* ⊕ *www.bartholomewparkwinery. com* ⊟ *Tasting $5* ⊙ *Daily 11–4:30.*

❽ Gundlach Bundschu looks a bit like a large gun bunker, but don't let that scare you away: a visit here is a heck of a lot of fun. Pop or rock plays on the tasting room's sound system instead of the typical classical music, but despite their lighthearted attitude, they're serious about crafting noteworthy wines, especially cabernet sauvignon. Next to the winery is a small stage for summer theater and music performances, and a climb up the hill from the tasting room yields a breathtaking valley view. ∎TIP→**You'll likely see a lot of Sonomans picnicking here: this spot is a favorite local hangout.** ⊠ *2000 Denmark St.* ☎ *707/938–5277* ⊕ *www.gunbun.com* ⊟ *Tasting $5–$10, tour free* ⊙ *Daily 11–4:30; tour weekends at noon, 1, 2, and 3, weekdays by appointment.*

WHERE TO STAY & EAT

$$–$$$$ ✕**Cafe La Haye.** Though the tiny storefront half a block off Sonoma's plaza might not catch your eye as you wander by, this spot is almost always packed with the food cognoscenti. It's a case of good things coming in small packages. The petite dining room, brightened by colorful art, looks into a minuscule kitchen. The menu is fittingly short, but each choice, such as quail with a bacon-shiitake–pine nut stuffing, is notably good. The wine list specializes in hard-to-find California bottles. The attentive, friendly service helps to secure plenty of repeat customers. ⊠ *140 E. Napa St.* ☎ *707/935–5994* ⊟ *AE, MC, V* ⊙ *Closed Sun. and Mon. No lunch.*

$$–$$$ ✕**Harvest Moon Cafe.** It's easy to feel like one of the fam-
★ ily at this little restaurant with an odd, zigzagging layout, and where diners seated at one of the two tiny bars chat with the servers like old friends. But Harvest Moon is very serious about the homey dishes on its daily changing menu, like a fat grilled pork chop with polenta and Brussels sprouts, seared ahi tuna with sautéed Swiss chard, and

a chicory Caesar salad dusted generously with Parmesan. Everything is so perfectly executed and the vibe so genuinely warm, that a visit here is deeply satisfying. ✉487 W. First St. ☎707/933–8160 ═AE, MC, V ☺Closed Wed. No lunch.

$$–$$$ ✗**LaSalette.** Chef-owner Manny Azevedo, born in the Azores and raised in Sonoma, serves dishes inspired by his native Portugal in this warmly decorated spot a few steps off Sonoma's plaza. Boldly flavored dishes such as *porco à alentejana*, a traditional pork with clams and tomatoes, might be followed by a dish of rice pudding with dried figs or a port from the varied list. ■TIP→**A small menu of crêpes, omelets, and baked goods like decadent** *sonhos* **(little cream-filled donuts), is served Wednesday through Sunday morning, when many other Sonoma restaurants are closed up tight** ✉452 E. 1st St. ☎707/938–1927 ═AE, D, MC, V.

$–$$$ ✗**The Girl & the Fig.** Maybe it's the down-to-earth bistro cuisine, or the high quality of the service, or the stellar wine list focused on Rhône varietals from both France and California. Whatever the winning combination, owner Sondra Bernstein's restaurant has succeeded marvelously in what was once the bar of the historic Sonoma Hotel. You can always find something with the signature figs in it here, from a salad with fresh figs to a chicken roasted with dried figs. Also look for duck confit with green lentils, steak frites, or Provençal shellfish stew. Brunch is a Sunday exclusive, with rib-sticking dishes such as hanger steak and eggs and a goat cheese frittata. ✉Sonoma Hotel, Sonoma Plaza, 110 W. Spain St. ☎707/938–3634 ═AE, D, DC, MC, V.

$–$$$ ✗**Meritage.** A fortuitous blend of southern French and northern Italian cuisine is the backbone of this restaurant, where chef Carlo Cavallo works wonders with house-made pastas. The warmly lighted dining room, with its sea of unusual sculpted-glass light fixtures, is more romantic than the lively bar area, where a sometimes raucous crowd slurps oysters while a TV flickers over the bar. ✉165 Napa St. W ☎707/938–9430 ═AE, MC, V ☺Closed Tues.

$–$$ ✗**Della Santina's.** A longtime favorite with a charming brick patio out back serves the most authentic Italian food in town. (The Della Santina family, which has been running the restaurant since 1990, hails from Lucca, Italy.) All the pastas are made in-house, while the roasted meats turn on a rotisserie. If they're available, don't miss the petrale sole and sand dabs. ✉*133 E. Napa St.* ☎*707/935–0576* ▭*AE, D, MC, V.*

$$$$ ✕▣ **The Fairmont Sonoma Mission Inn & Spa.** Pink, expensive, and popular, this sprawling Mission-style resort really seems to have it all, including two restaurants, multiple pools, tennis courts, and a world-class spa, easily the biggest in the Wine Country. The focus on fitness and rejuvenation extends to a 7,087-yard golf course winding through trees and vineyards, fitness classes, and guided hiking and biking excursions each morning. All of this is enough to work up an appetite for dinner at Santé, the resort's formal dining room that manages to be both rustic (wrought-iron chandeliers) and refined (Frette table linens). Chef Joseph Brown largely relies on local seasonal ingredients—cheeses made at nearby Cow Girl Creamery, Sonoma foie gras, or artichokes grown in Half Moon Bay—for his creative dishes. The guest rooms aren't terribly large but are supremely comfortable; some have fireplaces and patios or balconies. The staff stays on top of every detail. **Pros:** Enormous spa, excellent on-site restaurant, free shuttle to downtown Sonoma. **Cons:** Not as intimate as some similarly priced places, $15 valet parking. ✉*100 Boyes Blvd./ Rte. 12, 2 mi north of Sonoma, Boyes Hot Springs 95476* ☎*707/938–9000* ⊕*www.fairmont.com/sonoma* ⬩*168 rooms, 60 suites* ⬩*In-room: safe, refrigerator, Ethernet. In-hotel: 2 restaurants, room service, bars, golf course, pools, gym, spa, bicycles, concierge, laundry service, no-smoking rooms* ▭*AE, DC, MC, V.*

$$–$$$ ▣ **Inn at Sonoma.** They don't skimp on the little luxuries here: wine and cheese is served every evening in the lobby and the cheerfully painted rooms are equipped with Wi-Fi and warmed by gas fireplaces. In the closets you'll find fluffy terry robes, which come in handy for trips to the hot tub on the inn's upper level. A teddy bear perched on each feather comforter–topped bed holds a remote control to a small TV. Though the inn is just off heavily trafficked Broadway, good soundproofing makes it quieter than many of the hotels on Sonoma Plaza. (The town square is only a five-minute walk away.) Though rooms are not particularly large, you'd be hard pressed to find this much charm for the price elsewhere in town. **Pros:** Great last-minute specials, free sodas in the lobby, lovely hot tub. **Cons:** Friendly staff seems inexperienced. ✉*630 Broadway, 95476* ☎*707/939–1340* ⊕*www.innatsonoma.com* ⬩*19 rooms* ⬩*In-room:*

DVD, Wi-Fi. In-hotel: bicycles, no-smoking rooms =AE, *D, MC, V* ⦶CP.

$$ ☖**El Dorado Hotel.** Rooms in this remodeled 1843 building strike a spare, modern pose, with rectilinear four-poster beds and pristine white bedding, but the Mexican-tile floors hint at Sonoma's Mission-era past. Rooms are generally small, but high-tech features like flat-panel TVs are a nice touch, and a few have small balconies. Though its position smack-dab on Sonoma's plaza and on top of a bustling restaurant and bar is considered a boon by some, earplugs are advised for all but the hardiest sleepers. **Pros:** Stylish for the price, hip restaurant downstairs, central location. **Cons:** Indifferent staff, noisy, parking lot tends to fill up. ✉*405 1st St. W, 95476* ☎*707/996–3030* ⦶*www. eldoradosonoma.com* ⮫*27 rooms* ⟁*In-room: DVD, Wi-Fi. In-hotel: restaurant, bar, pool, no elevator, no-smoking rooms* =AE, *MC, V.*

NIGHTLIFE & THE ARTS

After hours you're apt to find locals at the bar at the rustic **Swiss Hotel** (✉*18 W. Spain St.* ☎*707/938–2884*), which looks much like it did a century ago, with the exception of the historic photographs of Sonoma added to the walls. To get in the spirit of things, ask for their signature secret-recipe drink, a Glariffee (a colder, sweeter variation of Irish coffee). For specialty cocktails and fairly pricey wines by the glass, head to the bar at the sleek and stylish **El Dorado Kitchen** (✉*405 1st St. W* ☎*707/996–3030*). If you're lucky, you might be able to nab a poolside seat. Opened in 2007, the **Harmony Lounge** (✉*480 1st St. E* ☎*707/996–9779*) has a full bar and sometimes books performances by local and touring jazz musicians.

The **Sebastiani Theatre** (✉*476 1st St. E* ☎*707/996–2020*), built on Sonoma's plaza in 1934 by Italian immigrant and entrepreneur Samuele Sebastiani, schedules first-run films, musical performances, and sometimes quirky theatrical performances.

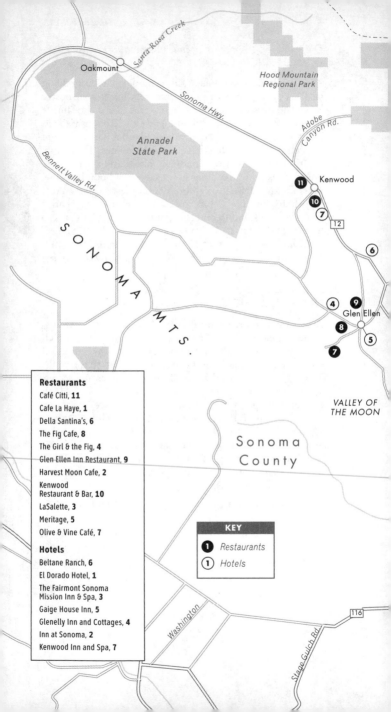

Restaurants

Café Citti, **11**

Cafe La Haye, **1**

Della Santina's, **6**

The Fig Cafe, **8**

The Girl & the Fig, **4**

Glen Ellen Inn Restaurant, **9**

Harvest Moon Cafe, **2**

Kenwood Restaurant & Bar, **10**

LaSalette, **3**

Meritage, **5**

Olive & Vine Café, **7**

Hotels

Beltane Ranch, **6**

El Dorado Hotel, **1**

The Fairmont Sonoma Mission Inn & Spa, **3**

Gaige House Inn, **5**

Glenelly Inn and Cottages, **4**

Inn at Sonoma, **2**

Kenwood Inn and Spa, **7**

KEY

1 *Restaurants*

① *Hotels*

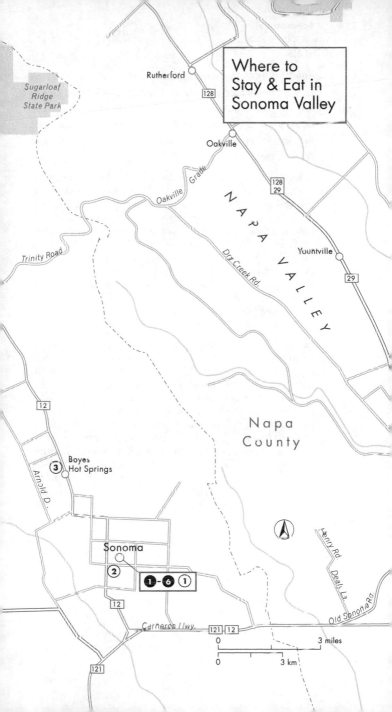

Where to
Stay & Eat in
Sonoma Valley

Sugarloaf
Ridge
State Park

Rutherford

128

Oakville

Oakville Grade

N A P A   V A L L E Y

128
29

Trinity Road

Dry Creek Rd.

Yountville

29

12

Napa
County

Boyes
Hot Springs

3

Arnold D.

Sonoma

2

1 - 6   1

12

Henry Rd

Deal Ln.

Old Sonoma Rd.

Cameron Hwy.

121   12

0   3 miles

0   3 km

121

SHOPPING

FARMERS' MARKET The **Sonoma Farmers' Market** overflows with locally farmed produce, artisanal cheeses, and baked goods. It's held year-round at Depot Park, just north of Sonoma Plaza, on Friday from 9 AM to noon. From April through October, it gets extra play on Tuesday evenings from 5:30 PM to dusk at Sonoma Plaza.

Sonoma Plaza is the town's main shopping magnet, with tempting boutiques and specialty food purveyors facing the square or just a block or two away. In addition to stocking more varieties of Sonoma Jack cheese than you probably knew existed, the **Sonoma Cheese Factory and Deli** (⊠*Sonoma Plaza, 2 Spain St.* ☎*707/996–1931*) sells a fine selection of wines and breads, making it a one-stop picnic-packing spot. There's a coffee and gelato bar in back. A block east of Sonoma Plaza, the **Vella Cheese Company** (⊠*315 2nd St. E* ☎*707/938–3232*) has been making superb cheeses, such as a raw milk cheddar and several varieties of jack, since 1931.

Lest you think that there's nothing but cheese to buy in Sonoma, take a spin around the plaza and make a few detours on the side streets to see what else is on offer. **Half-Pint** (⊠*Sonoma Plaza, 450 1st St. E* ☎*707/938–1722*) carries fashionable clothing and accessories for infants and children, like party dresses and too-cute booties for newborns. **Sign of the Bear** (⊠*Sonoma Plaza, 435 1st St. W* ☎*707/996–3722*) sells the latest and greatest in kitchenware and cookware, as well as a few Wine Country–themed items, like lazy Susans made from wine barrels. Half a block from the plaza, **Être** (⊠*156 East Napa St.* ☎*707/939–2700*) sells luxe housewares and gift items, like letterpress note cards, aromatic Diptyque candles, and decorative tchotchkes.

GLEN ELLEN

7 mi north of Sonoma on Rte. 12.

Numbers in the margin correspond to numbers on the Sonoma Valley map.

Craggy Glen Ellen epitomizes the difference between the Napa and Sonoma valleys. While small Napa towns such as St. Helena get their charm from upscale boutiques and restaurants lined up along well-groomed sidewalks, in Glen Ellen the crooked streets are shaded with stands of old oak trees and occasionally bisected by the Sonoma and Calabasas creeks. Tucked among the trees of a narrow canyon, where Sonoma Mountain and the Mayacamas pinch in the valley floor, Glen Ellen looks more like a town of the Sierra Foothills gold country than a Wine Country village.

Wine has been part of Glen Ellen since the 1840s, when a French immigrant, Joshua Chauvet, planted grapes and built a winery and the valley's first distillery. The winery machinery was powered by steam, and the boilers were fueled with wood from local oak trees. In 1881, Chauvet built a stone winery to house his operations. Other valley farmers followed Chauvet's example, and grape-growing took off. Wine was even made during Prohibition, when the locals took a liberal view of the 200 gallons each family was allowed to produce for personal consumption. There are still dozens of wineries in the area that beg to be visited, but sometimes it's hard not to succumb to Glen Ellen's slow pace and simply lounge poolside at your lodgings or linger over a leisurely picnic. The renowned cook and food writer M.F.K. Fisher, who lived and worked in Glen Ellen for 22 years until her death in 1992, would surely have approved.

Glen Ellen's most famous resident, however, was Jack London, who epitomized Glen Ellen's rugged spirit.

★ ❾ In the hills above town lies **Jack London State Historic Park**, once the author's Beauty Ranch, where he lived, wrote, and died in a small white farm cottage. Following his death, London's wife, Charmian, operated it as a dude ranch. After she died, in 1955, she willed the ranch to the state parks system. The park's 2-mi hiking trail along the edge of vineyards and through stands of oak trees takes you to London's grave and to the ruins of Wolf House, which burned under mysterious circumstances in 1913, days before the couple was to move into it. Shaded by huge redwood trees, the remains of London's house look like an ancient castle from a European fairy tale. The author's grave, though, is a simple affair: a small picket fence and a plaque mark the spot where his ashes rest. The author's South Seas artifacts and other personal effects are on view at the House of Happy Walls museum. ✉*2400 London Ranch Rd.* ☎*707/938–5216* 🚗*Parking $6* ☉*Park Nov.–*

Mar., daily 9:30–5; Apr.–Oct., daily 9:30–7. Museum daily 10–5.

VINEYARDS NEAR GLEN ELLEN

❿ Arrowood Vineyards & Winery is neither as old nor as famous as some of its neighbors, but winemakers and critics are quite familiar with the wines produced here by Richard Arrowood. A veranda with wicker chairs wraps around the gray-and-white building that looks like it would be at home on Cape Cod. Try the big but approachable cabernet sauvignons and excellent, inky syrahs, or, if you're fan of whites, the Côte de Lune Blanc, a blend of marsanne, roussanne, and viognier. A stone fireplace in the tasting room makes this an especially enticing destination in winter. ✉*14347 Sonoma Hwy./Rte. 12* ☏*707/935–2600* ⊕*www. arrowoodvineyards.com* 🍷*Tasting $5–$10, tour $30* ⊙*Daily 10–4:30; tour by appointment.*

★ **⓫** One of the best-known wineries in the Glen Ellen area is **Benziger Family Winery,** on a sprawling estate in a bowl with 360-degree sun exposure. Among the first wineries to identify certain vineyard blocks for particularly desirable flavors, Benziger is noted for its merlot, pinot blanc, chardonnay, and fumé blanc. The tours here are especially interesting (they're first come, first served). On a tram ride through the vineyards, guides explain the regional microclimates and geography and give you a glimpse of the extensive cave system. Tours depart several times a day, weather permitting, but are sometimes fully booked during the high season. ■TIP➔**Arrive before lunch for the best shot at joining a tour—and bring a picnic, since the grounds here are lovely.** ✉*1883 London Ranch Rd.* ☏*707/935–3000* ⊕*www.benziger.com* 🍷*Tasting $5–$10, tour $10* ⊙*Daily 10–5.*

OFF THE BEATEN PATH Just a 15-minute drive from Glen Ellen via curvy Bennett Valley Road, the visitor center at beautiful **Matanzas Creek Winery** sets itself apart with an understated Japanese aesthetic, with a tranquil fountain and a koi pond. Best of all, huge windows overlook a vast field of lavender plants. ■TIP➔**The best time to visit is in June, when the lavender blooms and perfumes the air.** The winery specializes in three varietals—sauvignon blanc, merlot, and chardonnay—though in 2005 they also started producing a popular dry rosé. After you taste the wines, ask for the self-guided garden-tour book before

Jack London Country

Rugged, rakish author and adventurer Jack London is perhaps best known for his travels to Alaska and his exploits in the South Pacific, which he immortalized in tales such as *Call of the Wild, White Fang,* and *South Sea Tales.* But he loved no place so well as the hills of eastern Sonoma County, where he spent most of his 30's and where he died, in 1916, at the age of 40.

In 1913 London rhapsodized about his beloved ranch near Glen Ellen, writing, "The grapes on a score of rolling hills are red with autumn flame. Across Sonoma Mountain wisps of sea fog are stealing. The afternoon sun smolders in the drowsy sky. I have everything to make me glad I am alive. I am filled with dreams and mysteries."

Between 1905 and 1916 London bought seven parcels of land totaling 1,400 acres, which he dubbed Beauty Ranch. When he wasn't off traveling, he dedicated most of his time to cultivating the land and raising livestock here. He also maintained a few acres of wine grapes for his personal use.

Much of the Beauty Ranch is now preserved as the Jack London State Historic Park, worth visiting not only for its museum and other glimpses into London's life but also for the trails that skirt vineyards and meander through a forest of Douglas fir, coastal redwoods, oak, and madrones. Here, London and his wife spent two years constructing their dream house, before it burned down one hot August night in 1913, just days before they were scheduled to move in.

A look at the remaining stone walls and fireplaces gives you a sense of the home's grand scale. Within, a fireproof basement vault was to hold London's manuscripts. Elsewhere in the park stands the unusually posh pigsty known to London's neighbors as the Pig Palace.

Outside the park, London-related attractions are relatively few. Downhill from the park entrance, the Jack London Saloon, which first opened in 1905, has walls covered with photographs and other London memorabilia.

Parts of Beauty Ranch are still owned by London's descendants, who grow cabernet sauvignon, zinfandel, and merlot on a portion of the property. For a taste of the wines made from these grapes, head a few miles north to Kenwood Vineyards, which uses them to produce Jack London Vineyard reserve wines.

taking a stroll. ⊠ *6097 Bennett Valley Rd.* ☎ *707/528–6464 or 800/590–6464* ⊕ *www.matanzascreek.com* ⌑ *Tasting $5, tour free* ⊙ *Daily 10–4:30; tour weekdays at 10:30 and 2:30, Sat. at 10:30 by appointment.*

WHERE TO STAY & EAT

$$–$$$ ✕ **Glen Ellen Inn Restaurant.** This cozy restaurant in a creekside house exudes romance, especially if you snag a seat in the shady garden or on the patio strung with tiny lights. The eclectic, frequently changing menu plucks elements from California, French, and occasionally Asian cuisines. For instance, you might try ginger-tempura calamari or a filet mignon with Maytag blue cheese. Desserts tend toward the decadent; witness the warm pecan bread pudding with a chocolate center that sites in a puddle of brandy sauce. The wine list is short but well chosen. ⊠ *13670 Arnold Dr.* ☎ *707/996–6409* ⊟ *AE, MC, V* ⊙ *No lunch Wed. or Thurs.*

$–$$ ★ Fodor'sChoice ✕ **The Fig Cafe.** Pale sage walls, yellow tablecloths, and casual but very warm service set a sunny mood in this little bistro that's run by the same team behind Sonoma's The Girl & the Fig. The restaurant's eponymous fruit shows up in all sorts of unexpected places—not only in salads and desserts, but even in an aperitif (the Champagne-based "fig royale") and on thin-crusted pizzas piled high with arugula. The small menu focuses on California and French comfort food, like steamed mussels served with terrific crispy fries, and a braised pot roast served with seasonal vegetables. Don't forget to look on the chalkboard for frequently changing desserts, such as butterscotch pots de crème. ■TIP➔ **The unusual no-corkage-fee policy makes it a great place to drink the wine you just discovered down the road.** ⊠ *13690 Arnold Dr.* ☎ *707/938–2130* ⊟ *AE, D, MC, V* ⌑ *Reservations not accepted* ⊙ *No lunch weekdays.*

¢–$ ✕ **Olive & Vine Café.** The menu changes every day at this casual café with wooden farmhouse tables. Take a look at the blackboard list, which is likely to include panini (like a barbecued pork sandwich with caramelized onions) or inventive seasonal dishes such as a refreshing watermelon gazpacho. But be sure to ask, too, about the items in the refrigerated case, like an updated three-bean salad or miniature pizzas with house-made tomato sauce. It's a good stop for picnic packers; you can also eat in the dining room, a soaring barnlike space in the Jack London Village complex, or tote your dishes out to the deck, where tables overlook a creek. At this writing, an attached wine bar was about to open. ✉14301 Arnold Dr. ☎707/996–9150 ⊟AE, MC, V ⌲Reservations not accepted ⊗Closed Mon. No dinner Wed. and Fri.–Sun.

$$$$ ★ Fodor'sChoice ☂**Gaige House Inn.** Gorgeous orchids and Asian objets d'art are just a few of the little luxuries in this understated B&B. Rooms in the main house, an 1890 Queen Anne, are mostly done in pale colors and each has its advantages. An upstairs room has wraparound windows to let in floods of light, for instance, while a smaller downstairs room opens onto the pool area. The most lavish rooms are the eight cottages, which have a pronounced Japanese influence, and massive granite soaking tubs overlooking a private atrium. In addition to the main pool and hot tub, surrounded by magnolia trees, a second, private hot tub is available to those who sign up. Though the staffers are helpful, service never seems fussy, and there's a bottomless jar of cookies in the kitchen. **Pros:** Beautiful lounge areas, very private cottages, three-course breakfast. **Cons:** Sound carries in the main house, a few rooms are small. ✉13540 Arnold Dr, 95442 ☎707/935–0237 or 800/935–0237 ⊕www.gaige.com ➪12 rooms, 11 suites ⌂In-room: safe (some), refrigerator, DVD (some), Ethernet (some), Wi-Fi (some). In-hotel: pool, no elevator, no-smoking rooms ⊟AE, D, DC, MC, V ⊚lBP.

$$ ☂**Glenelly Inn and Cottages.** On a quiet side street a few blocks from the town center, this sunny little establishment has a long history as a getaway. It was built as an inn in 1916, and the rooms, each individually decorated, tend toward a simple country style. Many have four-poster beds and touches such as a wood-burning stove or antique oak dresser; some have whirlpool tubs. All have puffy down comforters. Breakfast is served in front of the common room's cobblestone fireplace, as are cookies or other snacks in the afternoon. Innkeeper Kristi Hallamore Jeppesen has two children of her own, so this is an unusually kid-friendly inn. **Pros:** Children are welcome, quiet location, friendly innkeeper. **Cons:** Romantics may not appreciate presence of children, some rooms could use freshening up. ✉5131 Warm Springs Rd., 95442 ☎707/996–6720 ⊕www.glenelly.com ➪8 rooms, 2 suites ⌂In-room: no a/c (some), no phone (some), refrigerator (some), VCR (some),

no TV (some), Wi-Fi. In-hotel: no elevator, laundry facili-ties, no-smoking rooms ⊟*AE, D, MC, V* ⊚*BP.*

★ $-$$ ☷**Beltane Ranch.** On a slope of the Mayacamas range just a few miles from Glen Ellen, this 1892 ranch house stands in the shade of magnificent oak trees. The charmingly old-fashioned rooms, each individually decorated with antiques, have separate entrances, and some open onto a wraparound balcony ideal for whiling away lazy after-noons. The detached cottage, once the gardener's quar-ters, has a small sitting room. Formerly a turkey farm, the expansive property is traversed by an 8-mi hiking trail that's popular with guests. **Pros:** Reasonably priced, boun-tiful breakfast, beautiful grounds with ancient oak trees. **Cons:** Downstairs rooms get some noise from upstairs rooms, credit cards not accepted. ⊠*11775 Sonoma Hwy./ Rte. 12, 95442* ☏*707/996–6501* ⊕*www.beltaneranch.com* ☛*3 rooms, 3 suites* ⚭*In-room: no a/c, no TV. In-hotel: tennis court, no elevator* ⊟*No credit cards* ⊚*BP.*

NIGHTLIFE

Built in 1905, the **Jack London Saloon** (⊠*13740 Arnold Dr.* ☏*707/996–3100* ⊕*www.jacklondonlodge.com*) is decorated with photos of London and other London memorabilia.

SHOPPING

In the Jack London Village complex, the **Olive Press** (⊠*14301 Arnold Dr.* ☏*707/939–8900*) not only carries many local olive oils, serving bowls, books, and dining accessories but also presses fruit for a number of local growers, usually in the late fall. You can taste a selection of olive oils that have surprisingly different flavors.

KENWOOD

3 mi north of Glen Ellen on Rte. 12.

Numbers in the margin correspond to numbers on the Sonoma Valley map.

Blink and you might miss tiny Kenwood, which consists of little more than a few restaurants and shops, a couple of tasting rooms, and a historic train depot, now used for private events. But hidden in this pretty landscape of mead-

Best Tasting Room Snacks

Wine is meant to be drunk with food, many vintners would argue, so why is it that you have to taste wines all by themselves at most tasting rooms? Many wineries, in an attempt to show off their wines to best effect, have recently started hiring chefs to create complex wine-and-food pairings. We're not talking about a plate of cheese and crackers here (although some wineries will serve that, too), but elegantly prepared small plates that come hot out of the kitchen.

Many wineries organize occasional food-and-wine pairings on an irregular basis (check their Web sites for information), while others have made it a part of their regular wine-tasting program. Expect to pay about $25 to $50 for these pairings, which can range from a few rich bites to a light meal. Though the experience isn't exactly cheap, these tastings can often serve as a light lunch, especially on those days when you need some digestive downtime between a big B&B breakfast and your dinner reservations. The following wineries have a strong emphasis on food-and-wine pairings and regularly serve delicious hot dishes.

■ **J Vineyards and Winery.** Flights of four sparkling wines come with two bites each of paired appetizers ($25). Reserve wines are paired with more elaborate concoctions, or with caviar ($55), in the Bubble Room, where you are seated rather than standing. ✉*11447 Old Redwood Hwy.* ☎*707/431–3646* ⊕*www.jwine.com.*

■ **Mayo Family Winery Reserve Room.** This spot in Kenwood looks more like a small restaurant than a tasting room, with bar-height tables and vineyard views. Seven wines are paired with seven morsels of food, like a Russian River pinot noir with a hazelnut duck-liver pâté, or a chocolate truffle and blue cheese with a zinfandel port. ✉*9200 Sonoma Hwy.* ☎*707/833–5504* ⊕*www.mayofamilywinery.com.*

■ **St. Francis Winery.** In addition to the cheese and charcuterie pairing available daily, St. Francis also offers seated pairings of four wines with four small plates on Fridays, Saturdays, and Sundays from June through October. Reserve in advance for the $45 experience, which might match a seared scallop with a viognier or duck *rillettes* (a smooth pâté) and cherry compote with cabernet sauvignon. ✉*100 Pythian Rd.* ☎*800/543–7713* ⊕*www.stfranciswinery.com.*

4

ows and woods at the north end of Sonoma Valley are several good wineries, most just off the Sonoma Highway. A hodgepodge of varietals tend to be grown here at the foot of the Sugarloaf Mountains, from sauvignon blanc and chardonnay to zinfandel and cabernet.

⑫ Several wineries in the Kenwood area are small operations—some of them started within the last decade or so—that do not have tasting rooms of their own. At **The Wine Room,** you can sample the output of three such wineries. Since the tasting room is usually staffed by the owners and winemakers themselves, you can count on learning a lot about the wines being poured. ✉ *9575 Sonoma Hwy.* ☎ *707/833–6131* ⊕ *www.the-wine-room.com* ✍ *$5* ⊙ *Daily 11–5.*

VINEYARDS AROUND KENWOOD

⑬ On your way into **Kunde Estate Winery & Vineyards** you'll pass a terrace flanked with a reflecting pool and fountains, virtually coaxing you to stay for a picnic with views over the vineyard. The tour of the grounds includes its extensive caves, some of which stretch 175 feet below a chardonnay vineyard. Kunde is perhaps best known for its chardonnays, which range from crisp ones aged in stainless steel tanks to toastier ones that have spent time in French oak barrels. Tastings usually include sauvignon blanc, cabernet sauvignon, and zinfandel as well. If you skip the tour, take a few minutes to wander around the demonstration vineyard outside the tasting room. In the months before crush (usually in September), you can sample the different grapes on the vines and see if you can discern the similarities between the grapes and wines you just tasted. ✉ *10155 Sonoma Hwy./Rte. 12* ☎ *707/833–5501* ⊕ *www.kunde. com* ✍ *Tasting $5–$10, tour free* ⊙ *Daily 10:30–4:30, tour hourly Fri.–Sun. 11–3.*

⑭ **Kenwood Vineyards** makes some good-value red and white wines, as well as some showier cabernet sauvignons and zinfandels, many poured in the tasting room housed in one of the original barns on the property. The best of these come from Jack London's old vineyard, in the Sonoma Mountain appellation, above the fog belt of the Sonoma Valley (Kenwood has an exclusive lease). But what the wine connoisseurs keep coming back for is Kenwood's crisp sauvignon blanc. Most weekends the winery offers a free food-and-wine pairing, but there are no tours. ■ TIP→ **Free** tastings are a boon to those discovering that all those $10 tasting fees are starting to add up. ✉*9592 Sonoma Hwy./Rte. 12* ☎*707/833–5891* ⊕*www.kenwoodvineyards.com* 🍷*Tasting free* ⊙*Daily 10–4:30.*

⑮ At the foot of the Mayacamas Mountains stretch the impeccably groomed grounds of **Chateau St. Jean,** an old country estate once owned by a family of Midwestern industrialists. (A couple of ponds in the shape of Lakes Michigan and Huron speak to their loyalties.) Pick up a map as you enter: it will identify many of the flowers, trees, and hedges lining the neat pathways in the formal gardens. After a spin around the grounds, whose style harmonizes with the sprawling Mediterranean-style villa, go inside for a tasting of their fine chardonnay, fumé blanc, and reds that include a pinot noir, cabernet sauvignon, and syrah. An unusually large gift shop sells clothing and housewares, like a fully equipped picnic backpack, in addition to the usual wine-themed souvenirs. ✉*8555 Sonoma Hwy.* ☎*707/833–4134* ⊕*www.chateaustjean.com* 🍷*Tasting $10–$15* ⊙*Daily 10–5.*

⑯ Fleeing from subdivisions north of Santa Rosa, **Landmark Vineyards** decamped to the foothills of Sugarloaf Ridge in 1990. Rich, round chardonnay used to be the winery's main claim to fame, but in recent years critics have been taking note of its pinot noir as well. Stop here to taste the wines, but also take a close look at the building, which is a faithful reconstruction of a mission-period rancho—right on up to the shingle roof. Ask to borrow their boccie balls if you want to take advantage of the court in the picnic area. If you'll be visiting on a summer Saturday, call in advance to reserve a spot on the short horse-drawn wagon tour of the vineyard. ✉*101 Adobe Canyon Rd.* ☎*707/833–0053* ⊕*www.landmarkwine.com* 🍷*Tasting $5–$10* ⊙*Daily 10–4:30.*

★ ⑰ Named for Saint Francis of Assisi, founder of the Franciscan order, which established missions and vineyards throughout California, **St. Francis Winery** has one of the most scenic locations in Sonoma, nestled at the foot of Mount Hood. The visitor center beautifully replicates the California Mission style, with its red tile roof and dramatic bell tower (a plaque explains the bell was actually blessed in the St. Francis Cathedral in Assisi, Italy). Out back, a slate patio overlooks vineyards, lavender gardens, and hummingbirds flitting about the flower beds. The charm of the surroundings is matched by the wines, most of them red. Their reserve wines are all vineyard designates, made from grapes harvested from a single vineyard. Their other wines, many more modestly priced, are worth tasting, too. Consider paying a bit more ($25) to taste wines paired with artisanal cheeses and charcuterie. ✉ *100 Pythian Rd.* ☎ *800/543–7713* ⊕ *www.stfranciswinery.com* 🍷 *Tasting $10* ☉ *Daily 10–5.*

⓲ The strange purple-brick château of **Ledson Winery & Vineyards** sits incongruously amid vineyards, looking like a Victorian railway station in search of its town. The winery was originally designed by Steve Ledson as a home for his family, but when the outrageously ornate building started gaining intense interest during its construction, the family decided it made more sense to transform the building into a tasting room for their wines, first released in 1994. Ledson produces a number of varietals, including the obligatory pinot noir, syrah, zinfandel, and cabernet sauvignon, but also malbec, barbera, mourvèdre, primitivo, and several others. Particularly worth tasting are their chardonnay and an estate merlot, the first wine they released. A large deli next to the tasting room provides all you'll need to picnic under the oak trees. There's no tour. ✉ *7335 Sonoma Hwy./ Rte. 12* ☎ *707/537–3810* ⊕ *www.ledson.com* 🍷 *Tasting $5–$15* ☉ *Daily 10–5.*

WHERE TO STAY & EAT

$–$$$ ✕ **Kenwood Restaurant & Bar.** The menu changes constantly at Kenwood Restaurant, but you'll always find a great variety of French-inspired contemporary cooking, from a tender beef bourguignonne to hearty hamburgers to oysters on the half shell. The restaurant's at its best on warm afternoons and evenings, when you can enjoy the view of the vineyards from the patio, but the Sugarloaf Mountains can be glimpsed through the French doors from the dining room as well. The wine list is very good, especially when it comes to local bottlings, and you can also order cocktails from the full bar. ✉ *9900 Sonoma Hwy.* ☎ *707/833–6326* ▭ *MC, V* ☉ *Closed Mon. and Tues.*

¢–$$ ✕ **Café Citti.** Locals love this no-frills Tuscan-style trattoria, and they don't mind ordering at the counter before taking one of the seats indoor by the fireplace or out on the patio. Plain fare such as roast chicken, focaccia sandwiches, and pasta with your choice of sauce (marinara, puttanesca, or

A Great Drive in Sonoma Valley

It's easy to zip through the Sonoma Valley in a day—the drive from Sonoma at the south end to Kenwood to the north can be done in about 25 minutes—but once you start stopping at Sonoma's historic sites and the valley's wineries, your visit could easily be spread over two days. For a day trip of the highlights, start in the town of Sonoma. Do a lap around the historic plaza, then pick up picnic supplies at the Sonoma Cheese Factory. Once in your car, drive southeast on West Napa Street, which turns into East Napa Street. Turn right on East 8th Street and left onto Denmark Street, where you'll see the Gundlach-Bundschu winery sign. After a tasting, hike up the GunBun hill for your picnic.

Back in the car, head back to Sonoma Plaza and continue along West Napa Street (also Highway 12), following the signs pointing north on High-

way 12. About half an hour later, you'll pass the tiny town of Kenwood. Just north of Kenwood, on the right side of Highway 12, is St. Francis Winery, a very photogenic spot and a must for red-wine fans. Returning south on Highway 12, look for Kunde Estate just south of Kenwood, just a few minutes down the road. If you've managed to wrap up your wine tasting before 4 PM, continue south on Highway 12 and take the Arnold Drive exit into the picturesque town of Glen Ellen. From Arnold Drive turn right on London Ranch Road. After winding your way uphill for a few minutes you'll reach Jack London State Park. Take a short stroll through the grounds and a gander at some of the historic buildings near the parking area before the park closes at 5 PM. Return to Highway 12 and continue south to the town of Sonoma for dinner.

pesto) is served with the prepared salads displayed in the deli case. Everything is available to go, which means they do a brisk business in takeout for picnic packers. ✉*9049 Sonoma Hwy./Rte. 12* ☎*707/833–2690* ▭*MC, V.*

★ $$$$ ☷**Kenwood Inn and Spa.** Buildings resembling graceful old haciendas and mature fruit trees shading the courtyards convey the sense that this inn has been here for over a century. French doors opening onto terraces or balconies, fluffy feather beds, wood burning fireplaces, sumptuous velvet couches, and voluminous silk drapes give the uncommonly spacious guest rooms a particularly romantic air. A swimming pool, Jacuzzis, and saunas pepper three atmospheric courtyards, and you could easily spend an afternoon padding from one to another in your robe and slippers. The intimate spa draws on the local preoccupation, using the Caudalíe line of grape-derived products and treatments. In the dining room, open to inn guests only, the chef prepares traditional Italian dishes like fettuccine with a rich Bolognese sauce. **Pros:** Large rooms, attentive service, lavish furnishings. **Cons:** Expensive, restaurant isn't quite up to the level of the inn. ✉ *10400 Sonoma Hwy., 95452* ☎ *707/833–1293* ⊕ *www.kenwoodinn.com* ↩ *25 rooms, 4 suites* ♿ *In-room: no TV, Ethernet. In-hotel: restaurant, bar, pool, spa, no elevator, concierge, laundry service, no-smoking rooms.*

Northern Sonoma County

WORD OF MOUTH

"I would absolutely hands-down recommend a stay in Healdsburg and putter around the wineries here. There are few crowds, quiet bucolic country roads, much to recommend."

—heatherfife

NORTHERN SONOMA COUNTY IS A STUDY in contrasts. Urban Santa Rosa is northern Sonoma's workhorse: It has population of more than 150,000 residents but precious few visitors—not surprising, since there are far more office parks than wineries within its city limits. Fifteen miles north, on the other hand, ritzy Healdsburg buzzes with luxe hotels, hip wine bars, and some of the Wine Country's hottest restaurants. Just outside these towns, however, it's all rolling hills, with only the occasional horse ranch, orchard, or stand of oak trees interrupting the vineyards.

Lovely little Healdsburg is the most convenient home base for exploring most of this region. Not only does it have an easily walkable town center, swank hotels, and a remarkable restaurant scene, but it's smack-dab at the confluence of the Russian River, Dry Creek, and Alexander valleys, three of northern Sonoma's blockbuster appellations, which produce some of the country's best pinot noir, cabernet sauvignon, zinfandel, and sauvignon blanc.

The western stretches of Sonoma County, which reach all the way to the Pacific Ocean, are sparsely populated in comparison to the above destinations, with only the occasional vineyard popping up in between isolated ranches. A popular destination for weekending San Franciscans, who come to canoe down the Russian River and sun themselves on its banks, Guerneville isn't a big wine destination itself, but it's a convenient place for picking up River Road, then Westside Road, which passes through pinot noir paradise on its way to Healdsburg.

Although each of northern Sonoma's regions claims its own microclimate, soil types, and most-favored varietals, they do have something in common: peace and quiet. Northern Sonoma is far less crowded than Napa Valley and the larger tasting rooms in southern Sonoma. Though Healdsburg in particular is hardly a stranger to overnight visitors, it's rare to bump into more than a few others in most of northern Sonoma's tasting rooms.

GETTING AROUND NORTHERN SONOMA COUNTY

The quickest route to northern Sonoma from San Francisco is straight up U.S. 101 to Healdsburg, but the back roads offer the best rewards. Highway 116 (also called the Gravenstein Highway), west of 101, leads through the little towns of Forestville and Graton (both with a handful of great restaurants), before depositing you along the Russian River near Guerneville. Traffic along U.S. 101 is notoriously bad around Santa Rosa. Do whatever you can to avoid passing through during rush hour, especially on Friday afternoons, and be prepared for slow going at any time of day.

NORTHERN SONOMA COUNTY APPELLATIONS

The sprawling Northern Sonoma AVA covers about 329,000 acres, but is divided into about a dozen smaller subappellations. Three of the most important of these sub-appellations meet at Healdsburg: the Russian River Valley AVA, which runs southwest along the lower course of the river; the Dry Creek Valley AVA, which heads northwest from town; and the Alexander Valley AVA, which is east and north of Healdsburg.

The cool climate of the low-lying **Russian River Valley AVA** is perfect for fog-loving pinot noir grapes as well as chardonnay. Although 20 years ago this was a little-known appellation, with as much pastureland and redwood stands as vineyards, in recent years it has exploded with vineyards, and it's now one of Sonoma's most-recognized appellations.

Although it's a small region—only about 16 miles long and 2 miles wide—zin lovers know all about the **Dry Creek Valley AVA,** where coastal hills temper the cooling influence of the Pacific Ocean. But even more acres are planted with cabernet sauvignon, and you'll find a smattering of merlot, chardonnay, sauvignon blanc, syrah, and several other varietals growing in the diverse soils and climate (it's warmer in the north and cooler in the south).

The **Alexander Valley AVA** is an up-and-comer, still in the process of being planted with vines (you're still apt to see orchards and pasture in between vineyards). Winemakers are still experimenting to determine the varietals that grow best in the relatively warm climate and diverse soils here, but so far chardonnay, sauvignon blanc, zinfandel, and cabernet sauvignon seem to do well.

Also in this area are the Knights Valley, Chalk Hill, Green Valley, and Sonoma Coast AVAs.

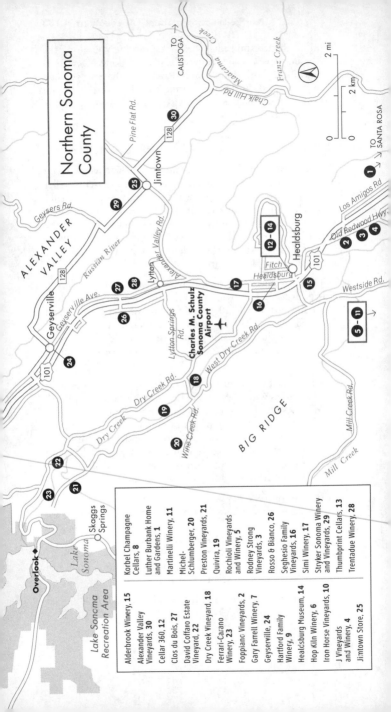

Northern Sonoma County

TO CALISTOGA →

TO SANTA ROSA →

ALEXANDER VALLEY

BIG RIDGE

Lake Sonoma

Skaggs Springs

Lake Sonoma Recreation Area

Overlook

Russian River

Dry Creek

Mill Creek

Franz Creek

Maacama Creek

Pine Flat Rd.

Geysers Rd.

Geyserville Ave.

Alexander Valley Rd.

Chalk Hill Rd.

Los Amigos Rd

Old Redwood Hwy

Westside Rd.

Mill Creek Rd.

Wine Creek Rd.

West Dry Creek Rd.

Dry Creek Rd.

Lytton Springs Rd.

Jimtown

Geyserville

Lytton

Healdsburg

Fitch Mountain

Charles M. Schulz Sonoma County Airport

2 mi

2 km

Aldenbrook Winery, **15**
Alexander Valley Vineyards, **30**
Cellar 360, **12**
Clos du Bois, **27**
David Coffaro Estate Vineyard, **18**
Dry Creek Vineyard, **18**
Ferrari-Carano Winery, **23**
Foppiano Vineyards, **2**
Gary Farrell Winery, **7**
Geyserville, **24**
Hartford Family Winery, **9**
Healdsburg Museum, **14**
Hop Kiln Winery, **6**
Iron Horse Vineyards, **10**
J Vineyards and Winery, **4**
Jimtown Store, **25**

Korbel Champagne Cellars, **8**
Luther Burbank Home and Gardens, **1**
Martinelli Winery, **11**
Michel-Schlumberger, **20**
Preston Vineyards, **21**
Quivira, **19**
Rochioli Vineyards and Winery, **5**
Rodney Strong Vineyards, **3**
Rosso & Bianco, **26**
Seghesio Family Vineyards, **16**
Simi Winery, **17**
Stryker Sonoma Winery and Vineyards, **29**
Thumbprint Cellars, **13**
Trentadue Winery, **28**

SANTA ROSA

8 mi northwest of Kenwood on Rte. 12.

Santa Rosa, the Wine Country's largest city, isn't likely to charm you with its office buildings, department stores, and almost perpetual snarl of traffic along U.S. 101. It is, however, home to a couple of interesting cultural offerings. Its chain motels and hotels are also handy if you're finding that everything else is booked up, especially since Santa Rosa is roughly equidistant from Sonoma, Healdsburg, and the Russian River Valley, three of the most popular wine-tasting destinations.

➊ The **Luther Burbank Home and Gardens** commemorates the great botanist who lived and worked on these grounds and single-handedly developed the modern techniques of hybridization. The 1.6-acre garden and a greenhouse show the results of some of Burbank's experiments to develop spineless cactus, fruit trees, and flowers such as the Shasta daisy. In the music room of his house, a modified Greek Revival structure that was Burbank's home from 1884 to 1906, a dictionary lies open to a page on which the verb "burbank" is defined as "to modify and improve plant life." (To see the house, you'll need to join one of the docent-led tours, which leave from the gift shop every half-hour.) ⊠*Santa Rosa and Sonoma Aves.* ☎*707/524–5445* ⊕*www.lutherburbank.org* ☜*Gardens free; tours $5* ☉*Gardens daily 8–dusk; museum and gift shop Apr.–Oct., Tues.–Sun. 10–4.*

WHERE TO STAY & EAT

$$–$$$$ ✕**John Ash & Co.** Patio seating and a cozy indoor fireplace make this spacious restaurant with vineyard views a draw in both summer and winter. The contemporary dishes cherry-pick influences from France, Italy, and even Asia, but the ingredients are largely local. Hog Island oysters come from Tomales Bay and in season you might find local king salmon with a miso crust and shiitake mushrooms. The wine list is impressive even by Wine Country standards, and a café menu offers bites in the bar between meals. ⊠*4330 Barnes Rd., River Rd. exit west from U.S. 101* ☎*707/527–7687* ⊟*AE, D, DC, MC, V* ☉*No lunch Sat.*

Beer Country

All over California, winemakers happily admit that "it takes a lot of beer to make fine wine." Lucky for them, there's no shortage of good local beer in the Wine Country.

The 1976 opening of the New Albion Brewery in Sonoma marks what many consider to be the renaissance of American craft brewing. With California in the forefront, microbreweries took off.

Many of California's brewers now take their inspiration from old British or European styles, tweaking them to sometimes extreme levels of intensity (and alcohol content!). You'll find monstrously malty porters, deep-golden lagers, and hefty wheat beers, plus lots of generously hopped—even triple-hopped—pale ales that finish with a distinctive kick.

Many breweries operate tasting rooms and tours, just as the wineries do. Look for brewpubs and local beer festivals to try more of the state's finest. Below are some of the best California breweries to visit.

Anderson Valley Brewing Company. Go for brewery tours, tasting room, and an 18-hole disc golf course at the home of Belk's Extra Special Bitter, Boont Amber Ale, and other consistent medal winners. ✉ 17700 Hwy. 253, Boon-

ville ☎ 707/895-2337 ⊕ www. avbc.com.

Bear Republic Brewing Company. Hops rule the Racer 5, Special XP Pale Ale, and specialty draft brews at this brewpub. ✉ 345 Healdsburg Ave., Healdsburg ☎ 707/433-2337 ⊕ www.bearrepublic.com.

Firestone Walker Brewing Company. Superb barrel-fermented ales are poured in the brewery tasting room. ✉ 1400 Ramada Dr., Paso Robles ☎ 805/238-2556 ⊕ www. firestonewalker.com.

Mendocino Brewing Company. The beer, such as the amber Red Tail Ale, is made in Ukiah, but you can taste it at the original brewery. ✉ 13351 S. Hwy. 101, Hopland ☎ 707/744-1361 ⊕ www. mendobrew.com.

Russian River Brewing Company. It's all about the double IPA and Belgian-style ales in this brewery's large pub. ✉ 725 4th St., Santa Rosa ☎ 707/545-2337 ⊕ www. russianriverbrewing.com.

Silverado Brewing Company. From a crisp blonde ale to a heartier oatmeal stout, the beers go well with the homey American food served at this St. Helena brewery. ✉ 3020 St. Helena Hwy., St. Helena ☎ 707/967-9876 ⊕ www. silveradobrewingcompany.com.

¢¢¢ ★ **Fodor'sChoice** ✕**Zazu.** A low wooden ceiling, rustic copper tables, and rock music on the stereo set a casual vibe at this roadhouse. It's a few miles from downtown Santa Rosa but the hearty, soulful cooking of owners Duskie Estes and John Stewart has passionate fans all over the Wine Country. Some of the produce for the salads comes from their own garden and the meats are house-cured, so the antipasto plate or a pizza with house-made pepperoni are both excellent choices. The small menu—a mix of Italian-influenced dishes and updated American classics—tends toward rich flavors, with seasonal items like fried rabbit with a cornmeal waffle and maple butter. ✉*3535 Guerneville Rd.* ☎*707/523–4814* ═*MC, V.*

$–$$$ ✕**Willi's Wine Bar.** Don't let the name fool you: instead of a sedate spot serving flights of bubbly with delicate nibbles, you'll find a cozy, casual restaurant where boisterous crowds snap up small plates from the globe-trotting menu. Asian-inflected dishes like the five-spice pork-belly pot stickers represent the East, while roasted bone marrow with toasted brioche and lobster gnocchi are some of the French- and Mediterranean-inspired foods from the West. Smack in the middle, oysters baked with artichokes and bacon are made with local ingredients. Wines are available in 2-ounce pours, making it easier to pair each of your little plates with a different type. ■TIP→ **The din inside can be deafening on busy nights. For a slightly quieter experience, ask for a table on the covered patio.** ✉*4404 Old Redwood Hwy.* ☎*707/526–3096* ═*D, MC, V* ⊙*Close Tues. No lunch Sun. and Mon.*

$$$$ 🛏**Vintners Inn.** Set on almost 100 acres of vineyards, this French provincial inn has large rooms, all with a patio or balcony and many with wood-burning fireplaces, and a trellised sundeck. Breakfast is complimentary, and the nearby John Ash & Co. restaurant is tempting for other meals. There's a surprisingly tranquil air here, considering how convenient it is to U.S. 101 and downtown Santa Rosa. **Pros:** Attentive service, large rooms, lovely grounds. **Cons:** Odd location next to the freeway and a power plant, Continental breakfast could be better. ✉*4350 Barnes Rd., River Rd. exit west from U.S. 101, 95403* ☎*707/575–7350 or 800/421–2584* ⊕*www.vintnersinn.com* ⇔*38 rooms, 6 suites* ⌂*In-room: safe, refrigerator, Wi-Fi (some). In-hotel: restaurant, room service, bar, no elevator, laundry service, concierge, no-smoking rooms* ═*AE, D, DC, MC, V* ⊙│*CP.*

5

NIGHTLIFE & THE ARTS

The **Wells Fargo Center for the Arts** (⊠*50 Mark West Springs Rd.* ☎*707/546–3600*) presents concerts, plays, and other performances by locally and internationally known artists—everyone from Dolly Parton to Andrew Dice Clay. For symphony, ballet, and other live theater performances throughout the year, call the **Spreckels Performing Arts Center** (⊠*5409 Snyder La.* ☎*707/588–3400*) in Rohnert Park, a short drive from downtown Santa Rosa.

RUSSIAN RIVER VALLEY

10 mi northwest of Santa Rosa.

Numbers in the margin correspond to numbers on the Northern Sonoma County map.

As the Russian River winds its way from Mendocino to the Pacific Ocean, it carves out a valley that's a near-perfect environment for growing certain grape varietals. Because of its low elevation, sea fogs push far inland to cool the land, yet in summer they burn off, giving the grapes enough sun to ripen properly. Fog-loving pinot noir and chardonnay grapes are king and queen here. The namesake river does its part by slowly carving its way downward through many layers of rock, depositing a deep layer of gravel that in parts of the valley measures 60 or 70 feet. This gravel forces the roots of grapevines to go deep in search of water and nutrients. In the process, the plants absorb a multitude of trace minerals that add complexity to the flavor of the grapes.

Visiting wineries in this rich viticultural region is a leisurely affair. Tall redwoods shade many of the two-lane roads that traverse this mostly rural area. Scenic Westside Road, with another winery visible at almost every bend of the road, roughly follows the curves of the Russian River from Healdsburg to Guerneville, wandering through vineyards, woods, and meadows along the way. Some visitors set up base camp in Guerneville, a popular destination for gay and lesbian travelers who stay in the rustic resorts and sunbathe on the bank of the river. But those on a mission to explore the area's food and wine usually choose to stay in Healdsburg *(⇨below)*, with its wealth of top restaurants, in-town tasting rooms, and easy access to most Russian River wineries.

VINEYARDS IN THE RUSSIAN RIVER VALLEY

❷ Established in 1896, **Foppiano Vineyards** primarily made bulk wine until 1970—visitors used to bring their own jugs to fill—but it has recently proven that it can produce quality wines under the "rock-and-roll winemaker," Bill Regan. (Regan's known for playing music by Eric Clapton and Jeff Beck as he works.) In the unassuming tasting room be sure to taste Foppiano's flagship wine, a hearty petite sirah, and the zinfandel, a good, modestly priced wine that just begs for a pizza or plate of pasta. The winery also produces sangiovese, cabernet sauvignon, pinot noir, and merlot. ✉ *12707 Old Redwood Hwy.* ☎ *707/433-7272* ⊕ *www. foppiano.com* ⌕ *Tasting free* ⊙ *Daily 10–4:30.*

❸ Although Rodney Strong, who founded this place in 1959, passed away in 2006, **Rodney Strong Vineyards** promises to continue producing intensely flavored reds. The 1970s cement building doesn't look particularly enticing from the exterior, but inside is an attractive octagonal tasting room ringed by a balcony overlooking the production facilities. An excellent self-guided tour leads along the balcony for a good view of the fermentation tanks and other machinery, but twice-daily guided tours are also available. Back at the bar, you can taste the fruits of the winery's high-tech labors. Symmetry, a red Bordeaux-style blend, is one of their most impressive offerings, but also taste the excellent pinot noir. (Strong was one of the first to plant pinot noir in the Russian River Valley.) The winery sponsors free outdoor concerts on the grounds during summer. ✉ *11455 Old Redwood Hwy.* ☎ *707/431-1533* ⊕ *www. rodneystrong.com* ⌕ *Tasting $5–$10* ⊙ *Daily 10–5; tour daily at 11 and 3.*

❹ Behind the bar in the tasting room, a dramatic steel sculpture studded with illuminated chunks of glass suggests a bottle of bubbly, cluing you in to the raison d'être of **J Vineyards and Winery** before your first sip. Their dry sparkling wines are made from pinot noir and chardonnay grapes planted in their Russian River vineyards. Still wines made with the same varietals are also good, if perhaps not as impressive as the sparklers. Your tasting fee brings you a flight of four wines, each matched with two bites of hors d'oeuvres. A similar but even more opulent tasting experience is available in the Bubble Room, where older vintages and smaller production wines are poured for a slightly higher fee. ✉ *11447 Old Redwood Hwy.* ☎ *707/431-3646*

5

⊕*www.jwine.com* ⌑*Tasting $25* ⊙*Daily 11–5; tour by appointment.*

★ ❺ **Rochioli Vineyards and Winery** claims one of the prettiest picnic sites in the area, with tables overlooking vineyards, which are also visible from the airy little tasting room hung with modern artwork. Production is small—about 14,000 cases annually—and fans on the winery's mailing list snap up most of the bottles, but the wines are worth stopping for. Because of the cool growing conditions in the Russian River Valley, the flavors of their cabernet sauvignon, chardonnay, and sauvignon blanc (from old vines) are intense and complex. Their pinot, though, is largely responsible for the winery's stellar reputation and has helped cement the Russian River's reputation as a pinot powerhouse. ✉*6192 Westside Rd.* ☎*707/433–2305* ⌑*Tasting free* ⊙*Daily 11–4.*

❻ As you wind along Westside Road it's hard to miss the odd-looking **Hop Kiln Winery**, where three stone towers rise from a barnlike building that was originally built for the production of America's *other* favorite beverage—beer. Built in 1905, the structure housed kilns for drying hops. Today, wine is stored in those old kilns, whose thick stone walls help keep the wine cool. Poke around the tasting room and you'll see old photos of the property, as well as original equipment such as railcar tracks running through the building. The picnic tables next to the duck pond are a good place to sip a bottle of their aptly named Big Red or the popular Thousand Flowers, a white blend. ✉*6050 Westside Rd.* ☎*707/433–6491* ⊕*www.hopkilnwinery.com* ⌑*Tasting free–$5* ⊙*Daily 10–5.*

★ ❼ Once you turn through the striking stone and metal gate at **Gary Farrell Winery,** a super-steep drive snakes up to the sleek, modern tasting room. From here, the views down the precipitous slope are a knockout. The wines are equally impressive: After building his reputation on pinot noir, Farrell is now followed for his zinfandel, especially his spicy, full-bodied zin from the Dry Creek Valley's Maple Vineyard. He also makes a fine cabernet sauvignon, sauvignon blanc, merlot, and chardonnay. The tour concludes with a pairing of their wines with cheeses made by a local artisanal cheese maker. ✉*10701 Westside Rd.* ☎*707/473–2900* ⊕*www.garyfarrellwines.com* ⌑*Tasting $5, tour $15* ⊙*Daily 11–4; tour daily at 10 by appointment.*

8 Technically, to be called Champagne, a wine must be made in the French region of Champagne or it's just sparkling wine. Whatever you call it, **Korbel Champagne Cellars** produces a tasty, reasonably priced bubbly as well as its own brandy, which is distilled on the premises. The wine tour clearly explains the process of making sparkling wine and takes you through the winery's ivy-covered 19th-century buildings. If you've already had wine making explained to you one too many times, a tour of the rose garden, where there are more than 250 varieties of roses, may be a welcome break. ✉*13250 River Rd., Guerneville* ☎*707/824-7000, 707/824-7316 wineshop* ⊕*www.korbel.com* 🍷*Tasting and tour free* ☼*Oct.–Apr., daily 9–4:30; May–Sept., daily 9–5. Tour Oct.–Apr., daily on the hr 10–3; May–Sept., weekdays every 45 mins 10–3:45, weekends at 10, 11, noon, 12:45, 1:30, 2:15, 3, and 3:45. Garden tour mid-Apr.–mid-Oct., Tues.–Sun.; call wineshop for times.*

9 Fans of pinot noir will surely want to stop at **Hartford Family Winery**, a surprisingly opulent winery off a meandering country road in Forestville. Here grapes from the coolest areas of the Russian River Valley, Sonoma coast, and other regions are turned into chardonnays, old-vine zinfandels, and single-vineyard pinots, the latter with unusual aging potential. ✉*8075 Martinelli Rd.* ☎*707/887-1756* ⊕*www.hartfordwines.com* 🍷*Tasting free* ☼*Daily 10–4:30.*

10 ★ **Fodor'sChoice** At the end of a meandering one-lane road off Highway 116 is **Iron Horse Vineyards**, whose sparkling wines smoothed the way of glasnost. Ronald Reagan served them at his summit meetings with Mikhail Gorbachev and George Herbert Walker Bush took some to Moscow for the signing of the START Treaty. Iron Horse also makes excellent chardonnay and pinot noir. Despite its fame, Iron Horse, founded in 1979, has avoided pretense—the winery buildings are of the simple Sonoma redwood-barn style—but the outdoor tasting area makes it a beautifully rustic stop. Enjoy views out over the predominantly cool and foggy Green Valley while you taste their impressive sparklers. ✉*9786 Ross Station Rd., near Forestville* ☎*707/887-1507* ⊕*www.ironhorsevineyards.com* 🍷*Tasting $10, tour free* ☼*Daily 10–3:30; tour daily at 10.*

★ **11** **Martinelli Winery**, housed in a 100-year-old hop barn with the telltale triple towers, has the feel of an old country store, with a wood-beam ceiling and an antique stove in the corner. The warm welcome you'll get from the tasting room staff might also remind you of another era. The Martinelli family has been growing grapes in the Russian River Valley since the late 1800s. Still, there's nothing old-fashioned about these sophisticated wines. Crafted by the acclaimed winemaker Helen Turley since 1993, the wines are typically big, complex, well balanced, and high in alcohol. Martinelli currently makes sauvignon blanc, chardonnay, gewürztraminer, muscat Alexandria, pinot noir, syrah, and an incredibly rich zinfandel, the wine that typically brings visitors to this back road in Windsor. ⊠*3360 River Rd.* ☏*707/525–0570* ⊕*www.martinelliwinery.com* ⊠*Tasting free* ⊘*Daily 10–5.*

OFF THE BEATEN PATH Just far enough off the beaten track to feel like a real find, **De Loach Vineyards** produces a variety of Russian River Valley sauvignon blancs, gewürztraminers, merlots, and zinfandels but is best known for chardonnay and, especially, pinot noir. Some of the pinot is made using open-top wood fermenters that are uncommon in Sonoma but have been used in France for centuries. The tour focuses on the estate vineyards outside the tasting room door, where you'll learn about the labor-intensive biodynamic farming methods they use, such as burying cow horns filled with cow manure in the vineyards. On summer weekends, local produce is sold on the front porch, conveniently near the picnic tables. (⊠*1791 Olivet Rd.* ☏*707/526–9111* ⊕*www.deloachvineyards.com* ⊠*Tasting $5–$10, tour free* ⊘*Daily 10–4:30; tour by appointment*)

WHERE TO STAY & EAT

$$$$ ★ ~~Fodor's~~Choice ╳The Farmhouse Inn. From the personable sommelier who arrives at the table to help you pick wines from the excellent list to the maître d' who serves cheeses from the cart with a flourish, the staff match the quality of the outstanding French-inspired cuisine. The signature dish, "rabbit, rabbit, rabbit," a rich trio of confit of leg, rabbit loin wrapped in applewood-smoked bacon, and roasted rack of rabbit with a mustard-cream sauce, is typical of the dishes that are simultaneously rustic and refined. The homemade desserts alone are worth the drive. A hand-painted mural surrounds the tranquil, country-style dining room. ■TIP➔ **Dinner here has become a particularly hot item since the restaurant was awarded a Michelin star in 2006,**

so reserve well in advance. ✉*7871 River Rd., Forestville* 📞*707/887–3300 or 800/464–6642* 🍴*Reservations essential* 🍽*AE, D, DC, MC, V* 🌙*Closed Tues. and Wed. No lunch.*

★ **Fodor's**Choice 🖼**The Farmhouse Inn.** Half hidden by roses and
$$$–$$$$ calla lilies in a glen right off River Road, this pale yellow 1873 farmhouse and adjacent cottages may have a woodsy setting, but the interior is anything but rustic. All of the well-appointed cottages have whirlpool tubs and flat-panel televisions, and most even have private saunas and wood-burning fireplaces. The two rooms in the farmhouse are on the small side but have dramatic infinity bathtubs. The spa specializes in side-by-side treatments for couples. It's worth leaving your supremely comfortable bed for the sumptuous breakfasts here. Best of all, the Farmhouse Inn is home to one of the very best restaurants in Sonoma; don't even think about eating elsewhere if you're here on a night the restaurant is open, Thursday through Monday. **Pros:** Secluded location, free DVDs and movie snacks, one of Sonoma's best restaurants on-site. **Cons:** Rooms closest to the street get a little road noise. ✉*7871 River Rd., Forestville 95436* 📞*707/887–3300 or 800/464–6642* ⊕*www.farmhouseinn. com* 🛏*8 rooms, 2 suites* 🛁*In-room: refrigerator, DVD, Wi-Fi. In-hotel: restaurant, pool, spa, no elevator, concierge, no-smoking rooms* 🍽*AE, D, DC, MC, V* 🍴*BP.*

$$–$$$$ ✕🖼**Applewood Inn & Restaurant.** On a knoll in the shelter
★ of towering redwoods and blossoming apple trees, this romantic inn has two distinct types of accommodations. Those in the original Belden House, where cozy chairs around a river-rock fireplace encourage loitering in the lounge area, are comfortable but modest in scale. Most of the 10 rooms in the newer buildings are larger and airier, decorated in sage green and terra-cotta tones. Readers rave about the accommodating service, soothing atmosphere, and the earthy Cal-Italian cuisine served in the cozy restaurant built to recall a French barn. ■TIP➔ **In winter, up the romance factor by asking for a table near the fireplace.** The owners are experts on local wines, and they can direct you to small, virtually unknown wineries of the Russian River Valley. **Pros:** Quiet, secluded location, decadent breakfast, owners Jim and Darryl are gracious hosts. **Cons:** Restaurant closed Monday and Tuesday. ✉*13555 Rte. 116, Guerneville 95421* 📞*707/869–9093 or 800/555–8509* ⊕*www.applewoodinn.com* 🛏*19 rooms* 🛁*In-room: no a/c*

5

(some), Wi-Fi. In-hotel: restaurant, pool, spa, no elevator, no-smoking rooms ⊟AE, MC, V ⊚BP.

$$ ⊡**Sebastopol Inn.** Simple but stylish rooms in a California country style are tucked behind an old train station; some have a patio or balcony with views over a wetlands preserve. The offbeat coffeehouse Coffee Catz, on the property, is convenient for light meals. **Pros:** Weekday discounts often available, short walk to Sebastopol's restaurants and shops. **Cons:** At least a 30-minute drive from most Russian River wineries, some will find the beds too firm. ✉*6751 Sebastopol Ave., Sebastopol 95472* ☎*707/829–2500* ⊕*www.sebastopolinn.com* ⇝*29 rooms, 2 suites* ⌂*In-room: refrigerator (some), Wi-Fi. In-hotel: restaurant, pool, spa, no elevator, laundry facilities, no-smoking rooms* ⊟*AE, D, DC, MC, V.*

SPORTS & THE OUTDOORS

At **Burke's Canoe Trips** (✉*River Rd. and Mirabel Rd., 1 mi north of Forestville* ☎*707/887–1222*), you can rent a canoe for a leisurely paddle 10 mi downstream to Guerneville. A shuttle bus will return you to your car at the end of the day. May through October is the best time for boating.

HEALDSBURG

17 mi north of Santa Rosa on U.S. 101.

Numbers in the margin correspond to numbers on the Northern Sonoma County map.

Just when it seems that the buzz about Healdsburg couldn't get any bigger, there's another article published in a glossy food or wine magazine about its posh properties like the restaurant Cyrus and the ultra-luxe Hotel Les Mars. But you don't have to be a tycoon to stay here and enjoy the town. For every ritzy restaurant there's a great bakery or relatively modest B&B. A whitewashed bandstand on Healdsburg's plaza hosts free summer concerts, where you might hear anything from bluegrass to Sousa marches. Add to that the fragrant magnolia trees shading the square and the bright flower beds, and the whole thing is as pretty as a Norman Rockwell painting.

The countryside around Healdsburg is the sort you dream about when you're planning a Wine Country vacation, with orderly rows of vines alternating with beautifully over-grown hillsides. Alongside the relatively untrafficked roads, country stores offer just-plucked fruits and vine-ripened tomatoes. Wineries here are barely visible, tucked behind groves of eucalyptus or hidden high on fog-shrouded hills.

Most visitors use Healdsburg as a base for visiting wineries in the surrounding hillsides and river valleys– it's ideally located at the confluence of the Dry Creek, Alexander, and Russian River valleys—but you could easily while away the day without setting foot outside of town. Around the old-fashioned plaza you'll find fashionable boutiques, art galleries, spas, hip tasting rooms, and some of the best res-taurants in the Wine Country, so don't forget to save some time to savor Healdsburg's particular pleasures.

In addition to several wineries on the outskirts of town, more than a dozen tasting rooms reside in the blocks sur-rounding the plaza, enabling you to sample wine all day without even getting in your car.

⑫ If you'd like to taste the wines of several different produc-ers in one fell swoop, stop by **Cellar 360**, which might be pouring wines from Chateau Souverain, Chateau St. Jean, Beringer, and several other wineries when you arrive. ✉*308B Center St.* ☎*707/433-2822* ⊙*Daily 11–6.*

⑬ The most stylish of the tasting rooms is **Thumbprint Cellars.** With its leather chairs, brown velvet curtains, and chic light fixtures, it could be a very hip friend's San Francisco living room. ✉*36 North St.* ☎*707/433-2393* ⊕*www.thumb-printcellars.com* ⊙*Daily 11–6.*

⑭ To take a short break from wine tasting, you can visit the **Healdsburg Museum,** which displays a collection of local his-torical objects, including baskets and artifacts from native tribes. Other exhibits cover the Mexican Rancho period, the founding and growth of Healdsburg in the 1850s, and the history of local agriculture. ✉*221 Matheson St.* ☎*707/431-3325* ⊕*www.healdsburgmuseum.org* ✉*Free* ⊙*Tues.–Sun. 11–4.*

VINEYARDS AROUND HEALDSBURG

⑮ Within walking distance of downtown Healdsburg if you don't mind a stroll of a little less than a mile, **Alderbrook Winery** is a cluster of olive-green buildings across U.S. 101 from the plaza. A fire warms the spacious but homey tasting room on chilly days. The standouts here include excellent Russian River Valley pinot noirs, which tend to sell out shortly after they're released, and dense Dry Creek Valley zinfandels. A small selection of picnic fixings and, conveniently, single glasses of wine, are available if you'd like to linger on the veranda or sit at one of the picnic tables in the grassy back yard. ⊠ *2306 Magnolia Dr.* ☎ *707/433–5987* ⊕ *www.alderbrook.com* ☜ *Tasting free–$5* ⊙ *Daily 10–5.*

🔟 Italian immigrant Edoardo Seghesio and his wife, Angela, planted zinfandel vineyards here in 1895 and added a winery in 1902. For years they and their descendants sold wine in bulk to other wineries, but they finally began bottling wines under their own name in the 1980s at **Seghesio Family Vineyards.** The majority of the grapes used by Seghesio are estate grown, in vineyards in the Alexander, Dry Creek, and Russian River valleys. Even though winemaker Ted Seghesio prefers his wines to be immediately drinkable, they have surprising depth and aging potential. Be sure to try the reserve zinfandel and the sangiovese, as well as their super-Tuscan blend called Omaggio, a blend of cabernet sauvignon and sangiovese. To make an afternoon of it, bring a picnic lunch and challenge your friends to a boccie game in the shade of the property's cork tree. ⊠ *14730 Grove St.* ☎ *707/433–3579* ⊕ *www.seghesio.com* ☜ *Tasting $5* ⊙ *Daily 10–5.*

🔟 Giuseppe and Pietro Simi, two brothers from Italy, began growing grapes in Sonoma in 1876, making **Simi Winery** one of the oldest in the Wine Country. Though operations are now strictly high-tech, the winery's tree-studded entrance area and stone buildings recall a more genteel era. Simi has long been known for crisp chardonnays, but these days its spicy, jammy cabernet sauvignon is getting attention. ⊠ *16275 Healdsburg Ave., Dry Creek Rd. exit off U.S. 101* ☎ *707/433–6981* ⊕ *www.simiwinery.com* ☜ *Tasting $5–$13, tour $10* ⊙ *Daily 10–5; tour daily at 11 and 2.*

WHERE TO STAY & EAT

$$$$ ★ **Fodor's**Choice ✕**Cyrus.** When glamorous Cyrus opened in 2005, it was widely hailed as one of the first restaurants in Sonoma that could hold a candle to the French Laundry. The high praise is richly justified. From the moment a cart with Champagne and caviar is wheeled up to your table to the minute your dessert plates are whisked away, you'll be coddled by polished servers and an expert sommelier.

The formal dining room, with its vaulted Venetian-plaster ceiling, is a suitably plush setting for chef Douglas Keane's creative, subtle cuisine. Three-, four-, and five-course tasting menus can be constructed any way you like—you can even order four desserts. Most opt to work their way through savories first, such as a terrine of foie gras with curried apple compote and duck with tamarind-glazed eggplant, before finishing up with an espresso gelato with an almond *dacquoise* pastry. ■TIP→If you haven't been able to finagle a reservation, or you just want a taste of the exquisite cuisine, you can order dishes à la carte in the bar, which also serves the finest cocktails in the Wine Country. ⊠*29 North St.* ☎*707/433–3311* ⚖*Reservations essential* ▤*AE, D, DC, MC, V* ☉*No lunch.*

$$-$$$ ✕**Barndiva.** Easily one of the hippest restaurants in all of Sonoma, Barndiva opened in 2004 and immediately made a splash with its sexy vibe, pricey specialty cocktails, and an inventive, if slightly difficult to decipher, color-coded menu divided into "light," "spicy," and "comfort" dishes. The seasonal menu might include a "light" pear, persimmon, fennel, and Asiago salad, "spicy" braised short ribs with horseradish mashed potatoes, and a "comforting" duck shepherd's pie. From the outside, the restaurant resembles a brand-new barn, but inside, it's more big-city than Mayberry, with dim lighting and well-dressed couples at the bar. During warmer months the beautiful patio more than doubles the number of seats. Service is friendly although not particularly expert. ⊠*231 Center St.* ☎*707/431–0100* ▤*AE, MC, V* ☉*Closed Mon. and Tues.*

$$-$$$ ✕**Bistro Ralph.** It may no longer be the hottest restaurant in Healdsburg, as it was in the 1990s, but chef Ralph Tingle's homey California cuisine clearly has a timeless appeal because his restaurant is still packed every night it's open. Typical dishes from the weekly changing menu include osso buco with saffron risotto and sautéed mahimahi with hedgehog mushrooms. The stark industrial space includes a stunning, gracefully curved wine rack, concrete floors, and a painted brick wall. Take a seat at the bar and chat with the locals, who love this place just as much as out-of-towners do, especially for the wicked martinis that are almost big enough to swim in. ⊠*109 Plaza St., off Healdsburg Ave.* ☎*707/433–1380* ▤*MC, V* ☉*Closed Sun.*

$$-$$$ ✕**Zin Restaurant and Wine Bar.** Concrete floors and large canvases on the walls create an industrial-chic mood here.

Owners and childhood friends Jeff Mall and Scott Silva planted their own garden to supply their restaurant with heirloom tomatoes, herbs, and peppers, which they match with the finest local meats and seafood. The American cuisine—such as smoked pork chop with homemade applesauce or the red beans and rice with andouille sausage—is hearty and highly seasoned. Portions are large, so consider sharing if you hope to save room for one of the decadent desserts, like the bread pudding with bourbon sauce. Of the roughly 100 bottles on the wine list, about half are zinfandels, naturally. ✉*344 Center St.* ☎*707/473–0946* ⊟*AE, DC, MC, V* ⊘*No lunch weekends.*

$–$$ ✕**Healdsburg Charcuterie.** This airy restaurant with a slightly Provençal feel serves a hodgepodge of cuisines, from an all-American chicken-salad sandwich to Italian favorites like a chicken *piccata* and fusilli pasta with a basil cream sauce. Some of the standout dishes, though, are French through and through, like the escargot in garlicky butter and a generous charcuterie plate that includes pâté, duck rillettes, salami, and cornichons. The vibe is casual rather than refined, but reasonable prices and ample portions makes it one of Healdsburg's better values for a sit-down meal. ■TIP➔**If you're planning a particularly lavish picnic, they'll pack up their food to go for you.** ✉*335 Healdsburg Ave.* ☎*707/431–7213* ⊟*AE, DC, MC, V.*

¢–$$ ✕**Bear Republic Brewing Company.** This wide-open hall of a brewpub on Healdsburg Plaza is a local favorite for a casual lunch or dinner of burgers, chicken wings, or pasta. Although the food is nothing out of the ordinary, the beers are good (if you like hoppy brews, try the Racer 5 IPA) and the service is fast. In warm weather, there's often a wait for the seats outdoors, but there's usually room in the spacious interior. This pub for people who like to socialize and can be a welcome relief from the serious demeanor of some other local spots. ✉*345 Healdsburg Ave.* ☎*707/433–2337* ⚲*Reservations not accepted* ⊟*AE, MC, V.*

¢–$$ ✕**Bovolo.** Husband-and-wife team John Stewart and Duskie Estes serve what they call "slow food...fast." Though you might pop into this casual café at the back of the Plaza Farms market for just a quick lunch, the staff will have spent hours curing the meats that star in the small menu of salads, pizzas, and sandwiches. For instance, the Salumist's Salad mixes a variety of cured meats with greens, white beans, and a tangy vinaigrette. At dinner, you can opt for a $27 three-course tasting menu of rustic Italian favorites or order a thin-crust pizza or antipasto plate. On warm days you can sit either in the spare dining room with sunny yellow walls or outdoors on the patio. ⊠*106 Matheson St.* ☎*707/431–2962* ◈*Reservations not accepted* ⊟*MC, V* ⊘*Closed Wed. No dinner Mon.–Thurs. in winter, no dinner Thurs. in summer.*

$$$$ ★ **Fodor'sChoice** ⊡**The Honor Mansion.** Each room is unique at this photogenic 1883 Italianate Victorian. Rooms in the main house preserve a sense of the building's heritage, while the larger suites out back are comparatively understated. Luxurious touches such as antiques and feather beds are found in every room, and suites have the added advantage of a deck; some even have private outdoor hot tubs. Outside the rooms, tall trees shade an outdoor sitting area and a koi pond, and there's a swimming pool out back, near the putting green and tennis, boccie, and croquet courts. Readers rave about the attentive staff, who coddle you with cookies, cappuccino, and other treats. **Pros:** Beautiful, tranquil grounds, personable innkeepers, homemade sweets available at all hours. **Cons:** Almost a mile from Healdsburg's plaza, along a moderately busy street. ⊠*14891 Grove St., 95448* ☎*707/433–4277 or 800/554–4667* ◈*www.honormansion.com* ◄*5 rooms, 8 suites* ◊*In-room: refrigerator, DVD (some), Wi-Fi. In-hotel: tennis court, pool, no elevator, no-smoking rooms* ⊟*AE, MC, V* ⊘*Closed 1 wk around Christmas* ◎|*BP.*

$$$$ ✕⊡**Hotel Healdsburg.** Across the street from Healdsburg's tidy town plaza, this spare, sophisticated hotel caters to travelers with an urban sensibility. Unadorned olive green walls, dark hardwood floors, and clean-lined furniture fill the guest rooms; the beds are some of the most comfortable you'll find anywhere. Spacious bathrooms continue the sleek style with monochromatic tiles and deep soaking tubs that are all right angles. The attached restaurant, Dry Creek Kitchen, is one of the best in Healdsburg; celebrity chef Charlie Palmer is the man behind seasonal dishes that largely rely on local ingredients and a wine list covering the best Sonoma vintners. **Pros:** Some rooms overlook the town plaza, free valet parking, extremely comfortable beds. **Cons:** Pricey, least expensive rooms are on the small side, street noise is a problem. ⊠*25 Matheson St., 95448* ☎*707/431–2800 or 800/889–7188* ◈*www.hotelhealdsburg.com* ◄*45 rooms, 10 suites* ◊*In-room: refrigerator, DVD, Ethernet, Wi-Fi (some). In-hotel: restaurant, room*

service, bar, pool, gym, spa, concierge, laundry service, no-smoking rooms, some pets allowed (fee) =AE, D, DC, MC, V |O|CP.

$$$$ ⊠**Hotel Les Mars.** In 2005, posh Healdsburg got even more chichi with the opening of this opulent hotel. The spacious rooms are elegant enough for French nobility, with 18th- and 19th-century antiques and reproductions. Most of the gleaming, white marble bathrooms have spa tubs in addition to enormous showers. And when you return at night to a box of chocolate truffles and crawl into your canopy bed covered in pristine Italian linens, you might wonder when you've ever had it so good. Rooms on the third floor have soaring ceilings that make them feel particularly large. Breakfast is served in the adjoining restaurant, Cyrus (⇨*above*), or in the library, sumptuously paneled with hand-carved black walnut. **Pros:** Just off Healdsburg's plaza, impeccable service, Bulgari bath products. **Cons:** Very expensive as it starts at over $500 per night, no parking lot. ⊠*27 North St., 95448* ☎*707/433–4211* ⊕*www. lesmarshotel.com* ⮡*16 rooms* &*In-room: safe, DVD, Wi-Fi. In-hotel: restaurant, bar, pool, gym, laundry service, no-smoking rooms* =AE, DC, MC, V |O|BP.

$$$–$$$$ ⊠**Madrona Manor.** The oldest continuously operating inn in the area, this 1881 Victorian mansion, surrounded by 8 acres of wooded and landscaped grounds, is straight out of a storybook. Rooms in the three-story mansion, the carriage house, and the two separate cottages are splendidly ornate, with mirrors in gilt frames and paintings covering every wall. Each bed is piled high with silk- and velvet-clad pillows. Romantic candlelight dinners are served in the formal dining rooms every night except Monday and Tuesday. **Pros:** Old-fashioned, romantic ambience, pretty veranda perfect for a cocktail. **Cons:** Breakfast could be better, decor might be too fussy for some. ⊠*1001 Westside Rd., central Healdsburg exit off U.S. 101, then left on Mill St., 95448* ☎*707/433–4231 or 800/258–4003* ⊕*www. madronamanor.com* ⮡*17 rooms, 5 suites* &*In-room: no TV, Wi-Fi. In-hotel: restaurant, bar, pool, no elevator, no-smoking rooms* =MC, V |O|BP.

$$–$$$ ⊠**Camellia Inn.** Built in 1869 and surrounded by the namesake camellias, this Italianate nine-room inn is only a couple of short blocks from the shops and restaurants of Healdsburg Plaza. The parlors downstairs are chockablock with ceramics and other decorative items, while rooms are individually decorated with antiques, such as an impressive mid-19th-century tiger-maple bed from Scotland. The inn-keepers are generous with their wine expertise—you might learn more about local wineries during happy hour on the swimming pool terrace than you will on many winery tours. The uncharacteristically modest rates for this pricey town attract loyal visitors that come year after year. ■TIP→**Those on a budget should ask about the cozy room with the bathroom across the hallway that goes for about half what the others do.** Pros: Great rates for the neighborhood, early evening wine-and-cheese hour, within easy walking distance of dozens of restaurants. Cons: Some rooms are slightly dated, some may find the look too frilly. ⊠*211 North St., 95448* ☎*707/433–8182 or 800/727–8182* ⊕*www.camelliainn. com* ⇆*8 rooms, 1 suite* ⌂*In-room: no TV. In-hotel: pool, no elevator, no-smoking rooms* ⊟*AE, D, MC, V* ⧦*BP.*

NIGHTLIFE & THE ARTS

As in many Wine Country towns, nightlife in Healds-burg tends to consist of lingering over a glass of dessert wine after a decadent dinner. There is a modest arts scene, though, and you can catch the occasional live music or theater performance at the **Raven Performing Arts Theater** (⊠*115 North St.* ☎*707/433–6335* ⊕*www.raventheater.org*).

Even if you think it's virtually sacrilege to drink anything other than wine in this neck of the woods, bartender Scott Beattie at **Cyrus** (⊠*29 North St.* ☎*707/433–3311*) will change your mind. At the bar of Healdsburg's hottest restaurant he mixes superb, inventive drinks with house-made infused syrups and seasonal ingredients like local Meyer lemons.

SHOPPING

Healdsburg is the most pleasant spot in Sonoma for an afternoon of window shopping, with dozens of boutiques, food markets, and tasting rooms clustered within easy walking distance around the bucolic main plaza.

Healdsburg's food fetish extends from the restaurants to the specialty grocers and markets. **Oakville Grocery** (⊠*124 Matheson St.* ☎*707/433–3200*) has a bustling Healds-burg branch filled with wine, condiments, and deli items. A terrace with ample seating makes a good place for an impromptu picnic, but you might want to lunch early or late to avoid the worst crowds. For more artisanal foods, pop into **Plaza Farms** (⊠*106 Matheson St.* ☎*707/433–2345*), where a few wineries share a market hall with the olive oil producer Da Vero, the chocolate maker Scharffen Berger, and Bellwether Artisan Creamery. To truly catch the Healdsburg spirit, go to the plaza early in the morning and order a fragrant sticky bun and a cup of coffee at the **Downtown Bakery & Creamery** (⊠*308A Center St.* ☎*707/431–2719*), a local cult favorite. The bakery uses local dairy products and fruit in their breads and decadent pastries.

There are plenty of nonedible temptations, too. French flea-market finds like burnished bronze candlesticks share the shelves with contemporary items like hand-painted silk pillows in the Lilliputian **21st Arrondissement** (⊠*309 Healdsburg Ave.* ☎*707/433–2166*). Possibly the most fashion-forward clothing shop on the plaza is **Out of Hand,** (⊠*333 Healdsburg Ave.* ☎*707/431–8178*) where flirty, feminine, youthful clothing fills the tiny shop.

A block off the plaza, the **Plaza Arts Center** (⊠*130 Plaza St.* ☎*707/431–1970*) displays work by local artists who also staff the gallery. In addition to the larger-scale paintings and photography, look for suitcase-friendly fine crafts, such as jewelry. **Spirits in Stone** (⊠*401 Healdsburg Ave.* ☎*707/723–7123*) is known for its popular Zimbabwe Shona sculpture; it also has a collection of African baskets, paintings, jewelry, and other art.

You'll have to get in your car to head north on Healdsburg Avenue to **Tip Top Liquor Warehouse** (⊠*90 Dry Creek Rd.* ☎*707/431–0841*), a nondescript spot that stocks an interesting selection of wines at fair prices. Though it's strongest in bottles from Sonoma, you'll also find a few Napa wines, including some rare cult cabernets.

FARMERS' MARKET During two weekly **Healdsburg farmers' markets,** you can buy locally made goat's cheese, fragrant lavender, and olive oil, in addition to the usual produce. On Saturday the market takes place one block west of the town plaza, at the corner of North and Vine streets, from 9 AM to noon, May through November. The Tuesday market takes place on the plaza itself from 4 to 7 PM, June through October. Townies turn out in droves for the open-air concert on the plaza from 6 to 8 PM from June through August, when several restaurants in the area offer outdoor dining or picnic dinner you can eat on the grass.

SPORTS & THE OUTDOORS

In summer, head for **Memorial Beach** (⊠*13839 Old Redwood Hwy.* ☎*707/433-1625*) on the Russian River, where you can swim in the pool created behind a seasonal dam. Parking costs $6 from Memorial Day weekend through Labor Day weekend; it's $5 during the rest of the year. Lifeguards are generally on duty in the summer.

SOAR/Russian River Adventures (⊠*20 Healdsburg Ave.* ☎*707/433-5599* ⊕*www.soar1.com*) rents inflatable canoes for leisurely trips down the Russian River. The $45-per-person fee includes a shuttle back to the starting point at the end of the day.

DRY CREEK VALLEY

Starting about 17 mi north of Santa Rosa on U.S. 101.

If you follow Healdsburg Avenue from downtown Healdsburg to Dry Creek Road and turn northwest, you'll soon feel like you've slipped back in time. Healdsburg looks totally urban in comparison to the pure, unspoiled countryside of Dry Creek Valley. Although the valley has become renowned for its wines, it preserves a rural simplicity rarely found in California's Wine Country today.

Dry Creek Road and the parallel West Dry Creek Road, brightened by wildflower-strewn shoulders in spring and early summer, offer tantalizing vineyard views as they skirt the hillside on the east side of the narrow valley. The winding roads can be quite narrow in places, forcing you to slow down—a good thing for the many bicyclists who navigate this route.

The valley's well-drained, gravelly floor is planted with chardonnay grapes to the south, where an occasional sea fog creeping in from the Russian River cools the vineyards, and with sauvignon blanc to the north, where the vineyards are warmer. The red decomposed soils of the benchlands bring out the best in zinfandel—the grape for which Dry Creek has become famous—but they also produce great cabernet sauvignon. And these soils seem well suited to Rhône varieties such as cinsaut, mourvèdre, and marsanne,

5

The Anderson Valley

If you're ready to take the road less traveled, turn off U.S. 101 at Cloverdale to wind your way west along Highway 128. Here you'll discover a wine country that's worlds away from the tour buses and faux-French châteaus of Napa.

Some combination of distance from San Francisco (the drive from the city takes about 2½ hours on a good day) and the hairpin switchback roads seems to have preserved the unpretentious, rustic nature of this region. Restaurants and B&Bs are relatively few and far between. And although the increasing attention to Anderson Valley wines has brought an uptick in tourism, this is still the spot to enjoy life in the slow lane.

At the western end of the valley, known to locals as the Deep End, cool fog and rainfall create ideal conditions for growing certain northern European varietals like chardonnay, riesling, gewürztraminer, and the Anderson Valley AVA's star, pinot noir. Further inland, where summer temperatures can be up to 15 degrees warmer than those of the Deep End, chardonnay and sauvignon blanc are the favored varietals.

Navigating the Anderson Valley is a cinch, since almost all the wineries are just off Highway 128, which winds its way west from U.S. 101. About 30 mi and 45 minutes after leaving U.S. 101 you'll roll through Boonville, the valley's biggest town, where you might want to get out, stretch your legs, and get lunch or stock up on picnic supplies before continuing west. This small farming town was once so isolated its residents invented a lingo all their own, known as Boontling, or Boont, for short. Few traces of this unique language survive, though you'll still find Bootling dictionaries sold in local shops.

Boonville is also a good option for spending the night, since you'll find fairly basic but attractive rooms with little touches like fresh wildflowers and down comforters at the **Boonville Hotel** (⊠ *Hwy. 128 at Lambert La.* ☎ *707/895–2210* ⊕ *www.boonvillehotel. com*). The hotel is also the site of the Anderson Valley's most exciting restaurant, whose menu focuses on organic ingredients and local produce.

Continuing west from Boonville, you'll pass through the towns of **Philo** and **Navarro,** little more than wide spots in the road. If you're visiting in summer or fall, stock up at one of the many fruit stands you'll see along the highway. Just past Navarro—2 mi before you would hit Highway 1—stand the magnificent giant trees of **Navarro River Redwoods State Park,** a lovely spot for a shady stroll.

Here are some of Anderson Valley's best wineries to visit, from east to west.

Goldeneye Winery. The owners of the Napa Valley's well-respected Duckhorn Vineyards have been making pinot noir here from local grapes with very satisfying results. Leisurely tastings take place in a restored farmhouse, or you can take your glass to the shady back patio, which overlooks a vineyard. ✉ *9200 Hwy. 128* ☎ *707/895-3203* ⊕ *www. goldeneyewinery.com.*

Navarro Vineyards. This winery produces an unusually diverse array of wines for the region, including cabernet sauvignon, chardonnay, a dry rosé, and, of course, pinot noir. The unusual Alsatian-style gewürztraminers, though, are the winery's most impressive offering. The cheeses and smoked salmon for sale inspire more than a few picnics at the tables overlooking the vineyards. ✉ *5601 Hwy. 128* ☎ *707/895-3686* ⊕ *www. navarrowine.com.*

Roederer Estate. From the looks of this unassuming tasting room, it would be hard to guess that this is an outpost of a renowned French Champagne maker. Only estate-grown grapes go into the sparkling wines, which are generally considered among the very best sparklers made in the United States. They share characteristics of the finest Champagne, with a creamy, full-bodied character and fine, tiny bubbles. ✉ *4501 Hwy. 128* ☎ *707/895-2288* ⊕ *www. roedererestate.net.*

Husch Vineyards. The setting here—a converted late-19th-century barn, with a rusted antique car in the yard and picnic tables spread out under the trees—makes a tasting feel particularly "down home." Established in 1971, this is the oldest winery in the Anderson Valley. ✉ *4400 Hwy. 128* ☎ *707/895-3216* ⊕ *www. huschvineyards.com.*

Handley Cellars. The winery produces a splendid chardonnay from Anderson Valley grapes, a delicately blushing pinot gris, an exotically fruity gewürztraminer, and some very good sparkling wines. Your attention may also be caught by the winery's impressive, large-scale works of international folk art collected by Milla and her father, such as a 14th-century granite Ganesh figure. ✉ *3151 Hwy 128* ☎ *707/895-3876* ⊕ *www. handleycellars.com.*

which need heat to ripen properly. Grapes like this valley so much that they grow wild in roadside thickets, the way blackberries cluster elsewhere in the West.

The Dry Creek Valley is so picture-perfect it would be a shame to pass up the opportunity to picnic at one of the wineries. For prepared sandwiches, bread, terrific cheeses, and other picnic supplies, stop by the **Dry Creek General Store** (⊠ *3495 Dry Creek Rd.* ☎ *707/433–4171*) established in 1881 and still a popular spot for locals to hang out on the porch.

VINEYARDS IN THE DRY CREEK VALLEY

🔟⁸ **Dry Creek Vineyard,** where fumé blanc is the flagship wine, also makes well-regarded zinfandels and a zesty, refreshing dry chenin blanc that critics often claim is one of the best white wine values in Sonoma. Dry Creek has a delightful grassy picnic area brightened by flowers and is a perfect place to hang out on a hot summer's day. Conveniently, a general store and deli with plenty of picnic fixings is just steps down the road, but you could also pick up some cheese and bread in the tasting room. ⊠ *3770 Lambert Bridge Rd.* ☎ *707/433–1000* ⊕ *www.drycreekvineyard. com* ⊠ *Tasting $5–$10* ⊙ *Daily 10:30–4:30.*

🔟⁹ Named after a legendary kingdom sought by Spanish explorer Vasquez de Coronado after he was told its streets were paved with gold, **Quivira** blends the old and the new. Its winery looks like an unassuming wood-and–cinder block barn, but in 2005 it got a high-tech touch when it was covered with solar panels. Here they produce some of the more interesting reds in the Dry Creek Valley. Though it is known for its dangerously drinkable and fruity zinfandel and its red blend Steelhead Red, the intensely flavored syrahs and petite sirahs are also worth checking out. If the weather's warm, the limited production mourvèdre rosé, available only at the winery, is great to sip in the picnic area, shaded by redwood and olive trees. ⊠ *4900 W. Dry Creek Rd.* ☎ *707/431–8333* ⊕ *www.quivirawine.com* ⊠ *Tasting $5, tour $10* ⊙ *Daily 11–5; tour by appointment.*

🔟⁰ ★ **Fodor's**Choice Down a narrow road at the westernmost edge of the Dry Creek Valley, **Michel-Schlumberger** is one of Sonoma's finest producers of cabernet sauvignon, aptly described by the winery's tour guide as a "full, rich big mouthful of wine." The tour is required, but it's casual, friendly—and free. You'll wander up a gravel pathway into the edge of their lovely benchland vineyards before swinging through the barrel room in the California Mission-style building that once served as the home of the winery's founder, Jean Jacques Michel. The tour concludes with a taste of their coveted cabernet, plus some very fine chardonnay, syrah, and pinot noir. ✉4155 *Wine Creek Rd.* ☎707/433–7427 *or* 800/447–3060 ⊕*www.michelschlumberger.com* ☕*Tasting and tour free* ☉*Tasting and tour daily at 11 and 2 by appointment.*

㉑ ★ Fodor'sChoice Once you wind your way down the private drive, flanked by vineyards, to **Preston Vineyards,** you'll be welcomed by the sight of a few farmhouses encircling a shady yard prowled by several friendly cats. In summer, a small selection of organic produce grown in their gardens is sold from an impromptu stand on the front porch, and bread and olive oil made on the premises are available year-round. Their down-home style is particularly in evidence on Sundays, the only day of the week that tasting-room staffers sell a 3-liter jug of Guadagni Red—a zinfandel, cinsaut, and carignane blend filled from the barrel right in front of you. Owners Lou and Susan Preston are committed to organic growing techniques and use only estate-grown grapes in their wines. ■TIP→**Preston only produces 8,000 or so cases of wine a year, most sold at the winery, so be sure to stock up if you find something you like.** ✉9282 *West Dry Creek Rd.* ☎707/433–3372 ⊕*www.prestonvineyards. com* ☕*Tasting $5* ☉*Daily 11–4:30.*

★ ㉒ David Coffaro himself tends to every aspect of the winemaking process at **David Coffaro Estate Vineyard,** where the tasting room resembles an enormous garage (where barrels take the place of cars), and Coffaro's beloved Raiders memorabilia lines the wall behind the bar. Rather than single-varietal wines, Coffaro crafts unique blends, mixing up, for example, cabernet, petite sirah, petite verdot, and tannat, a varietal that's popular in Europe's Basque region but rarely grown in the United States. ■TIP→**Though it is generally open daily 11–4, call ahead to ensure someone is available to pour for you; you'll often be treated to a barrel tasting.** ✉7485 *Dry Creek Rd.* ☎707/433–9715 ⊕*www. coffaro.com* ☕*Tasting and tour free* ☉*Daily 11–4, tour Friday at 11 and 1 by appointment.*

㉓ Known for its Disney-esque Italian villa, which has as many critics as it does fervent fans for its huge size and general over-the-top-ness, **Ferrari-Carano Winery** is Dry Creek's oddball. The wines here are a bit less grand than the setting, but the chardonnays, fumé blancs, syrahs, and cabernet sauvignons are generally quite good. The tour covers not only the wine-making facilities and underground cellar but also the manicured gardens, where you can see a cork tree and learn about how cork is harvested. ■ TIP→ **If the crowds are a bit much at the main tasting bar, consider paying an extra fee to taste their reserve wines in the** *enoteca* **(wine bar) downstairs.** ✉ *8761 Dry Creek Rd., Dry Creek Valley* ☎ *707/433–6700* ⊕ *www.ferrari-carano.com* 🖥 *Tasting $5–$10, tour free* ⊙ *Daily 10–5; tour Mon.–Sat. at 10 by appointment.*

WHERE TO STAY

$–$$ 🖥 **Best Western Dry Creek Inn.** The lackluster location of this Spanish Mission–style motel near U.S. 101 nevertheless means quick access to downtown Healdsburg and other Wine Country hot spots. Deluxe rooms are slightly more spacious than the standard rooms, but both types are kept spotless. The newest accommodations, the Tuscan Rooms, are more expensive, but come equipped with amenities like flat-panel TVs, spa tubs, and DVD players. A casual family restaurant is next door. **Pros:** Free Wi-Fi, free laundry facilities, frequent discounts available on Web site. **Cons:** Thin walls, basic furnishings in standard rooms. ✉ *198 Dry Creek Rd., Healdsburg 95448* ☎ *707/433–0300 or 800/222–5784* ⊕ *www.drycreekinn.com* 🛏 *163 rooms* ⌂ *In-room: refrigerator, Ethernet. In-hotel: restaurant, pool, gym, laundry facilities, no-smoking rooms, some pets allowed (fee)* ⊟ *AE, D, DC, MC, V* 🍴 *CP.*

ALEXANDER VALLEY

Starting about 17 mi north of Santa Rosa on U.S. 101.

The lovely Alexander Valley, which extends northeast of Healdsburg to the Mendocino County line north of Cloverdale, is one of Sonoma's least-visited regions. Driving through the rolling hills along Highway 128, you're more likely to have to slow down for tandem bicyclists than for other drivers. And you might find you're the only visitor in the tasting room at some of the small, family-owned wineries. Though most Californians couldn't find the Alexander Valley on a map if pressed, this appellation got a boost in

2006, when film- and winemaker Francis Ford Coppola bought the old Chateau Souverain here and opened a tasting room.

There are a wide variety of soils and microclimates in this neck of the woods. It is warmer than the Russian River appellation, and its small side valleys become very hot in summer. Sea fogs only occasionally drift in from the Santa Rosa Plain, and though they cool the land, they burn off more quickly than on the lower river. As recently as the 1980s the valley was mostly planted to walnuts, pears, prunes, and bulk grapes, so one might argue that experimentation here has hardly begun. So far, chardonnay, sauvignon blanc, zinfandel, and cabernet sauvignon seem to do well in places. Italian grapes such as sangiovese or the Rhône varieties, which do so well in the Dry Creek Valley, may make great wines in the warmer parts of the Alexander Valley. Stay posted for a decade or two. This valley is sure to be full of surprises.

24 Though most visitors to the Alexander Valley establish their home base in Healdsburg, you might end up passing through the town of **Geyserville**. Not long ago, it was a dusty farm town with little to offer wine tourists besides a grocery store. Though Geyserville is still little more than a crossroads with a few small markets and a good restaurant or two, the storefront tasting room **Locals** (⊠*21023A Geyserville Ave.* ☎*707/857–4900*) is definitely worth a stop for serious wine tasters. Local winemakers, critics, and tourists come here to taste wines produced by nine small wineries that do not have tasting rooms of their own, including Hawley Wines, Hart's Desire, Eric Ross, and others. There's no fee for tasting, and the extremely knowledgeable staff is happy to pour you a flight of several wines so you can compare, say, several different cabernet sauvignons.

25 The Alexander Valley's best picnic-packing stop is the **Jimtown Store** (⊠*6706 Hwy. 128* ☎*707/433–1212*), which has great espresso and a good selection of deli items, including their signature Brie-and-chopped-olive sandwich. While you're here, take a few minutes to browse through their gifts, which include both housewares and old-fashioned toys like sock monkeys.

VINEYARDS IN THE ALEXANDER VALLEY

26 In 2006, filmmaker-winemaker-publisher-hotelier Francis Ford Coppola snapped up a majestic French-style château, formerly Chateau Souverain and now called **Rosso & Bianco,** to showcase his less-expensive wines. (His Napa winery, Rubicon, focuses on the high-end vintages). It's still very much a work in progress: at this writing, visitors can taste wines like the summery Sofia Rosé, a soft, fruity wine made from pinot noir grapes, as well as reserve chardonnay, pinot noir, syrah, and merlot. You can also size up Coppola's Oscar trophies on display near the well-stocked gift shop. A casual café serves pizzas and salads, with a sea of red umbrellas on the terrace overlooking the vineyards. Major renovations scheduled to continue through most of 2008 will result in the addition of a boccie ball court, a high-end restaurant, and lots of Coppola memorabilia (the desk from *The Godfather* and costumes from *Bram Stoker's Dracula,* for example). ⊠ *400 Souverain Rd.* ☎ *707/433–8282* ⊕ *www.rossobianco.com* ⊜ *Tasting $5–$10, tour $10* ⊙ *Daily 11–5; tour daily at 12:30 and 2:30.*

27 Despite the name, there's no French connection at **Clos du Bois**: the name was suggested by the first owner's children, who thought the ho-hum title "Woods Vineyard" would sound better in Gallic. Although the large, airy, modern tasting room and gift shop here aren't particularly atmospheric, the winery is worth a stop for its in-depth tour that takes you through a demonstration vineyard and usually includes a barrel tasting in the cellar. Though you may be familiar with their inexpensive, approachable Classic wines, also look for their more intense Proprietary Series. ■TIP→ **Their shop sells half-bottles—a good choice for picnickers who want to pick up some cheese from the deli case and take a seat under the gazebos outside.** ⊠ *19410 Geyserville Ave.* ☎ *707/857–1651* ⊕ *www.closdubois.com* ⊜ *Tasting $5, tour $10* ⊙ *Daily 10–4:30; tour daily at 11 and 2 by appointment.*

28 When Leo and Evelyn Trentadue decided to move to a rural location in 1959, they found their new home in a neglected Alexander Valley prune and pear orchard. True to their Tuscan heritage, the family planted classic Italian grape varietals at **Trentadue Winery.** They still produce wines that are 100-percent sangiovese and carignane, something of a rarity in the area, but now they've added merlot, cabernet sauvignon, petite sirah, and zinfandel to their lineup. When

A Great Drive in Northern Sonoma County

Healdsburg is the area's hub, so plan on starting a day's drive here, nabbing an early breakfast in the town plaza. From downtown Healdsburg, take Healdsburg Avenue to Dry Creek Road and turn west. Almost as soon as you pass under the U.S. 101 freeway bridge, you'll feel like you're in the true countryside, free of urban sprawl. Turn left on Lambert Bridge Road, then right on West Dry Creek Road, taking your time on this scenic track. Drive past the NO OUTLET sign and veer right on the narrow lane alongside Peña Creek until you see an old barn on your left and the Preston Vineyard sign on the right. After visiting Preston, return the way you came until you reach Yoakim Bridge Road. Turn left there, then right on Dry Creek Road and left on Canyon Road. Just after Canyon Road crosses U.S. 101, turn right on Highway 128, which will lead you through Geyserville to Jimtown. Pick up picnic fixings at the Jimtown Store, then backtrack along Highway 128 less than a mile to the dramatic tasting room at Stryker Sonoma, where you

can taste their wines and enjoy your picnic.

Backtrack southeast on Highway 128; at the Jimtown Store, turn left on Alexander Valley Road. Veer left at Healdsburg Avenue to return to downtown Healdsburg, where you can taste wine at one of its many tasting rooms before dinner.

If you're lucky enough to have a second day, stock up on sandwiches at the Oakville Grocery before leaving Healdsburg. Drive south on Healdsburg Avenue and turn right on Mill Street. After it crosses U.S. 101 it turns into Westside Road. Wind along Westside Road—looking out for the many cyclists along this route—for about 20 minutes to Gary Farrell, where you can see much of the Russian River Valley below you from the tasting room. Return to Healdsburg by winding back the way you came along Westside Road, stopping to taste at whichever of the many tasting rooms appeals to you: Rochioli pours pinots that have their ardent admirers, and Hop Kiln is housed in an unusual historic building.

5

visiting their ivy-covered Tuscan-style villa, be sure to taste their most celebrated wine, the La Storia Red Meritage, a blend of merlot, cabernet sauvignon, and cabernet franc. ✉*19170 Geyserville Ave.* ☎*707/433-3104* ⊕*www.trenta-due.com* 🍷*Tasting free–$5* ☉*Daily 10–5.*

★ **㉙** You can catch a tempting glance of the **Stryker Sonoma Winery and Vineyards** tasting room from Highway 128, and the building becomes even more intriguing as you approach it. Dramatic horizontal concrete louvers frame the barrel room. Inside the tasting room, vaulted ceilings and seemingly endless walls of windows onto the vineyards suggest you've entered a cathedral to wine. The wines are almost as impressive as the architecture: most of their bottles are single varietals, such as chardonnay, pinot noir, merlot, zinfandel, and cabernet sauvignon. The two exceptions are Bordeaux-style blends, including the powerful E1K Red Blend, which, unfortunately, is not usually poured in the tasting room. ✉*5110 Hwy. 128* ☎*707/433–1944* ⊕*www.strykersonoma.com* 🍷*Tasting free–$10* ⊙*Daily 10:30–5.*

㉚ Off Highway 128 is the 1841 homestead of Cyrus Alexander, for whom the valley is named, now the site of **Alexander Valley Vineyards.** The Wetzel family bought the land from Alexander's heirs in 1963 and restored the historic adobe to serve as their family home. But the Wetzels also planted vineyards, and in 1975 they built a winery with adobe blocks and weathered wood. Today when you visit, the yellow labs belonging to Hank Wetzel, who oversees the winery operations, are likely to lope up to meet you. Head into the tasting room to taste the splendid Sin Zin, which is fairly low in alcohol for a California zinfandel and full of ripe cherry flavor, as well as their round, rich chardonnay. After tasting, you can wander up a grassy hill behind the winery to the cemetery of the Alexander family or grab a bottle and head for the picnic tables. ✉*8644 Hwy. 128* ☎*707/433–7209* ⊕*www.avvwine.com* 🍷*Tasting free–$5* ⊙*Daily 10–5; tour by appointment.*

WHERE TO STAY & EAT

★ ✗**Santi.** This outstanding restaurant would get much more
$$–$$$ notice if it weren't hidden away in the two-block town of Geyserville. As it is, the cozy dining room behind the brick facade feels like a find. The Italian fare is heartwarmingly old-school; for instance, the salamis and sausages are made in-house. Marinated sardines served with celery hearts and toasted almonds are a good example of the rustic style of cooking. ✉*21047 Geyserville Ave.* ☎*707/857–1790* ▭*AE, D, DC, MC, V* ⊙*No lunch Sat.–Tues.*

Central Coast

WORD OF MOUTH

"San Luis Obispo would be a central place to stay. You'd be close to the Paso Robles area and the Edna Valley area and not too far from the northern Santa Barbara County wineries as well."

—sequess

ALONG SOME 250 MILES of rolling seaboard, the Central Coast's wine region reaches from San Jose in the north to Santa Barbara in the south. Not too long ago this region was defined by its farmland and cattle and dairy ranches, and it's still largely agricultural. Since California's wine boom in the 1980s, however, much local agriculture has morphed into viticulture—cabernet sauvignon and chardonnay instead of strawberries and broccoli.

Central Coast wine making came fully into its own by the turn of the 21st century, with hundreds of wineries turning out premium bottles and earning a global reputation for excellent pinot noir, zinfandel, and chardonnay, among many other varietals. That status was affirmed in 2006, when two cabernet sauvignons from Ridge Vineyards, in the Santa Cruz Mountains, took the top honors at a re-creation of the famous 1976 Judgment of Paris tasting—the tasting that put California on the international wine map. Despite the recent uptick in tourism here, however, the wineries of the Central Coast still seem sleepier than those in Napa and Sonoma. You'll rarely find gridlock on the main roads, and tour buses are few and far between.

The climate along the Central Coast is mostly ideal for wine grapes, much like that in southern France, Italy, and Spain. Vines thrive on a diet of brilliantly sunny days and cool, often foggy nights; on aridly hot summers and gentle, wet (but not too wet) winters. Of course, the weather varies up and down this long strip of coastline raked by mountain ranges, and soil conditions differ from place to place. To recognize these variations in terroir, the Central Coast's five county appellations encompass some two dozen AVAs.

The same things that make the Central Coast a great place for wine growing make it a beautiful place to visit. The ocean-edged landscape of open lowland is backed by forested peaks. Wild, ranched, or farmed, the land remains mostly rural, and in spring, wildflowers blanket the meadows. Some of the most scenic stretches of California's Highway 1 wind along the Central Coast. The road links small, pretty cities such as Carmel-by-the-Sea, San Luis Obispo, and Santa Barbara; relaxed beach towns such as Santa Cruz; and spectacular landmarks such as Monterey Bay. The speedier north-south route, U.S. 101, emerges from the congested Silicon Valley to cut straight through the heart of the fertile (if featureless) Salinas Valley. The freeway then connects the major dots of south Central Coast wine country: Paso Robles, Templeton, Edna Valley, Santa Maria, and the Santa Ynez Valley.

GETTING AROUND THE CENTRAL COAST

The Central Coast wine region spreads out over a large area—it's about 250 mi from the Santa Cruz Mountains to the wineries of Santa Barbara County—so plan to spend some time in your car if you'd like to see more than a narrow slice of it.

U.S. 101 is the quickest thoroughfare through the region, running all the way from San Francisco to Santa Barbara along an inland route. On this route you'll speed primarily through flat agricultural land, although between San Francisco and San Jose it's all urban sprawl, and traffic can slow to a crawl during commute hours.

Roughly parallel to U.S. 101, Highway 1 along the coast is a less efficient north-south route through the region—most of the wineries are found a dozen or more miles inland, and the winding, usually two-lane road is much slower than U.S. 101—but the spectacular views of the Pacific Ocean, especially between San Simeon and Big Sur, make it worth the trip if you're not in a hurry and not prone to car sickness.

Santa Cruz can be reached via Highway 1 from San Francisco, or by taking Highway 17 from U.S. 101 near San Jose through the redwood-filled Santa Cruz Mountains. Take your time on Highway 17 and other routes through the mountains, which twist and turn as they climb through the trees.

The town of Monterey is on the coast along Highway 101, but can also be reached by Highway 68 from U.S. 101.

U.S. 101 runs directly through Paso Robles, intersecting with the east–west Highway 46, the main route to the AVA's east side and west side wineries. U.S. 101 links Paso in the north with San Luis Obispo in the south.

U.S. 101 continues south from Paso Robles and San Luis Obispo to the northern Santa Maria Valley. Just north of Los Olivos, Highway 154 leads southeast from U.S. 101 into the heart of Santa Barbara wine country, through Los Olivos and Santa Ynez.

CENTRAL COAST APPELLATIONS

A host of microclimates in the **Santa Cruz Mountains AVA,** thanks to the varying elevation and distance from the ocean, mean that many grapes are fair game on the steep slopes here. Cool weather varietals like pinot noir and chardonnay are popular on the Pacific side, while cabernet can thrive in the warmer pockets.

The **Monterey County AVA** is one of the cooler Central Coast regions, which means that chardonnay and pinot are in plentiful supply, but syrah, merlot, cabernet, and sauvignon blanc are popular, too. Of the county's seven subappellations, two of the most important are the tiny **Carmel Valley AVA,** where granite terraces around Carmel Valley Village are planted in cabernet sauvignon and merlot, and the large **Monterey AVA,** which spreads over about 36,000 acres, centered in the Salinas Valley.

In San Luis Obispo County, the booming **Paso Robles AVA** is basking in the wine-world limelight at the moment, and many new wineries are springing up every year. Vineyards in the hills west of Paso Robles are cooled by ocean breezes, while those on flatter east side of town are warmer and drier. Both sides are known for big, fruity cabernet sauvignon and zinfandel, as well as Rhône varietals such as syrah, grenache, and mourvèdre. To the south, the small **Edna Valley AVA** grows chardonnay and pinot in its clay-rich vineyards that are cooled by morning fog.

The rolling hills of up-and-coming **Santa Barbara County AVA** are divided into the three following subappellations. The **Santa Maria Valley AVA** may have a small number of wineries, but it has a big reputation for its pricey pinots, which are cultivated during a long growing season. In the slightly warmer **Santa Ynez Valley AVA,** pinot and chardonnay are joined by syrah and other Rhône varietals. The **Sta. Rita Hills AVA,** between Buellton and Lompoc, falls almost entirely within the Santa Ynez Valley appellation.

SANTA CRUZ MOUNTAINS

62 mi south of San Francisco on U.S. 101, Highway 85, and Highway 17.

Numbers in the margin correspond to numbers on the Santa Cruz Mountains map.

The Santa Cruz Mountains AVA, flanked by Silicon Valley suburbs and the Santa Clara Valley AVA on one side and beach towns on the other, lies only about 60 mi from San Francisco. The rugged area is cut by steep, redwood-studded canyons that shelter small vineyards and even smaller wineries. Visiting the wineries of the Santa Cruz Mountains requires some white-knuckle driving on twisting roads, but the scenery is gorgeous, and the tiny family-owned operations you'll find at the end of the road make it worth the trip.

Though this AVA is small—there are fewer than 1,500 acres of vineyards and fewer than 60 wineries here—it's still one of California's oldest and most important. Wine grapes were first planted here in the 1850s, but most vineyards and wineries fell victim to Prohibition and competition from more prolific regions. In the 1970s, growing respect for high-quality California wine began to bring vintners back to the Santa Cruz Mountains, and now wineries such as Ridge and David Bruce turn out truly world-class pinot noir, cabernet sauvignon, and chardonnay.

The Santa Cruz Mountains may make excellent wine, but tough growing conditions mean that the AVA doesn't make a whole lot of it. The slopes are steep and rocky, with poor soil, and the weather is tricky. The range is also tall enough (from 2,000 feet to nearly 4,000 feet in elevation) to intercept weather systems drifting in from the Pacific Ocean. As a result, the AVA has two distinct growing climates: vineyards east of the ridge often bask in sunshine while sea fog chills those west of the ridge. On the cooler, wetter western face, fog slows the ripening of grapes, especially at lower elevations.

The most convenient home base for visiting the wineries of the Santa Cruz Mountains is the town of Santa Cruz. Long known for its surfing and its amusement-filled beach boardwalk, the town is a mix of grand Victorian-era homes and rinky-dink motels. The opening of the University of California campus in the 1960s swung the town sharply to the left: Tie-dye, yoga, and social progressivism arrived with the faculty and students, many of whom have settled here permanently, and the counterculture thrives here.

Even visitors who are eager to get out to the vineyards in the surrounding mountains might want to take a morning off to swim at one of the town's soft sand beaches or visit the **Santa Cruz Beach Boardwalk,** which celebrated its 100th anniversary in 2007. Its Looff carousel and classic wooden Giant Dipper roller coaster, both dating from the early 1900s, are surrounded by high-tech thrill rides, arcade games, a mini-golf course, and easygoing kiddie rides with ocean views. You have to pay to play, but you can wander the entire boardwalk for free while blowing your diet on corn dogs and chowder fries. ✉*Along Beach St.* ☎*831/423–5590 or 831/426–7433* ⊕*www.beachboardwalk.com* 💲*$29, day pass for unlimited rides* ⊙*Late May–early Sept., daily; early Sept.–late May, weekends only, weather permitting; call for hrs.*

❷ One of Santa Cruz's few wine-related attractions, **Vinocruz** is the spot for a one-stop tasting of Santa Cruz Mountain wines. They pour vintages from more than 65 local wineries, including small operations that don't have their own tasting rooms. On weekends, winemakers come to introduce their wines; those tastings cost an extra $5. The slick, contemporary space in Abbott Square off Cooper Street in historic downtown was once part of an old jail. ✉*725 Front St. #101* ☎*831/426–8466* ⊕*www. vinocruz.com* 💲*$9* ⊙*Mon.–Thurs. 11–7, Fri. and Sat. 11–8, Sun. 11–6.*

VINEYARDS IN THE SANTA CRUZ MOUNTAINS

At the western fringe of the San Francisco Peninsula's inland suburbs, housing developments quickly give way to wooded foothills. Wineries only a few miles off I-280, in **Woodside and Cupertino,** perch far above the sprawl. Farther south, Highway 9 and Highway 17 cut roughly parallel north–south paths through the densely wooded Santa Cruz Mountains. Between them, several remote wineries work to capture the essence of the terroir in the **Los Gatos** area. And a few wineries in and around the town of **Santa Cruz** itself round out the wineries in the Santa Cruz Mountains.

WOODSIDE & CUPERTINO

❸ Pinot noir and chardonnay ripen slowly in the vineyards at **Thomas Fogarty Winery and Vineyards,** at the crest of the Santa Cruz Mountains. The results are intense and aromatic; a merlot redolent of berries, cocoa, and toast is particularly worth a try. Beyond the estate-grown wines, there are gewürztraminer, cabernet sauvignon, and other varietals from Monterey County grapes. The multilevel winery takes in a lofty view over the Bay Area. ✉*19501 Skyline*

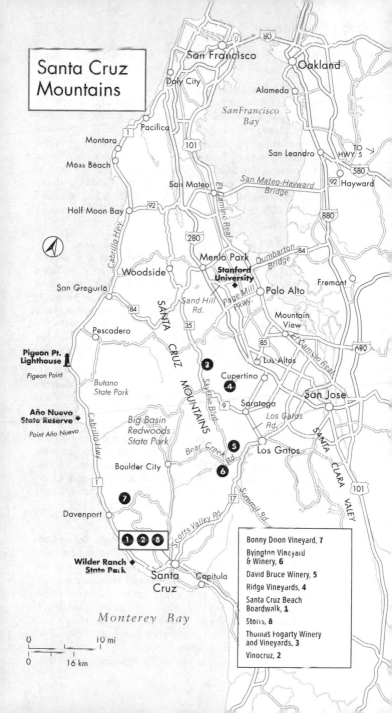

Santa Cruz Mountains

Bonny Doon Vineyard, **7**

Byington Vineyard
& Winery, **6**

David Bruce Winery, **5**

Ridge Vineyards, **4**

Santa Cruz Beach
Boardwalk, **1**

Storrs, **8**

Thomas Fogarty Winery
and Vineyards, **3**

Vinocruz, **2**

Blvd., Woodside ☎*650/851–6777* ⊕*www.fogartywinery. com* 🍷*Tasting $6–$12* ⊙*Wed.–Sun. 11–5:30.*

❹ At 2,300 feet above sea level, and with a wall of windows taking in the panorama from the tasting room, aptly named **Ridge Vineyards** is famous for its sturdy, well-structured Monte Bello cabernet sauvignon. A 1971 bottle outshone similar French and California vintages to win the 2006 Judgment of Paris tasting, a re-creation of the historic 1976 event, and a 2000 bottle topped the young wine category. ■TIP➔ **Fair warning for the drive: the road to the winery is a white-knuckler.** ✉*17100 Monte Bello Rd., Cupertino* ☎*408/867–3233* ⊕*www.ridgewine.com* 🍷*Tasting free–$5* ⊙*Weekends 11–4.*

LOS GATOS

★ ❺ Pinot noir, made from both local grapes as well as fruit sourced elsewhere, is the soul of the operation at **David Bruce Winery.** Overall, the results are boldly elegant, with intense cherry flavors and a supple finish. ■TIP➔ **Renovations in the works could cause some disruptions to their hours, so call ahead to confirm they'll be open before making the trip.** ✉*21439 Bear Creek Rd., Los Gatos* ☎*408/354–4214* ⊕*www.davidbrucewinery.com* 🍷*Tasting free* ⊙*Weekdays noon–5, weekends 11–5.*

❻ The view from the manicured grounds of **Byington Vineyard & Winery** ranges across the slopes of the western Santa Cruz Mountains all the way to the distant Pacific Ocean—if there's no fog. From the estate vineyards comes an earthy pinot noir; the Santa Cruz Mountains chardonnay is characteristically zippy. After your tasting at the Italianate stone winery, hang out at the boccie court, umbrella-shaded tables, and outdoor grills (bring your own grill tools). ✉*21850 Bear Creek Rd., Los Gatos* ☎*408/354–1111* ⊕*www.byington.com* 🍷*Tasting free* ⊙*Daily 11–5.*

SANTA CRUZ

★ ❼ Randall Grahm, the founder of iconoclastic **Bonny Doon Vineyard,** grooves to the same different drummer followed by tie-died, surfy Santa Cruz. Fanciful labels bear punny names such as Le Cigare Volante and Domaine des Blagueurs Syrah-Sirrah. The winery grows its estate grapes biodynamically, in Soledad, Monterey County. And they've embraced the screw-cap instead of the cork. Here's your chance to taste oddball grapes such as lemony white erbaluce and robust, red madiran; Bonny Doon also does a solid job with more familiar riesling, sangiovese, and Rhône

A Great Drive in the Santa Cruz Mountains

If you're starting your exploration of the Central Coast from San Francisco, but don't want to drive for four hours or more to get to your first winery in the Paso Robles area or further south, try this drive, which will have you sipping wine in no time. It's a quick hop down I-280 from San Francisco to the northernmost Central Coast AVA, the Santa Cruz Mountains. From I-280 in Cupertino, take Foothill Boulevard up to Montebello Road and make world-renowned Ridge Vineyards your first stop.

After trying the Ridge's outstanding cabernet, continue on the red wine trail to the David Bruce Winery. The quickest route is to go back to I-280, take it to Highway 17, and drive south into the mountains to Bear Creek Road. (In this case trying to take a scenic route isn't such a pleasure, since the roads between the two wineries are tortuous, steep, and slow.)

From David Bruce, continue on Bear Creek Road to reach Highway 9. Head south on this highway to reach Bonny Doon Vineyard, where you can taste wines made with less-familiar grapes. From Highway 9, wend west on Felton-Empire Road to Pine Flat Road, and you're there. From the winery, head south on Pine Flat Road, which turns into Bonny Doon Road. If you turn left when you hit the coast, onto Highway 1, you'll soon be in Santa Cruz, a mellow place to spend the night before heading farther south.

varietals. The tasting room often has a party atmosphere. ✉ *10 Pine Flat Rd., Santa Cruz* ☎ *831/425-4518* ⊕ *www. bonnydoonvineyard.com* 🍷 *Tasting $5* ⊙ *Daily 11-5.*

❽ Right in the town of Santa Cruz, the **Storrs** tasting room is in a restored 1806 lumber mill, among shops and design studios. The winery carefully matches grape varieties to the microclimates in its Santa Cruz Mountains vineyards, focusing on chardonnay, pinot noir, and zinfandel. Apple and pear flavors burst from the chardonnay, balanced with slight minerality and toasty oak. ✉ *303 Potrero St., Santa Cruz* ☎ *831/458-5030* ⊕ *www.storrswine.com* 🍷 *Tasting free* ⊙ *Daily noon-5.*

6

WHERE TO STAY & EAT

$$–$$$ ✕**Gabriella Café.** The work of local artists hangs on the walls of this petite, romantic café in a tile-roof cottage. The kitchen uses organic produce from area farms to serve up simple, seasonal Italian dishes like steamed mussels, braised lamb shank, or grilled portobello mushrooms. ✉*910 Cedar St., Santa Cruz* ☎*831/457–1677* ═*AE, MC, V.*

★ **$–$$** ✕**O'mei.** This is Chinese food like you've never had it. Imagine oolong-smoked chicken wok-cooked with cremini mushrooms and rosemary or impossibly fluffy fried potatoes topped with house-cured bacon and black date sauce. Service in the tasteful dining room is excellent; you can also order takeout. ✉*2316 Mission St., Santa Cruz* ☎*831/425–8458* ═*AE, D, DC, MC, V* ☻*No lunch weekends.*

★ **$–$$** ✕**Soif.** Wine reigns at this sleek bistro and wine shop that takes its name from the French word for thirst. The lengthy wine list includes selections from near and far, dozens of which you can order by the taste or glass. Infused with the tastes of the Mediterranean, small plates and mains are served at the copper-top bar, the big communal table, and private tables. A jazz combo or solo pianist plays some evenings. ✉*105 Walnut Ave., Santa Cruz* ☎*831/423–2020* ═*AE, MC, V* ☻*No lunch.*

¢ ✕**Zachary's.** This noisy café filled with students and families defines the funky essence of Santa Cruz. It also dishes up great breakfasts: stay simple with sourdough pancakes, or go for the Mike's Mess—eggs scrambled with bacon, mushrooms, and home fries, then topped with sour cream, melted cheese, and fresh tomatoes. ■TIP→ **If you arrive after 9 AM, expect a long wait for a table; lunch is a shade calmer, but closing time is 2 PM.** ✉*819 Pacific Ave., Santa Cruz* ☎*831/427–0646* ⚐*Reservations not accepted* ═*MC, V* ☻*Closed Mon. No dinner.*

$$$$ ▦**Pleasure Point Inn.** Tucked in a residential neighborhood at the east end of town, this modern B&B sits right across the street from the ocean and a popular beach (surfing lessons are available). The four rooms include such amenities as minibars and Wi-Fi; some have fireplaces. Lounge in the hot tub on the large rooftop sundeck overlooking the Pacific, or take a surfing lesson on the beach below. ■TIP→ **Because this is a popular romantic getaway spot, it's best not to bring kids. Pros:** Fantastic views, ideal for checking the swells, quirky neighborhood. **Cons:** Several miles from major attractions. ⊠2-3665 E. Cliff Dr., Santa Cruz 95062 ☎831/475–4657 or 877/557–2567 ⊕www.pleasurepointinn.com ⋙4 rooms ♿In-room: no a/c, safe, refrigerator, DVD, Wi-Fi. In-hotel: beachfront, no elevator, no-smoking rooms ⊟MC, V ⊚CP.

$$$–$$$$ ⚐**Babbling Brook Inn.** Though it's smack in the middle of Santa Cruz, this B&B has lush gardens, a running stream, and tall trees that make you feel like you're in a secluded wood. All rooms have fireplaces (though a few are electric) and feather beds; most have private patios. Complimentary wine, cheese, and fresh-baked cookies are available in the afternoon. **Pros:** Close to UCSC, walk to downtown shops, woodsy feel. **Cons:** Near high school, some rooms close to busy street. ⊠1025 Laurel St., Santa Cruz 95060 ☎831/427–2437 or 800/866–1131 ⊕www.babblingbrookinn.com ⋙11 rooms, 2 suites ♿In-room: no a/c, VCR. In-hotel: no elevator, no-smoking rooms ⊟AE, D, DC, MC, V ⊚BP.

$$–$$$$ ⚐**West Cliff Inn.** Perched on the bluffs across from Cowell's
★ Beach, this posh nautical-themed inn commands sweeping views of the boardwalk and Monterey Bay. Built in 1877, the Italianate three-story Victorian emerged from a top-to-bottom renovation in 2007 in classic California beach style with color schemes that hint of ocean, sky, and reflected light. All rooms have a comfy king bed, fireplace, and fancy marble tile bathrooms, many with spa tubs and some with sitting areas. For ultimate privacy, ask for the room with its own patio and hot tub. Ask for a room facing the bay for the best views. In the morning, fill up on a lavish breakfast in the elegant dining room and gaze at surfers and seals catching the waves below. **Pros:** Killer views, walk to beach, close to downtown. **Cons:** Boardwalk noise, street traffic. ⊠174 West Cliff Dr., Santa Cruz 95060 ☎800/979–0910 ⊕www.westcliffinn.com ⋙7 rooms, 2 suites ♿In-room: DVD, Wi-Fi. In-hotel: no-smoking rooms ⊟AE, D, MC, V ⊚BP.

$$–$$$ ⚐**Sea & Sand Inn.** The main appeal of this aging motel perched on a waterfront bluff is its location: every room has an ocean view, and the boardwalk is just down the street. Blond-wood furniture and floral fabrics create a vaguely country look; some rooms have private hot tubs or fireplaces. A few studios and suites include kitchenettes. **Pros:** Beach is steps away, friendly staff, tidy landscaping. **Cons:** Tight parking lot, fronting a busy road, can be noisy.

✉*201 W. Cliff Dr., Santa Cruz 95060* ☎*831/427–3400*
⊕*www.santacruzmotels.com* ⌖*15 rooms* ☖*In-room:
kitchen (some), VCR (some), Wi-Fi. In-hotel: no elevator,
no-smoking rooms* ▤*AE, MC, V* ⫽*CP.*

NIGHTLIFE & THE ARTS

★ Renowned in the international jazz community, and drawing performers such as Herbie Hancock, Pat Metheny, and
Charlie Hunter, the nonprofit **Kuumbwa Jazz Center** (✉*320–
2 Cedar St.* ☎*831/427–2227* ⊕*www.kuumbwajazz.org*)
bops with live music most nights. A Santa Cruz version of
a SoHo loft, **The Attic** (✉*931 Pacific Ave.* ☎*831/460–1800*
⊕*www.theatticsantacruz.com*) combines an art lounge,
restaurant, tea house, gallery, and performance venue in
a sprawling second-floor space in the heart of downtown.
Hang out with a cool, artsy crowd and tune into cutting-
edge culture: music, poetry readings, dance, and theater.

SPORTS & THE OUTDOORS

There aren't many places in the world where you can
go surfing in the morning and wine tasting in the afternoon, but Santa Cruz is one of the best places to experience this rare combination of pleasures. Surfers gather
for spectacular waves and sunsets at **Pleasure Point** (✉*E.
Cliff and Pleasure Point Drs.*). If you're a newcomer to
the sport, visit **Club-Ed Surf School and Camps** (✉*Cowell
Beach, at Coast Santa Cruz Hotel* ☎*831/464–0177 or
800/287–7873* ⊕*www.club-ed.com*). Your first private or
group lesson ($85 and up) includes all equipment. The
most welcoming place in town to buy or rent surf gear is
Paradise Surf Shop (✉*3961 Portola Dr.* ☎*831/462–3880*
⊕*www.paradisesurf.com*).

MONTEREY COUNTY

125 mi south of San Francisco on U.S. 101.

*Numbers in the margin correspond to numbers on the
Monterey County map.*

When people think of Monterey County, they commonly
think of craggy coastline, sea otters, and maybe the Pebble Beach golf courses with their magnificent ocean views.

When wine buffs think of Monterey, however, they conjure up inland valleys scored with row upon row of vines.

Novelist John Steinbeck, a native of Monterey County, made the area's hardworking people famous in books such as *Cannery Row*, about Monterey's sardine-canning industry, and *Grapes of Wrath*, about migrant farm workers in the Salinas Valley during the Great Depression. The area's fortunes have improved since Steinbeck's day, but many locals still depend upon the generous land, sea, and climate for their livelihood.

A few coastal Monterey vineyards have ventured into cool-climate viticulture, but most of the county's grape growers and wineries concentrate in the Carmel and Salinas valleys. The Carmel Valley AVA runs southeast from Monterey Bay into the Santa Lucia Highlands AVA, whose mountains cut off the Salinas Valley from the Pacific Ocean. The Carmel and Salinas valleys get plenty of sun and cool sea breezes, and fog can roll in anytime, especially at night. Higher elevation distinguishes viticultural conditions in the Carmel Valley from those in the Salinas Valley. Over the undulating terrain of the Salinas Valley, pockets of warm or cold air and variable levels of sun and fog generate many microclimates.

If you want to be be in the center of Monterey County's vineyards, the most convenient place to stay is **Carmel Valley Village**, a tiny town about 13 mi southeast of the coast via Carmel Valley Road. In addition to opulent hotels, the town has several crafts shops and art galleries, as well as tasting rooms for numerous local wineries. To pick up fresh veggies, ready-to-eat meals, gourmet groceries, flowers and gifts, stop at the 32-acre **Earthbound Farm** (⌂7250 *Carmel Valley Rd.* ☎831/625–6219 ⊕*www.ebfarm.com*), the world's largest grower of organic produce. Check out the kid's garden, cut your own herbs, and stroll through the chamomile aromatherapy labyrinth. On Saturdays from April through December the farm offers special events, from bug walks to garlic braiding workshops.

If money is no object, you might consider staying in the self-consciously charming town of **Carmel-by-the-Sea** (often referred to as simply "Carmel," and not to be confused with Carmel Valley Village), whose population quadruples with tourists on weekends and in summer. The town's greatest attraction is its rugged coastline, with pine and cypress forests and countless inlets, but browsing the shops along the cobblestone streets downtown comes in a close second. Buildings still have no street numbers (street names are written on discreet white posts) and consequently there is no mail delivery (if you really want to see the locals, go to the post office). Artists started this community, and their legacy is evident in the numerous galleries.

The coastal town of **Monterey** is also within easy striking distance of many of the county's wineries—about 30 minutes from Carmel Valley Village and its surrounding wineries. As one of the most touristed towns on the Central Coast, it's got tons of lodgings, from no-frills motels to luxurious hotels, and plenty of non-wine-related tourist attractions.

🕐 ❿ The mournful barking of sea lions provides a steady soundtrack at **Fisherman's Wharf**, an undeniably touristy but entertaining area lined with souvenir shops, seafood restaurants, and whale-watching tour boats. ⊠*End of Calle Principal* ☎*831/649–6544* ⊕*www.montereywharf.com.*

The waterfront **Cannery Row** was once crowded with sardine canneries processing, at their peak, nearly 200,000 tons of the smelly silver fish a year. Through the years, however, the old tin-roof canneries have been converted into restaurants, art galleries, and malls with shops selling T-shirts, fudge, and plastic sea otters. ⊠*Cannery Row, between Prescott and David Aves.* ⊕*www.canneryrow.com.*

⓫ ★ **Fodors**Choice Monterey's most impressive attraction by far 🕐 is the world-renowned **Monterey Bay Aquarium.** The minute you hand over your ticket at this extraordinary aquarium you're surrounded by sea creatures. The beauty of the exhibits here is that they are all designed to give a sense of what it's like to be in the water with the animals—sardines swim around your head in a circular tank, and jellyfish drift in and out of view in dramatically lighted spaces that suggest the ocean depths. The only drawback to the experience is that it must be shared with the throngs of people that crowd the place daily. ⊠*886 Cannery Row* ☎*831/648–4888, 800/756–3737 in CA for advance tickets* ⊕*www.montereybayaquarium.org* ⊠*$24.95* ⊘*Late May–early Sept., daily 9:30–6; early Sept.–late May, daily 10–6.*

⓬ Before leaving town to visit the wineries, you might want to stop by **A Taste of Monterey.** Without driving the county's back roads, you can taste the wines of 40 area vintners. Purchase a few bottles and pick up a map and guide to the county's wineries and vineyards. ⊠*700 Cannery Row, Suite KK* ☎*831/646–5446 or 888/646–5446* ⊕*www.tastemonterey. com* ⊙*Daily 11–6.*

VINEYARDS IN MONTEREY COUNTY

A small number of wineries within a few miles of the town of Monterey brave the elements to grow cool-weather varietals like chardonnay and pinot noir. South of Monterey the Carmel River runs through the narrow Carmel Valley. The mountainside vineyards here are quite cool, so they produce more intense fruit with higher acid levels than do vineyards elsewhere in the county. Some of the wineries are hard to reach, so they operate tasting rooms in the more accessible lower valley, many in tiny Carmel Valley Village. Farther inland and to the south, in the heart of the Salinas Valley, the gritty town of Soledad is more famous for its vast produce farms and its state prison than for grapes, but it is the address of two Monterey County wine scene mainstays.

BARGAIN WINE TOUR Why risk driving while wine tasting? Hop aboard the **Carmel Valley Grapevine Express** (☎*888/670–2871* ⊕*www.mst.org*) a bus operated by Monterey–Salinas Transit that travels between downtown Monterey and Carmel Valley Village, with stops near wineries, restaurants, and shopping centers. Buses depart daily every hour from 11 to 6. At $4.50 for a ride-all-day pass, it's an incredible bargain.

MONTEREY

⓭ The founder of **Ventana Vineyards/Meador Estate,** Doug Meador, is a master in the art of cold-climate viticulture and a leader in the region's emergence as a wine producer. His most successful wines, made from locally grown grapes, are whites such as chardonnay, sauvignon blanc, and gewürztraminer; the off-dry (slightly sweet) riesling balances apricot flavors with mouthwatering acidity. Reds include merlot, cabernet franc, and syrah. The tasting room occupies an old stone house that's an easy five-minute drive east of downtown Monterey. ⊠*2999 Monterey–Salinas Highway, Monterey* ☎*831/372–7415* ⊕*www. ventanawines.com* ⊠*Tasting free* ⊙*Oct.–May, daily 11–5; June–Sept., daily 11–6.*

6

CLOSE UP

The 17-Mile Drive

Although most of the wineries in the Monterey area are a dozen or so miles inland, where the grapes are protected from the worst of the cold winds whipping off the Pacific Ocean, most visitors to Monterey County spend at least half a day getting a gander of the spectacular coastline.

The most jaw-dropping stretch of California's long coast is the justly famous **17-Mile Drive**, between Carmel-by-the-Sea and Pacific Grove, where palatial late-20th-century estates are interspersed with wild coastal vistas.

Some sightseers balk at the $8.75-per-car fee collected at the gates—this is the only private toll road west of the Mississippi—but most find the drive well worth the price. An alternative is to grab a bike. ■TIP→ **Cyclists tour for free, as do those with confirmed lunch or dinner reservations at one of the hotels.**

Dotting the drive are rare Monterey cypress, trees so gnarled and twisted that Robert Louis Stevenson described them as "ghosts fleeing before the wind."

Along the way you can take in views of the impeccable greens at **Pebble Beach Golf Links** (✉ *17-Mile Dr. near Lodge at Pebble Beach* ☎ *800/654–9300* ⊕ *www. pebblebeach.com*) over a drink or lunch at the Lodge at Pebble Beach.

Many of the stately homes along 17-Mile Drive reflect the classic Monterey or Spanish Mission style typical of the region. A standout is the **Crocker Marble Palace,** about a mile south of the Lone Cypress (⇨ *below*). It's a private waterfront estate inspired by a Byzantine castle, easily identifiable by its dozens of marble arches.

The most-photographed tree along 17-Mile Drive is the weather-sculpted **Lone Cypress,** which grows out of a precipitous outcropping above the waves about 1½ mi up the road from Pebble Beach Golf Links. You can stop for a view of the Lone Cypress at a parking area, but you can't walk out to the tree.

Sea creatures and birds—as well as some very friendly ground squirrels—make use of **Seal Rock,** the largest of a group of islands about 2 mi north of Lone Cypress.

Bird Rock, the largest of several islands at the southern end of the Monterey Country Club's golf course, teems with harbor seals, sea lions, cormorants, and pelicans.

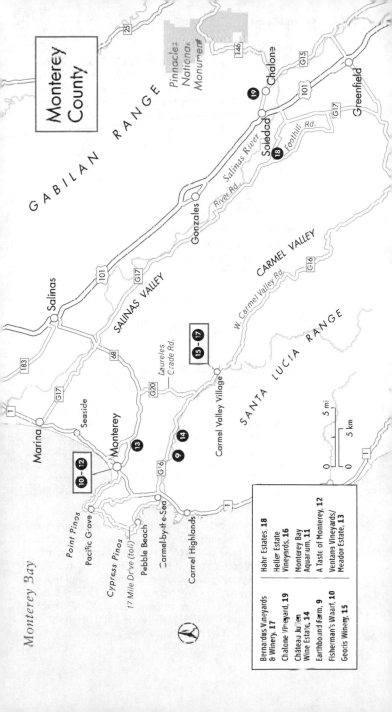

Monterey County

Monterey Bay

GABILAN RANGE

Pinnacles National Monument

SANTA LUCIA RANGE

SALINAS VALLEY

CARMEL VALLEY

Point Pinos
Pacific Grove
Cypress Point
17 Mile Drive (toll)
Pebble Beach
Carmel-by-the-Sea
Carmel Highlands
Marina
Seaside
Monterey
Salinas
Gonzales
Soledad
Chalone
Greenfield
Carmel Valley Village
W. Carmel Valley Rd.
Laureles Grade Rd.
River Rd.
Salinas River
Foothill Rd.

13
10 – 12
15 – 17
14
9
19
18

Bernardus Vineyards & Winery, **17**	Hahn Estates **18**
Chalone Vineyard, **19**	Heller Estate Vineyards, **16**
Château Julien Wine Estate, **14**	Monterey Bay Aquarium, **11**
Earthbound Farm, **9**	A Taste of Monterey, **12**
Fisherman's Wharf, **10**	Ventana Vineyards/ Meador Estate, **13**
Georis Winery, **15**	

0   5 mi
0   5 km

CARMEL VALLEY

⑭ Taking its cue from French châteaus, **Château Julien Wine Estate** has a postcard prettiness. But the effect is more than just show: the wines made here from Monterey County grapes—sauvignon blanc, pinot grigio, chardonnay, gewürztraminer, merlot, cabernet sauvignon, syrah, sangiovese, and zinfandel—are first rate. The views are captivating, and you can sip and snack at a cobblestoned picnic area. ✉ *8940 Carmel Valley Rd., Carmel Valley* ☎ *831/624–2600* ⊕ *www.chateaujulien.com* ✑ *Tasting $5, tour free* ⊙ *Weekdays 8–5, weekends 11–5; tour weekdays at 10:30 and 2:30 by appointment, weekends at 12:30 and 2:30 by appointment.*

⑮ **Georis Winery** makes only cabernet sauvignon and merlot grown on its 28 acres of vineyards. Opulent and tannic, these reds have attracted a devoted following; they really are meant for aging. The tasting room, with plump leather chairs and a fireplace, is tucked in the back of an old adobe that it shares with Talbott Vineyards; there are tables on the garden patio. ✉ *4 Pilot Rd., Carmel Valley* ☎ *831/659–1050* ⊕ *www.georiswine.com* ✑ *Tasting $15–$20* ⊙ *Daily 11–5.*

⑯ Gilbert Heller's 120 acres of certified-organic dry-farmed vineyards at **Heller Estate Vineyards** rely on underground springs for their water. The result is luscious wine that stands up well to aging (though the refreshing, dry merlot rosé is best young). Friendly servers in the simple Carmel Valley Village tasting room pour estate-grown wines such as chenin blanc, chardonnay, pinot noir, and cabernet sauvignon. Outside are a picnic area and a sculpture garden filled with work by Heller's wife, Toby. ✉ *69 West Carmel Valley Rd., Carmel Valley* ☎ *831/659–6220* ⊕ *www.hellerestate.com* ✑ *Tasting $5* ⊙ *Mon.–Thurs. 11–5:30, Fri.–Sun. 11–6.*

⑰ Inspired by the vineyards of Bordeaux, **Bernardus Vineyards & Winery** grows cabernet sauvignon and merlot high in the untamed hills above Carmel Valley. Marinus, a proprietary blend of the two, is the full-bodied signature bottle, full of black cherry and toast notes that lead to a long finish. Chardonnay grown elsewhere in Monterey County has a pineapple tang and appley sweetness. ✉ *5 West Carmel Valley Rd., Carmel Valley* ☎ *831/659–1900* ⊕ *www.bernardus.com* ✑ *Tasting $5–$10* ⊙ *Daily 11–5.*

SOLEDAD

⑱ Founded as Smith & Hook Winery in 1974, **Hahn Estates**, a former ranch along the east-facing slopes of the Santa Lucias, is above the fog line and perfect for growing cabernet sauvignon. The winery continues to produce noteworthy cabs, as well as viognier, chardonnay, cabernet franc, and merlot. Hahn also continues to make pricier premium wines, such as a challenging cabernet sauvignon, under the Smith & Hook label. Tasting takes place in a low-slung house with views over the valley; outside, there's a wide deck with tables and umbrellas. ⊠*37700 Foothill Rd., Soledad* ☏*831/678–2132* ⊕*www.hahnestates.com* ⊠*Tasting free* ⊙*Weekdays 11–4, weekends 11–5.*

⑲ ★ **Fodor's**Choice A Frenchman planted **Chalone Vineyard** with chenin blanc grapes in 1919—just in time for Prohibition—and other owners added chardonnay, pinot blanc, and pinot noir vines in the 1940s. By the early 1960s, the vines were barely alive, but Dick Graff resurrected them and began making some exceptionally fine wine, now including estate syrah and viognier. These are among the very few American wines grown in the revered limestone-based soil type on which Burgundy built its eminence. The on-site winery, added in 1974, remains the sole production facility in the Chalone AVA. The tasting room lies east of U.S. 101 on the road to Pinnacles National Monument, within sight of the dramatic remains of a prehistoric volcano. ⊠*Stonewall Canyon Road, off Hwy. 146, Soledad* ☏*831/678–1717* ⊕*www.chalonevineyard.com* ⊠*Tasting $5* ⊙*Weekends 11:30–5, weekdays by appointment.*

6

WHERE TO STAY & EAT

CARMEL VALLEY

$$–$$$$ ✕**Will's Fargo.** On the main street of Carmel Valley Village since the 1920s, this restaurant calls itself a "dressed-up saloon." Steerhorns and gilt-frame paintings adorn the walls of the Victorian-style dining room; you can also eat on the patios. The menu is mainly steaks, including a 24-ounce porterhouse. ⊠*16 E. Carmel Valley Rd.* ☏*831/659–2774* ▤*AE, DC, MC, V.*

$–$$ ✕**Café Rustica.** Italian-inspired country cooking is the focus at this lively roadhouse. Specialties include roasted meats, pastas, and thin-crust pizzas from the wood-fired oven. ■TIP➔**Because of the tile floors, it can get quite noisy inside; opt for a table outside if you want a quieter meal.** ⊠*10 Del-*

fino Pl. ☎*831/659–4444* ⚘*Reservations essential* ▤*MC,*
V ⊘*Closed Wed.*

¢ ✕**Wagon Wheel Coffee Shop.** This local hangout decorated
with wagon wheels, cowboy hats, and lassos serves up terrific hearty breakfasts, including date-walnut-cinnamon
French toast and a plate of trout and eggs. The lunch menu
includes a dozen different burgers and other sandwiches.
✉*Valley Hill Center, Carmel Valley Rd. next to Quail
Lodge* ☎*831/624–8878* ▤*No credit cards* ⊘*No dinner.*

★ **$$$$** ✕▥**Bernardus Lodge.** As soon as the valet whisks away
your car, you're handed a glass of wine at this luxury spa
resort, a sign of the pampering to come. The spacious guest
rooms, if not exactly the pinnacle of modern style, have
vaulted ceilings, fireplaces, patios, and bathtubs for two,
and are stocked with fresh flowers, snacks, and compli-
mentary wine. The owners want to provide all the com-
forts of home, but few homes have come with a spacious
pool area and a lawn for croquet or boccie. The restaurant
Marinus ($$$$; jacket recommended) is perhaps the best
in the Monterey Bay area, with a menu that changes daily
to highlight local produce. Reserve the chef's table in the
kitchen and you can talk to him as he prepares your meal.
Pros: Exceptional personal service, outstanding food and
wine, no fee to use spa faciltities. **Cons:** Room decor is a bit
pedestrian for the price. ✉*415 Carmel Valley Rd., 93924*
☎*831/659–3131 or 888/648–9463* ⊕*www.bernardus.com*
⇲*56 rooms, 1 suite* ⚘*In-room: safe, refrigerator, DVD
(some), Wi-Fi. In-hotel: 2 restaurants, room service, bar,
tennis courts, pool, gym, spa, concierge, laundry service,
no-smoking rooms* ▤*AE, DC, MC, V.*

$$$$ ✕▥**Quail Lodge.** What began as the Carmel Valley Country Club—a hangout for Frank Sinatra, among others—is
now a private golf club and resort in the valley's west side.
Winding around swimming pools and putting greens, the
buildings' exteriors recall the old days, but indoors the
luxury is totally updated with a cool, modern feel: plasma
TVs swing out from the walls, the toiletries include giant
tea bags to infuse your bath with herbs, and each room has
a window seat overlooking a private patio. The Covey at
Quail Lodge ($$$–$$$$; jacket recommended) serves con-
temporary California cuisine in a romantic lakeside din-
ing room. One of the lodge's recreation offerings is a rare
treat: a Land Rover off-road driving lesson along a tailor-
made trail. **Pros:** Located on golf course, pastoral views.

Cons: Some rooms need updating, about a 5-mi drive to Carmel Valley Village. ⊠ *8205 Valley Greens Dr., 93923* 🕿 *831/624–1581 or 800/538–9516* ⊕ *www.quaillodge. com* ⇨*83 rooms, 14 suites* △*In-room: safe, refrigerator, Wi-Fi. In-hotel: 2 restaurants, room service, bars, golf course, tennis courts, pools, gym, spa, bicycles, concierge, laundry service, public Internet, no-smoking rooms* ⊟*AE, DC, MC, V.*

$$–$$$ ⚟**Carmel Valley Lodge.** This small inn has rooms surrounding a garden patio, and separate one- and two-bedroom cottages with fireplaces and full kitchens. Open-beam ceilings, Shaker-style furnishings, and plaid easy chairs give the rooms a casual, almost rustic air. **Pros:** Peaceful property, friendly staff, close to village. **Cons:** Rooms may appear too rustic for some. ⊠ *8 Ford Rd., at Carmel Valley Rd., 93924* 🕿 *831/659–2261 or 800/641–4646* ⊕ *www.valleylodge. com* ⇨*19 rooms, 4 suites, 8 cottages* △*In-room: no a/c, kitchen (some), refrigerator, VCR, Wi-Fi. In-hotel: pool, public Internet, no-smoking rooms, some pets allowed (fee)* ⊟*AE, MC, V* ⊚*CP.*

CARMEL

$$$–$$$$ ✕**Casanova.** This cozy restaurant, formerly a home, seems to coax its guests into celebration and romance. Chairs are painted in various colors, accordions hang from the walls, and tiny party lights dance along the low ceilings. The entrées include antipasti and your choice of appetizers, which all but mandate you to sit back and enjoy a long meal. The seasonal menu focuses on dishes from southern France and northern Italy, such as veal *piccata* (sauteed, with a lemony sauce). Private dining and a special menu are offered at Van Gogh's Table, a special table imported from France's Auberge Ravoux, the artist's final residence. ⊠ *5th Ave. between San Carlos and Mission Sts.* 🕿 *831/625–0501* △*Reservations essential* ⊟*AE, MC, V.*

$$–$$$$ ✕**Bouchée.** With its copper bar, the dining room feels more
★   urban than most of Carmel; perhaps this is why Bouchée is the "cool" place in town to dine. Local ingredients get an innovative spin, as in a Reuben sandwich made with veal sweetbreads. The stellar wine list sources the selection at adjoining Bouchée Wine Merchant. ⊠ *Mission St. between Ocean and 7th Aves.* 🕿 *831/626 7880* △*Reservations essential* ⊟*AE, MC, V* ⊘*Closed Mon. No lunch.*

$$–$$$ ✕**Flying Fish.** Simple in appearance yet bold with its flavors, this Japanese–California seafood restaurant has quickly

established itself as one of Carmel's most inventive eateries. Among the best entrées is the almond-crusted sea bass served with Chinese cabbage and rock shrimp stir-fry. The warm, wood-lined dining room is broken up into very private booths. The entrance is a bit hard to spot; go down the steps near the gates to Carmel Plaza. ⊠*Mission St. between Ocean and 7th Aves.* ☎*831/625–1962* ▤*AE, D, MC, V* ⊗*Closed Tues. No lunch.*

¢–$ ✕**Tuck Box.** This bright little restaurant is in a cottage right out of a fairy tale, complete with a stone fireplace that's lighted on rainy days. Handmade scones are the house specialty, and are good for breakfast or afternoon tea. ⊠*Dolores St. between Ocean and 7th Aves.* ☎*831/624–6365* ▤*No credit cards* ⊗*No dinner.*

$$$$ ★ **Fodor's**Choice ✕▥**L'Auberge Carmel.** This elegant inn is like an Armani suit: no splashy labels, just impeccable, understated style. Guest rooms are punctuated by original black-and-white photos; the bathrooms are especially posh with their huge soaking tubs and heated floors. Lolling in the sun-soaked brick courtyard can make you feel like a movie star. A highlight is the intimate **Restaurant L'Auberge** ($$$$). The single, prix-fixe tasting menu consists of endless courses, each one a marvel imagined by chef Walter Manske. The deconstructed lobster taco, for example, consists of a tortilla strip balanced atop a tiny glass of clear tomato and cilantro essence, a cube of lobster, and a shot of lime ice drenched in fine tequila. **Pros:** In town yet off the main street, four blocks to beach, full-service luxury. **Cons:** Not best choice for kids, touristy area. ⊠*Monte Verde at 7th Ave., 93921* ☎*831/624–8578* ⊕*www.laubergecarmel.com* ⇨*20 rooms* ⌂*In-room: safe, DVD. In-hotel: restaurant, room service, bar, concierge, no-smoking rooms* ▤*AE, D, MC, V* ⏍*CP.*

★ $$$$ ▥**Tradewinds Inn.** Its sleek decor inspired by the South Seas, this converted motel encircles a courtyard with waterfalls, a meditation garden, and a fire pit. Each room has a tabletop fountain and orchids, to complement antique and custom furniture from Bali and China. Some private balconies afford a view of the bay or the mountains. The chic boutique hotel, owned by the same family since it opened in 1959, is on a quiet downtown side street. **Pros:** Serene, walk to restaurants, friendly service. **Cons:** No pool, longish walk to beach. ⊠*Mission St. at 3rd Ave., 93921* ☎*831/624–2776 or 800/624–6665* ⊕*www.carmel-*

tradewinds.com ↩*26 rooms, 2 suites* &*In-room: no a/c, safe, refrigerator, Wi-Fi. In-hotel: concierge, no-smoking rooms, some pets allowed (fee)* ═*AE, MC, V* ⊙*CP.*

$$-$$$ ⊡**Mission Ranch.** The property at Mission Ranch is gorgeous and includes a sprawling sheep pasture, bird-filled wetlands, and a sweeping view of the ocean. The ranch is nicely decorated but low-key, with a 19th-century farmhouse as the central building. Other accommodations include rooms in a converted barn, and several cottages, many with fireplaces. Though the ranch belongs to movie star Clint Eastwood, relaxation, not celebrity, is the focus here. **Pros:** Farm setting, pastoral views, great for tennis buffs. **Cons:** Drive to heart of town, busy parking lot. ⊠*26270 Dolores St., 93923* ☎*831/624–6436 or 800/538–8221* ⊕*www. missionranchcarmel.com* ↩*31 rooms* &*In-room: no a/c, refrigerator (some). In-hotel: restaurant, bar, tennis courts, gym, no-smoking rooms* ═*AE, MC, V* ⊙*CP.*

$-$$ ⊡**Sea View Inn.** In a residential area a few hundred feet from the beach, this restored 1905 home has a double parlor with two fireplaces, Oriental rugs, canopy beds, and a spacious front porch. Rooms are individually done in cheery colors and country patterns; taller guests might feel cramped in those rooms tucked up under the eaves. Afternoon tea and evening wine and cheese are offered daily. Because of the fragile furnishings and quiet atmosphere, families with kids will likely be more comfortable elsewhere. **Pros:** Quiet, private, close to beach. **Cons:** Small building, some rooms with shared bath, uphill trek to heart of town. ⊠*Camino Real between 11th and 12th Aves., 93921* ☎*831/624–8778* ⊕*www.seaviewinncarmel.com* ↩*8 rooms, 6 with bath* &*In-room: no a/c, no phone, no TV. In-hotel: no-smoking rooms* ═*AE, MC, V* ⊙*CP.*

MONTEREY

$$$$ ✕**Fresh Cream.** For years this dining room with a view of glittering Heritage Harbor has provided one of the most refined dining experiences in Monterey. The wine list is carefully chosen, the service is attentive yet restrained, and everything carries an air of luxury. The menu centers around imaginative variations on classic French cuisine, such as lobster and prawns with white corn bisque. Though there's no explicit dress policy, men will feel more comfortable in a jacket. ⊠*99 Pacific St., Suite 100C* ☎*831/375–9798* ⚲*Reservations essential* ═*AE, D, DC, MC, V* ⊙*No lunch.*

$$–$$$ ✕**Montrio Bistro.** This quirky, converted firehouse, with its
★ rawhide walls and iron indoor trellises, has a wonderfully
sophisticated menu. Chef Tony Baker uses organic, often
local, produce and meats to create imaginative dishes such
as baby-artichoke risotto and whole stuffed quail with
savory French toast and apple-blackberry reduction. Like-
wise, the wine list draws primarily on California, and many
bottles come from the Monterey area. ✉*414 Calle Principal* ☎*831/648–8880* ⚑*Reservations essential* ▭*AE, D,
DC, MC, V* ⊘*No lunch.*

$$–$$$ ✕**Tarpy's Roadhouse.** Fun, dressed-up American favor-
ites—a little something for everyone—are served in this
renovated early-1900s stone farmhouse several miles outside town. The kitchen cranks out everything from Cajun-
spiced prawns to meat loaf with marsala-mushroom gravy
to grilled ribs and steaks. Eat indoors by a fireplace or outdoors in the courtyard. ✉*2999 Monterey–Salinas Hwy.,
Hwy. 68* ☎*831/647–1444* ▭*AE, D, DC, MC, V.*

★ **$$$$** ▥**Old Monterey Inn.** This three-story manor house was the
home of Monterey's first mayor, and today it remains a
private enclave within walking distance of downtown.
Lush gardens are shaded by huge old trees and bordered
by a creek. Rooms are individually decorated with tasteful
antiques; many have fireplaces, and all have feather beds.
Those with private entrances have split doors; you can open
the top half to let in cool air and the sound of birds. The
extensive breakfast is delivered to the rooms, and wine,
cheese, and cookies are served each afternoon in the parlor.
Pros: Gorgeous gardens, refined luxury, serene property.
Cons: Must drive to attractions and sights, fills quickly.
✉*500 Martin St., 93940* ☎*831/375–8284 or 800/350–
2344* ⊕*www.oldmontereyinn.com* ⌂*6 rooms, 3 suites, 1
cottage* ⚭*In-room: no a/c, VCR, Wi-Fi. In-hotel: no elevator, concierge, no-smoking rooms* ▭*MC, V* ⊚*BP.*

$$$–$$$$ ▥**Monterey Plaza Hotel and Spa.** This full-service hotel com-
mands a waterfront location on Cannery Row, where you
can see frolicking sea otters from the wide outdoor patio
and many room balconies. The architecture blends early
California and Mediterranean styles, and also echoes ele-
ments of the old cannery design. Meticulously maintained,
the property offers both simple and luxurious accommo-
dations. On the top floor, the spa offers a full array of
treatments, perfect after a workout in the penthouse fit-
ness center. **Pros:** On the ocean, resort amenities, attentive

service. **Cons:** Touristy area, heavy traffic. ✉*400 Cannery Row, 93940* ☎*831/646–1700 or 800/334–3999* ⊕*www. montereyplazahotel.com* ⇔*280 rooms, 10 suites* ⌂*In-room: no a/c, DVD, Ethernet. In-hotel: 2 restaurants, room service, gym, spa, concierge, laundry service, public Internet, no-smoking rooms* ⊟*AE, D, DC, MC, V.*

$ ▣**Monterey Bay Lodge.** Location (on the edge of Monterey's El Estero Park) and superior amenities give this cheerful facility an edge over other motels in town. Lots of greenery, indoors and out, views over El Estero Lake, and a secluded courtyard with a heated pool are other pluses. **Pros:** Walk to beach and playground, quiet at night, good family choice. **Cons:** Near busy boulevard. ✉*55 Camino Aguajito, 93940* ☎*831/372–8057 or 800/558–1900* ⊕*www. montereybaylodge.com* ⇔*43 rooms, 2 suites* ⌂*In-room: safe, refrigerator, VCR (some), Wi-Fi. In-hotel: restaurant, pool, no elevator, no-smoking rooms, some pets allowed (fee)* ⊟*AE, D, DC, MC, V.*

NIGHTLIFE & THE ARTS

★ The **Monterey Jazz Festival** (☎*831/373–3366* ⊕*www.montereyjazzfestival.org*), the world's oldest, attracts jazz and blues greats from around the world to the Monterey Fairgrounds on the third full weekend of September. Beyond the annual jazz festival, the **Sunset Center** (✉*San Carlos St. at 9th Ave.* ☎*831/624–3996* ⊕*www.sunsetcenter.org*), in Carmel-by-the-Sea, is the area's top venue for the performing arts, with concerts, lectures, and headline acts.

In the heart of downtown Monterey, **Monterey Live** (✉*414 Alvarado St.* ☎*831/646–1415* ⊕*www.montereylive.org*) presents jazz, rock, and comedy acts, including some big names, nightly. In Carmel Valley Village, the Wild West–themed bar at the **Running Iron Restaurant and Saloon** (✉*24 W. Carmel Valley Rd.* ☎*831/659–4633*) is a laid-back spot for a draft beer.

SPORTS & THE OUTDOORS

Throughout most of the year, the Monterey Bay area is a haven for those who love tennis, golf, surfing, fishing, biking, hiking, scuba diving, and kayaking. In the rainy winter months, when the waves grow larger, adventurous surfers flock to the water. The **Monterey Bay National Marine Sanctuary** (☎*831/647–4201* ⊕ *montereybay.noaa.gov*), home to mammals, seabirds, fishes, invertebrates, and plants, encompasses a 276-mi shoreline and 5,322 square mi of ocean. Ringed by beaches and campgrounds, it's a great place for kayaking, whale-watching, scuba diving, and other water sports.

GOLF

Though the greens fees are often astronomical and tee times are hard to come by, golfers are willing to do whatever it takes to play on one of the justifiably famous courses near Pebble Beach. **Pebble Beach Golf Links** (⊠*17-Mile Dr. near Lodge at Pebble Beach* ☎*831/624–3811, 831/624–6611, or 800/654–9300*) attracts golfers from around the world, despite greens fees of $450. Nonguests can reserve a tee time only one day in advance on a space-available basis (up to a year for groups); resort guests can reserve up to 18 months in advance.

Poppy Hills (⊠*3200 Lopez Rd., at 17-Mile Dr.* ☎*831/625–2035*), a splendid 18-hole course designed in 1986 by Robert Trent Jones Jr., has greens fees of $130–$160. Individuals may reserve up to one month in advance, groups up to a year.

Spyglass Hill (⊠*Stevenson Dr. and Spyglass Hill Rd.* ☎*831/624–3811, 831/624–6611, or 800/654–9300*) is among the most challenging Pebble Beach courses. With the first five holes bordering on the Pacific and the other 18 reaching deep into the Del Monte Forest, the views offer some consolation. Greens fees are $300. Reservations may be made up to one month in advance (18 months for guests).

AROUND PASO ROBLES

115 mi southeast of Monterey via Highway 68 and U.S. 101.

Numbers in the margin correspond to numbers on the Paso Robles map.

The Cuesta Ridge of the Santa Lucia Range divides San Luis Obispo County into northern and southern parts. The county's largest city, San Luis Obispo, sits in a pretty valley south of the Cuesta Grade, just a few miles inland from the ocean. A handful of AVAs, such as Edna Valley, shoulder in among the coastal ranges and valleys that stretch north and south of town. But the star of the show is without a doubt Paso Robles, California's fastest-growing AVA.

With more than 100 wineries, 25,000 acres of vineyard, and a surge of interest from the wine establishment, the Paso Robles AVA is booming. Between 2002 and 2007, the number of wineries almost doubled. Paso Robles first gained fame for its grapes, however, at the end of Prohibition. In the 1920s Polish concert pianist Ignace Paderewski, a major celebrity of his era, bought 2,000 acres here, planted petite sirah and zinfandel, and began winning prizes for his wine. Zinfandel remains one of Paso's strengths, joined by cabernet sauvignon in the 1960s and 1970s. Cab now accounts for a third of the AVA's grape tonnage, with merlot about one-fifth of the crop. In short, this is prime red-wine country.

But this is also an area of tremendous variety: close to 40 kinds of grapes are grown here. Rhône grapes have been so successful that the AVA has become a stronghold of the Rhône Rangers, an industry organization dedicated to promoting American-grown Rhône varieties such as grenache, marsanne, mourvèdre, roussanne, syrah, and viognier. Italian grapes such as dolcetto and barbera, and Spaniards such as tempranillo and touriga, show great promise here, too. A long growing season makes for high production, 65 to 75 percent of which is sold to wineries in Napa, Sonoma, and other areas.

Paso Robles experiences the widest temperature swings of any California AVA, especially on the east side, which is farther from the ocean. There, flatter topography allows for large-scale commercial viticulture, while the west side wineries are smaller and less accessible, tucked into hollows and perched on hillsides in the coastal mountains. North to south, Paso Robles has still more variations: the AVA tends to be warmest in the north, near San Miguel; coolest in its middle, where ocean air rushes through the Templeton Gap (a cleft in the Coast Range); and warm in the south. It's little wonder, then, that in tasting rooms and watering holes, the potential division of Paso Robles into two or more AVAs is a hotly debated topic. One proposal under consideration would result in the creation of a whopping 11 subappellations.

The most convenient home base for exploring all this viticultural territory is the town of **Paso Robles,** which has its own attractions for visitors. The Old West town, complete with opera house, emerged in the 19th century—grand Victorian homes went up, followed in the 20th century by Craftsman bungalows. A 2003 earthquake demolished or weakened several beloved downtown buildings, but historically faithful reconstruction has proceeded rapidly.

A mix of down-home and up-market restaurants, bars, antiques stores, tasting rooms, and little shops fills the streets around oak-shaded City Park, where special events of all kinds—custom car shows, an olive festival, Friday night summer concerts—take place on many weekends. Still, Paso (as the locals call it) more or less remains cowboy country: each year in late July and early August, the city throws the two-week California Mid-State Fair, complete with livestock auctions, carnival rides, and corn dogs.

⑳ The lakeside **River Oaks Hot Springs & Spa**, on 240 hilly acres near the intersection of U.S. 101 and Highway 46E, is a great place to relax before and after wine tasting or festival going. Soak in a private indoor or outdoor hot tub fed by natural mineral springs, or indulge in a massage or facial. ⊠*800 Clubhouse Dr.* ☎*805/238–4600* ⊕*www. pasohotsprings.com* ⊠*Hot tubs $13 to $20 per person per hr* ⊙*Sun.–Thurs. 9–9; Fri. and Sat. 9–10.*

★ ㉑ While touring the idyllic west side of Paso Robles, take a break from wine by stopping at **Willow Creek Olive Ranch** (⊠*8530 Vineyard Dr.* ☎*805/227–0186* ⊕*www.pasolivo. com*). Find out how they make their Tuscan-style Pasolivo olive oils on a high-tech Italian press, and taste the widely acclaimed results.

Although Paso is clearly where much of the wine-making magic happens in the region, don't discount **San Luis Obispo**, a friendly college town about a 30-minute drive to the south. About halfway between San Francisco and Los Angeles, San Luis Obispo—nicknamed SLO—spreads out below gentle hills and rocky extinct volcanoes. Its main appeal lies in its architecturally diverse and lively downtown, especially several blocks of Higuera Street. The pedestrian-friendly district bustles with shoppers, restaurant-goers, and students from California Polytechnic State University, known as Cal Poly. SLO is less a vacation destination than a pleasant stopover along Highway 1; still, it's a nice place to stay while touring the wine country south of town, stretching along Highway 227 toward Lake Lopez in the inland mountains.

㉗ In downtown SLO, the San Luis Obispo Vintners Association operates **Taste**, a wine bar and information center that's open daily. You can taste from among 70 Edna Valley and Arroyo Grande Valley wines; staff provides information about the wine, the appellations, and the wineries. To start tasting, head to the cash register and buy a user's card; the cost of each tasting gets deducted from this. ✉*1003 Osos St.* ☎*805/269-8278* ⊕*www.taste-slo.com* ⊙*Mon.–Sat. 11–9, Sun. 11–5.*

㉓ While touring the Edna Valley wine country, around SLO, be sure to stop at **Old Edna** (✉*Hwy. 227 at Price Canyon Rd.* ☎*805/544-8062* ⊕*www.oldedna.com*), a peaceful, 2-acre site that once was the town of Edna. Browse for gifts and antiques, pick up sandwiches at the deli, and stroll along Old Edna Lane.

VINEYARDS AROUND PASO ROBLES

The section of the Paso Robles AVA that's **east of the Salinas River** covers open, gently rolling land on loamy, nutrient-deficient soil. Since the east side receives less of the ocean's moderating influence, it's generally hotter by day and colder by night than the west side. All of this adds up to great conditions for chardonnay and cabernet sauvignon. **West of the Salinas River,** the Paso Robles AVA gets hilly and wooded as it rises up the Santa Lucia slopes. Those mountains help bring down the rain, which is soaked up by soils rich in calcium carbonate. Zinfandel and Rhône varieties such as syrah do particularly well over here. West of U.S. 101, Highway 46 rides the city line between Paso Robles to the north and **Templeton** to the south. It's a minor technicality as far as wine is concerned, because the wineries on either side of the road have a lot in common. Twenty-two miles south of Templeton, **San Luis Obispo** benefits from relatively moderate temperatures. It shares this good-for-grapes climate with two valleys that extend south of town, Edna and Arroyo Grande, each now its own AVA.

EAST SIDE PASO ROBLES

★ ㉔ Local heavyweight **Meridian Vineyards**, established in 1988 by winemaker Chuck Ortman, is now part of the global company Beringer Blass Wine Estates. Meridian has extensive vineyard holdings on the Central Coast: chardonnay comes from Santa Barbara County and the Edna Valley, while the east Paso Robles vineyards surrounding the hilltop winery provide cabernet sauvignon, syrah, and zinfan-

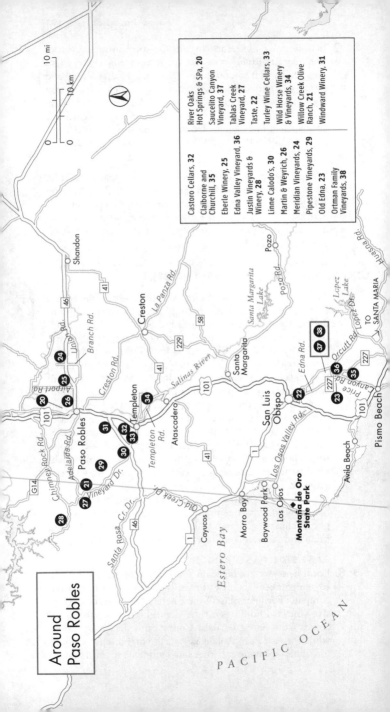

Around Paso Robles

Castoro Cellars, **32**	River Oaks Hot Springs & Spa, **20**
Claiborne and Churchill, **35**	Saucelito Canyon Vineyard, **37**
Eberle Winery, **25**	Tablas Creek Vineyard, **27**
Edna Valley Vineyard, **36**	Taste, **22**
Justin Vineyards & Winery, **28**	Turley Wine Cellars, **33**
Linne Calodo's, **30**	Wild Horse Winery & Vineyards, **34**
Martin & Weyrich, **26**	Willow Creek Olive Ranch, **21**
Meridian Vineyards, **24**	Windward Winery, **31**
Pipestone Vineyards, **29**	
Old Edna, **23**	
Ortman Family Vineyards, **38**	

PACIFIC OCEAN

0   10 mi
0   10 km

del. Limited-release and reserve wines, sold only from the winery, can be sampled here. The picnic area, shaded by giant oaks, has sweeping vineyard views. ✉ *7000 Hwy. 46 East, Paso Robles* ☎ *805/237–6000* ⊕ *www.meridianvineyards.com* 🖭 *Tasting $5* ⊙ *Daily 10–5.*

㉕ A bronze sculpture of a boar guards the entrance to **Eberle Winery,** an east-side institution. Gary Eberle, a founding father of the Paso Robles wine renaissance, has been making wine in the area since the 1970s. His barbera, cabernet sauvignon, chardonnay, viognier, zinfandel, sangiovese, syrah, and Côtes-du-Rôbles blend are among the best the region has to offer, and his late-harvest muscat canelli is exquisite. You can bring your own food and picnic on a deck that has panoramic views of estate vineyards, and take one of the daily cave tours. ✉ *Hwy. 46 East and Airport Rd., Paso Robles* ☎ *805/238–9607* ⊕ *www.eberlewinery.com* 🖭 *Tasting and tour free* ⊙ *Oct.–Mar., daily 10–5; Apr.–Sept., daily 10–6; cave tours every half-hour.*

㉖ It's hard to miss the elaborate, faux-Tuscan **Martin & Weyrich** tasting room overlooking Highway 46 East near U.S. 101. This winery, established in 1981, specializes in classic Italian grape varieties such as nebbiolo, the spicy red Piedmontese grape. Martin & Weyrich also grows sangiovese, muscat canelli, pinot grigio, and malvasia bianca but its pride and joy is the "Super Tuscan"–style Cabernet Etrusco, a blend of 85-percent cabernet sauvignon and 15-percent sangiovese. ✉ *2610 Buena Vista Dr., Paso Robles* ☎ *805/238–2520* ⊕ *www.martinweyrich.com* 🖭 *Tasting $4–$10* ⊙ *Apr.–Sept., daily 10–6; Oct.–Mar., Sun.–Thurs. 10–5, Fri.–Sat. 10–6.*

6

WEST SIDE PASO ROBLES

㉗ ★ **Fodor'sChoice** Tucked in the far-west hills of Paso Robles, **Tablas Creek Vineyard** makes some of the area's finest wine. The vineyards are planted with Rhône varieties using vines imported from their partner, Château de Beaucastel, a highly regarded Châteauneuf-du-Pape *domaine* in the Rhône Valley. Organically grown and hand-harvested syrah, grenache, roussanne, viognier, and other grapes— including the little-known counoise and picpoul blanc— are blended or bottled as single varietals. With complex, multilayered, and well-balanced aromas and flavors, the red and white versions of their signature Esprit de Beaucastel blend have classic Rhône style with a Central Coast twist. Tastings include a generous 10 or so pours, and the twice-daily tours include a chance to graft your own grape-vine. ✉9339 Adelaida Rd., Paso Robles ☎805/237–1231 ⊕www.tablascreek.com ⌁Tasting $5, tour free ⊙Daily 10–5; tour daily at 10:30 and 2 by appointment.

★ ㉘ Small but swank **Justin Vineyards & Winery** has become one of Paso's better-known places, primarily thanks to the cult following for Isosceles, a hearty blend of cabernet sauvignon, cabernet franc, and merlot. Two other red blends, Justification and Obtuse, are rich and fruity. Deborah's Room restaurant serves lunch on weekends and prix-fixe dinners nightly (reservations required). There's even an on-site B&B, Just Inn. Justin lies at the western end of Paso Robles, 15 mi from town via lovely, winding roads. ✉11680 Chimney Rock Rd., Paso Robles ☎805/238–6932 ⊕www.justinwine.com ⌁Tasting $5, tour $10 ⊙Daily 10–5; tour daily at 10:30 and 2:30 by appointment.

㉙ Sustainable viticulture gets an extra twist at **Pipestone Vineyards**—Jeff Pipes and Florence Wong planted and maintain their vineyard according to feng shui principles, too. At this small family operation, tasting-room conversations with the owners, who do almost everything themselves, provide an up-close, unvarnished look at wine making. Syrah, grenache noir, and viognier grown just outside go into full-bodied wines. If the crisp, deep-strawberry rosé of grenache hasn't sold out, grab a bottle to drink with your picnic. ✉2040 Niderer Rd., Paso Robles ☎805/227–6385 ⊕www.pipestonevineyards.com ⌁Tasting $5, tour free ⊙Thurs.–Mon. 11–5; tour by appointment.

㉚ The massive, mouth-filling wines at **Linne Calodo** take Paso Robles to Napa's outer limits, emulating the extreme styles that have brought some Napa boutique outfits a cult following. Ultra-ripe fruit explodes in red Rhône and zinfandel blends. Names like Problem Child and Slacker underscore the audacious approach. The one white in the portfolio, a perplexing Rhône blend called The Contrarian, seems like an afterthought. ✉3845 Oakdale Rd., Paso Robles ☎805/227–0797 ⊕www.linnecalodo.com ⌁Tasting $7 ⊙Daily 11–5.

㉛ The Paso Robles AVA gained a reputation for superlative pinot noir starting in the early 1970s. Continuing that tradition are Marc Goldberg and Maggie D'Ambrosia, owners of **Windward Winery,** who in 1989 purchased 15 acres just north of Templeton in Paso Robles. Here cool winds sweeping through the Templeton Gap, creating just the right conditions for cultivating the particularly persnickety pinot noir grape. They introduced their first vintage—pinot is the only wine they make—in 1993, and have had great success in recent years. The shady lath house next to the tasting room, partially built into the hillside, is the one of the coolest spots in the area for a picnic, and has views of their vineyards to boot. ✉ *1380 Live Oak Rd., Paso Robles* ☎ *805/239-2565* ⊕ *www.windwardvineyard.com* 🍷 *Tasting $5–$10* ⊙ *Daily 10:30–5.*

TEMPLETON

㉜ A popular wine-touring spot off Highway 46 West, the large tasting room and grounds of **Castoro Cellars** frequently hold concerts and other special events. Husband-and-wife team Niels and Bimmer Udsen founded this Mediterranean-style winery in 1983 with the goal of making, in their words, "dam fine wine" (*il castoro* is Italian for beaver). Their heady zinfandel, creamy chardonnay, and intensely aromatic merlot are very easy to drink; Castoro also makes quite a few other varietals from estate vineyards and locally bought grapes. ✉ *1315 North Bethel Rd., Templeton* ☎ *805/238-0725* ⊕ *www.castorocellars.com* 🍷 *Tasting free* ⊙ *Daily 10–5:30.*

★ **㉝** **Turley Wine Cellars** is a happy instance of a great second act. Their old-vine zinfandel vineyard, planted in the 1920s, turned out decent wine for many years, but renowned winemaker and consultant, Larry Turley (cofounder of Frog's Leap in the Napa Valley), with the help of his sister Helen, bought and refurbished the winery and truly tapped its potential. In 1995 Helen left for her own winery, and Turley Wine Cellars has continued to thrill its cult following with zinfandels that are deep in color, intense in flavor, and full bodied. The wines are hard to find, so a visit to the source is a rare opportunity. ✉ *2900 Vineyard Dr., Templeton* ☎ *805/434-1030* ⊕ *www.turleywinecellars.com* 🍷 *Tasting $10* ⊙ *Daily 9–5.*

★ **㉞** **Wild Horse Winery & Vineyards,** founded in 1983, is off the beaten path but well worth searching out for the extraordinary quality of its wines. It's a local favorite for pinot noir, chardonnay, cabernet sauvignon, and especially a yummy, sophisticated merlot. Always experimenting with less familiar varieties, such as malvasia bianca, tempranillo, or verdelho, Wild Horse bottles consistently enjoyable wine. Some of the unusual varietals and reserves are available nowhere else but here. The tasting room, which overlooks vineyards planted on gently rolling hills, is east of U.S. 101 via Vineyard Drive and Templeton Road. The last part of the road is unpaved gravel. ⊠*1437 Wild Horse Winery Ct., Templeton* ☎*805/434–2541* ⊕*www.wildhorsewinery.com* 🍷*Tasting free* ☉*Daily 11–5.*

AROUND SAN LUIS OBISPO

★ ㉟ In an unusual winery built of straw bales (finished in stucco), **Claiborne and Churchill** founders Claiborne Thompson and Fredericka Churchill make Alsatian-style wines that are a departure for the Edna Valley. Their signature dry gewürztraminer and dry riesling are deeply aromatic whites—the gewürztraminer with a typical touch of spice and the riesling with a big dollop of acid-balanced fruit. Small batches of pinot gris and dry muscat round out the Alsatian list. ⊠*2649 Carpenter Canyon Rd., San Luis Obispo* ☎*805/544–4066* ⊕*www.claibornechurchill.com* 🍷*Tasting $5* ☉*Daily 11–5.*

㊱ Persuaded that the Edna Valley's singular soil is well suited for producing chardonnay and perhaps pinot noir, Dick Graff of Monterey County's Chalone Vineyard established **Edna Valley Vineyard.** The vineyards produce fine chardonnay, but success has been less easily achieved with the pinot noir. From the soaring picture windows of the tasting room, or from the picnic patio outside, you can look across the valley. ⊠*2585 Biddle Ranch Rd., San Luis Obispo* ☎*805/544–5855* ⊕*www.ednavalleyvineyard.com* 🍷*Tasting $5–$10, tour free* ☉*Daily 10–5; tour weekdays at noon, weekends at 11, noon, 1, 2, and 3.*

㊲ **Saucelito Canyon Vineyard** grows some of its grapes on 3 acres of vines planted in the early 1880s; their newer vines are more than a quarter-century old. It's possible this renowned old-vine zinfandel survived Prohibition because the vineyards are tucked so far up in the Arroyo Grande Valley. (The tasting room, in the heart of the Edna Valley, is easy to reach.) Bill and Nancy Greenough acquired the land in 1974 and now make zins that combine the best of the old (subtle and complex) with the best of the not-so-old (fruity and bold) in wines that are full of berry flavors and have a silky, almost thick mouth feel. ⊠*3080 Biddle Ranch Rd., San Luis Obispo* ☎*805/543–2111* ⊕*www.saucelito-canyon.com* 🍷*Tasting $5 (includes Ortman Family Vineyards)* ☉*Spring–fall, daily 10–5; winter, Thurs.–Mon. 10–5 or by appointment.*

⑲ After a major success with Meridian Vineyards in Paso Robles, Chuck Ortman is turning his hand to a small, family venture with **Ortman Family Vineyards.** With his son, Matt, he handcrafts vineyard-designated and blended chardonnay and pinot noir, among other varietals, sourced from the Edna Valley, Paso Robles, and Santa Rita Hills. Their chardonnay nicely balances pear and pineapple flavors with toasty vanilla, and the pinot noir has intense plum and berry notes touched with spice. The tasting room shares a building with Saucelito Canyon's. ⊠*3080 Biddle Ranch Rd., San Luis Obispo* ☎*805/543-2111* ⊕*www. ortmanvineyards.com* ⊅*Tasting $5 (includes Saucelito Canyon Vineyard)* ⊗*Apr.–Dec., daily 10–5; Jan.–Mar., Thurs.–Mon. 10–5.*

WHERE TO STAY & EAT

PASO ROBLES

$$$–$$$$ ✕**Bistro Laurent.** Owner-chef Laurent Grangien has cre-
★ ated a handsome, welcoming French bistro in an 1890s brick building across from City Park. He focuses on traditional dishes such as osso buco, cassoulet, rack of lamb, goat-cheese tart, and onion soup, but always offers a few updated dishes as daily specials. Wines come from around the world. Le Petit Marcel, a tiny nook next door to the main restaurant, is open just for lunch Monday through Saturday. ⊠*1202 Pine St.* ☎*805/226-8191* ⊟*MC, V* ⊗*Closed Sun. and Mon. No lunch.*

$$$–$$$$ ✕**McPhee's Grill.** The grain silos across the street and the floral oilcloths on the tables belie the sophisticated cuisine at this casual chophouse. In an 1860s building in the tiny cow town of Templeton (just south of Paso Robles), the restaurant serves creative, contemporary versions of traditional Western fare—such as oak-grilled filet mignon and cedar-planked salmon. House label wines, made especially for McPhee's, are quite good. ⊠*416 Main St., Templeton* ☎*805/434-3204* ⊟*AE, D, MC, V.*

★ **Fodor's**Choice ✕**Artisan.** A bit of the big city in small-town
$$–$$$$ Paso Robles, this urbane newcomer (it opened in late 2006) is all the rage. Mid-century-inspired light fixtures and large black-and-white photographs on the walls set a mood that's stylish but not stuffy, and a fitting venue for the seasonal menu of robust contemporary American food. The tuna tartare veers from the ordinary, served on a bed of fried green tomatoes, while other dishes tend toward the

CLOSE UP

A Great Drive Around Paso Robles

The west side of Paso Robles is a terrific area for a slower-paced, intimate winery experience. Starting from town, pack a picnic lunch and drive north, turning west onto 24th Street. As it leaves town, 24th Street turns into Nacimiento Lake Road; in about 1½ mi you reach a Y. Bear left onto Adelaida Road and drive 9 hilly, winding miles out to Tablas Creek for their morning tour. Next up: some knockout red wines at Justin Winery. Get back on Adelaida, drive 2 mi, and turn left at the T onto Chimney Rock Road. About 1½ mi along you'll find Justin, where you can tour, taste, and picnic.

To try some particularly hard-to-find wines at the source, head back to Adelaida, take a right onto Vineyard Drive, and cross Highway 46 into Templeton to reach Turley Wine Cellars. (Although Turley's just 10 mi away, the drive takes about 40 minutes since the roads are so twisty.) From Turley, continue on Vineyard, which turns into Templeton Road when it crosses U.S. 101, and after nearly 5 mi keep an eye out on your left for Wild Horse Winery Court, the half-mile driveway for Wild Horse. After sipping their merlot, backtrack on Templeton Road and, before you hit the 101, turn right onto Main Street. The street passes through Templeton's Old West–style town center, then picks up the freeway north of town.

If you've still got some juice, drive about 1½ mi north on U.S. 101 and take the first exit, onto Highway 46 West. Another 1½ mi brings you to Arbor Road (there's a big, white B&B on the corner); turn right and in about half a mile take a left onto Live Oak Road. On this road, you can stop by Windward. Finish your day by backtracking to Highway 101 and returning to downtown Paso Robles for dinner.

---

traditional (flat-iron steak with fries, barbecued baby back ribs). The wine list, heavy on Paso-area wines, includes several flights as well as wines by the bottle and glass. ⊠*1401 Park St.* ☎*805/237–8084* ⊟*AE, D, MC, V.*

$$–$$$ ✕ **Villa Creek.** With a firm nod to the Southwest, chef Tom Fundero conjures distinctly modern magic with locally and sustainably grown ingredients. The seasonal menu has included butternut-squash enchiladas and braised rabbit with mole *negro* (black mole sauce), but you might also find duck breast with sweet-potato latkes. Central Coast wines dominate the list, with a smattering of Spanish and

French selections. All brick and bare wood, the dining room can get loud when winemakers start passing their bottles from table to table, but it's always festive. ■TIP→For lighter appetites or wallets, the bar serves smaller plates—not to mention a killer marqarita ⊠1114 Pine St. ☎805/238–3000 ⊟AE, D, MC, V ⊗No lunch Sun. and Mon.

¢–$$ ✕**Panolivo.** Scrumptious French bistro fare draws a loyal crowd of locals to this cheery downtown café with butter-yellow walls. For breakfast, try the house-made muesli or quiches, or build your own omelet. For lunch, choose among traditional French dishes like a quiche with a side of French onion soup or a roast chicken. For lighter fare, you can fill up on a sandwich, like the *croque monsieur* (grilled ham-and-cheese sandwich), or a salad. A display case full of glistening fruit tarts and chocolate-filled pastries tempts many to indulge in dessert. ⊠1344 Park St. ☎805/239–3366 ⊟AE, D, MC, V ⊗No dinner

$$$$ ★ FodorsChoice ⊡**Hotel Cheval.** An equestrian theme pops up everywhere in this stylish, sophisticated, European-style inn just a half-block from the main square and a short walk from some of Paso's best restaurants. Each of the 16 spacious rooms is named after a famous racehorse (whose history and picture hang on the wall) and include custom furnishings, king beds with exquisite linens and ethereal down comforters, and original works of art. Most rooms have fireplaces and window seats; some have vaulted cedar ceilings. ■TIP→On Friday and Saturday nights, ask for a free ride in the carriage drawn by a Belgian draft horse; the driver and footman will deliver you to and from your dinner destination in Paso. Pros: Attentive but unobtrusive service, attractive interior courtyard area with wood-burning fireplaces, large flat-panel TVs. Cons: No pool or hot tub, some rooms don't have bathtubs. ⊠1021 Pine St., 93446 ☎805/226–9995 ⊕www.hotelcheval.com ⊷16 rooms ⅋In-room: DVD, Ethernet, Wi-Fi. In-hotel: bar, no elevator, no-smoking rooms ⊟AE, D, MC, V ❏CP.

$$$$ ⊡**Summerwood Inn.** Verdant gardens and vineyards envelop Summerwood Winery's elegant, friendly B&B in tranquillity. Four-poster and sleigh beds, lace and floral fabrics, thick robes, and nightly turn-down service bring comfort to the individually designed rooms. All have gas fireplaces and balconies or decks with vineyard views; some have vaulted ceilings or jetted tubs. Order what you like for breakfast and sip Summerwood wines in the evening.

6

Pros: Convenient wine-touring base, super-friendly staff, delicious breakfast. **Cons:** Across from winery on a main highway, can be noisy during the day. ✉ *2130 Arbor Rd., 1 mi west of U.S. 101 at Hwy. 46W and Arbor Rd., 93446* ☎ *805/227-1111* ⊕ *www.summerwoodwine.com* ⇆ *9 rooms* ♻ *In-room: Wi-Fi. In-hotel: no-smoking rooms, no elevator* ☰ *AE, DC, MC, V* ⦿ *BP.*

$–$$ ⚏ **Paso Robles Inn.** On the site of a luxurious old spa hotel by the same name, the inn is built around a lush, shady garden with a hot mineral pool. The water is still the reason to stay here, and each deluxe room (new and old) has a spring-fed hot tub in its bathroom or on its balcony. Have breakfast in the circular 1940s coffee shop, and on weekends dance with the ranchers in the Cattlemen's Lounge. **Pros:** Private spring-fed hot tubs, historic property, across from park and town square. **Cons:** Fronts a busy street, rooms vary in size and quality. ✉ *1103 Spring St., 93446* ☎ *805/238-2660 or 800/676-1713* ⊕ *www.pasoroblesinn. com* ⇆ *92 rooms, 6 suites* ♻ *In-room: refrigerator, Ethernet. In-hotel: restaurant, bar, pool, public Wi-Fi, no-smoking rooms* ☰ *AE, D, DC, MC, V.*

★ ¢–$ ⚏ **Adelaide Inn.** Family-owned and -managed, this clean, friendly oasis with meticulous landscaping offers spacious rooms and everything you need: coffeemaker, iron, hair dryer, and peace and quiet. In the lobby, complimentary muffins and newspapers are set out in the morning; cookies come out in the afternoon. The motel has been around for decades, but nearly half the rooms were built in 2005. It's a tremendous value, so it books out weeks or even months in advance. A short walk from the fairgrounds, the Adelaide is tucked behind a conglomeration of gas stations and fast-food outlets just west of the U.S. 101 and Highway 46E interchange. **Pros:** Great bargain, attractive pool area, ideal for families. **Cons:** Near busy intersection and freeway. ✉ *1215 Ysabel Ave., 93446* ☎ *805/238-2770 or 800/549-7276* ⊕ *www.adelaideinn.com* ⇆ *109 rooms* ♻ *In-room: refrigerator, Ethernet, Wi-Fi. In-hotel: pool, laundry facilities, laundry service, no-smoking rooms, no elevator* ☰ *AE, D, DC, MC, V* ⦿ *CP.*

SAN LUIS OBISPO

$$$–$$$$ ✕ **The Park Restaurant.** Chef-owner Meghan Loring presents
★ food that she describes as "refined rustic" in one of the county's more sophisticated restaurants. The always-evolving menu relies on seasonal ingredients sourced from local

producers. You might find sweet pea–asparagus soup with mint cream, or organic rib eye with panko-crusted shiitakes. The well-crafted wine and beer list includes local and international selections. Service is skillful in the spare, white-tablecloth dining room and on the tree-rimmed patio. ⊠*1819 Osos St.* ☎*805/545–0000* ▤*AE, MC, V* ✆*Closed Mon. No lunch.*

$–$$ ✕**Novo Restaurant and Bakery.** In the colorful dining room or on the large creek-side deck, this animated downtown eatery will take you on a culinary world tour. The salads, small plates, and entrées gesture to all sorts of cuisines, from Moroccan (a quail salad with chile-powered *harissa* vinaigrette) to Thai (green or red curries). The wine and beer list also covers the globe and includes local favorites. ■TIP➜**A late-night menu is served until 1 AM Thursday through Saturday, a rarity in this area.** ⊠*726 Higuera St.* ☎*805/543–3986* ▤*MC, V.*

¢–$$ ✕**Mo's Smokehouse BBQ.** Barbecue joints abound on the Central Coast, but this one excels. A variety of southern-style sauces seasons tender hickory-smoked ribs and shredded meat sandwiches; sides such as baked beans, coleslaw, homemade potato chips, and garlic bread extend the pleasure. ⊠*1005 Monterey St.* ☎*805/544–6193* ▤*AE, MC, V.*

$$–$$$$ ▥**Apple Farm.** Decorated to the hilt with floral bedspreads and watercolors by local artists, this Victorian country-style hotel is one of the most popular places to stay in town. Each room has a gas fireplace and fresh flowers; some have canopy beds and cozy window seats. There's a working gristmill in the courtyard; within the inn are a restaurant serving American food (the hearty breakfasts are best), a food and wine shop, a bakery, and a gift shop. **Pros:** Flowers everywhere, convenient to U.S. 101, creek-side setting. **Cons:** Hordes of tourists stop here during the day, may be too floral for some tastes. ⊠*2015 Monterey St., 93401* ☎*800/374–3705* ⊕*www.applefarm.com* ⚲*66 rooms, 3 suites* ♿*In-hotel: restaurant, pool, spa, public Wi-Fi, no-smoking rooms* ▤*AE, D, MC, V.*

$$–$$$ ▥**Garden Street Inn.** From this fully restored 1887 Italianate–Queen Anne, the only lodging in downtown SLO, you can walk to many restaurants and attractions. The individually decorated rooms are filled with antiques; some have stained-glass windows, fireplaces, and decks. Each evening, wine and hors d'oeuvres are served in the intimate dining room; there's also a lavish homemade breakfast. **Pros:** Easy

6

walk to downtown, nice wine-and-cheese reception. **Cons:** City noise filters through some rooms, not a great place for families. ⊠*1212 Garden St., 93401* ☎*805/545–9802 or 800/488–2045* ⊕*www.gardenstreetinn.com* ⌂⌐*9 rooms, 4 suites* ⌂*In-room: no TV (some), Wi-Fi. In-hotel: no-smoking rooms, no elevator* ⊟*AE, D, MC, V* ⧉|*BP.*

$–$$$ ⊡**Petit Soleil.** A cobblestone courtyard, country-French custom furnishings, and Gallic music piped through the halls evoke a Provençal mood at this cheery inn on upper Monterey Street's motel row. The owners are serious about the details: the individually themed rooms are sprinkled with lavender water and have CD players and L'Occitane bath products. Rates include wine and appetizers at cocktail hour and a full homemade breakfast in the sun-filled patio or dining room. **Pros:** French details throughout, scrumptious breakfast, cozy rooms. **Cons:** On busy avenue, cramped parking. ⊠*1473 Monterey St., 93401* ☎*805/549–0321 or 800/676–1588* ⊕*www.petitsoleilslo.com* ⌂⌐*15 rooms, 1 suite* ⌂*In-room: no a/c, Wi-Fi. In-hotel: no-smoking rooms, no elevator* ⊟*AE, MC, V* ⧉|*BP.*

¢–$ ⊡**Peach Tree Inn.** Extra touches such as rose gardens, a porch with rockers, and flower-filled vases turn this modest, family-run motel into a relaxing creek-side haven. Four rooms have king and sofa beds with private patios overlooking the creek. You can use the refrigerator and microwave in the sunny breakfast room, and snacks are available all day and evening. **Pros:** Bargain rates, cozy rooms, decent breakfast. **Cons:** Near busy intersection and freeway, basic amenities. ⊠*2001 Monterey St., 93401* ☎*805/543–3170 or 800/227–6396* ⊕*www.peachtreeinn.com* ⌂⌐*37 rooms* ⌂*In-room: VCR, Ethernet, Wi-Fi. In-hotel: no-smoking rooms, no elevator* ⊟*AE, D, DC, MC, V* ⧉|*CP.*

NIGHTLIFE

Sleepy Paso Robles doesn't have a thriving nightlife scene, and most wine bars and restaurants wind down well before midnight. You can sip wine until 10 PM, 11 PM on Fridays and Saturdays, at the contemporary-but-classic feeling **Pony Club** (⊠*1021 Pine St.* ☎*805/226–9995* ⊕*www.hotelcheval. com*) in the Hotel Cheval. Inside is a zinc bar shaped like a horseshoe, but on warm nights the tables on the patio are equally attractive for nibbling on pâté and drinking local wines.

SPORTS & THE OUTDOORS

For an aerial view of vineyards, ranches, and mountains, make an advance reservation with **Let's Go Ballooning!** Flights carrying up to four passengers launch at sunrise and last about an hour. ✉*Paso Robles Airport, 4912 Wing Way* ☎*805/458–1530* ⊕*www.slohalloon.com* 💰*$189 per person* ☺*Daily.*

SANTA BARBARA COUNTY

88 mi south of Paso Robles on U.S. 101; 128 mi north of Los Angeles on U.S. 101 and Highway 154.

Only about 100 mi north of Los Angeles, Santa Barbara has long been a weekend and summer retreat for Angelenos, so it was only a matter of time before the county's wines started showing up at high-end restaurants in Santa Monica and Beverly Hills. Then, in 2004, the the region got a huge shot in the arm courtesy of Hollywood, when the hit movie *Sideways,* set in the Santa Barbara wine country, brough tremendous attention to the region. Tourism and demand for local wines skyrocketed, and tasting rooms quickly filled up.

Though now an up-and-coming wine region, Santa Barbara County got off to a modest start. The Franciscan padres who colonized the region in the late 1700s planted grapes for sacramental wine. In 1884, a French immigrant planted 150 acres of French grapes on Santa Cruz Island. But none of those early vineyards survived. All was quiet until 1962, when Pierre Lafond of Quebec opened the Santa Barbara Winery downtown. It was an unpretentious place, making fruit wines as well as grape wines in its first years—the sort you'd take to the beach with a picnic.

In northern Santa Barbara County, another hint of things to come appeared in 1964, when local farmer Uriel Nielson planted vines in the Santa Maria Valley. A few vineyards soon popped up in the Santa Ynez Valley. The local wine industry, however, didn't take off until the 1980s and 1990s, when so many wineries were established in the Santa Ynez Valley that some locals feared the region might turn into another Napa Valley.

North of the city of Santa Barbara, a series of valleys and ridges runs roughly west–east from the coast into the mountains. These include the Santa Maria Valley, the Santa

Ynez Valley, and the Sta. Rita Hills, the county's three designated AVAs. The region's topography channels ocean air and fog through the valleys, creating one of California's cooler wine-growing climates. Inland, days are warmer and sunnier and nights chillier than they are closer to the shore, where the sea moderates temperatures. A variety of soil types adds to the diversity that allows Santa Barbara County to grow quite a range of grape varieties.

■TIP→ **To really experience the relaxed way of life of the Santa Barbara Wine Country, you should plan to stay in Santa Ynez, Solvang, or Los Olivos, three small towns in the center of a cluster of wineries.**

Founded in 1882, the tiny town of **Santa Ynez** still has many of its original frontier buildings. You can walk through the three-block downtown area in just a few minutes, shop for antiques, and hang around the old-time saloon. At some of the eponymous valley's best restaurants, you just might bump into one of the many celebrities who own nearby ranches. The pretty village of **Los Olivos,** in the Santa Ynez Valley, was once on the Spanish-built El Camino Real (Royal Highway) and later a stop on major stagecoach and rail routes. It's so sleepy today, though, that TV's *Return to Mayberry* was filmed here. A row of tasting rooms, art galleries, antiques stores, and country markets lines Grand Avenue.

㊴ At **Los Olivos Tasting Room & Wine Shop** (✉ *2905 Grand Ave.* ☏ *805/688–7406* ✇ *www.losolivoswines.com*), you can sample locally produced wines and pick up winery maps.

㊵ Historic Heather Cottage, originally an early-1900s doctor's office, houses the **Daniel Gehrs Tasting Room** (✉ *2939 Grand Ave.* ☏ *800/275–8138* ✇ *www.dgwines.com*). Here you can sample Gehrs's various varietals, produced in limited small-lot quantities.

You'll know you've reached the town of **Solvang** when the architecture suddenly changes to half-timber buildings and windmills. This incongruous faux-Danish village was settled in 1911 by a group of Danish educators (the flatlands and rolling green hills reminded them of home), and even today, more than two-thirds of the residents are of Danish descent.

Although Solvang has attracted tourists in the mood for some kitsch or a smorgasbord for decades, in recent years it has become more sophisticated, with galleries, upscale restaurants, and wine-tasting rooms. A good way to get your bearings is to park your car in one of the many free public lots and stroll around town. Stop in at one of the visitor centers—at 2nd Street and Copenhagen Drive, or Mission Drive (Highway 246) at 5th Street—for maps and helpful advice on what to see and do. Don't forget to stock up on Danish pastries from the town's excellent bakeries before you leave.

41 Often called the "Hidden Gem of the Missions," Solvang's **Mission Santa Inés** has an impressive collection of paintings, statuary, vestments, and Chumash and Spanish artifacts in a serene blufftop setting. You can take a self-guided tour through the museum, sanctuary, and tranquil gardens. ✉ *1760 Mission Dr.* 📞 *805/688–4815* ⊕ *www.missionsantaines.org* 💲 *$3* ⊘ *Daily 9–5.*

VINEYARDS IN SANTA BARBARA COUNTY

Fogs frequently drift into the **Santa Maria Valley** from the ocean, making the western part of the AVA too cold for grapes. Cool-climate grapes like chardonnay and pinot noir thrive on the warmer slopes east of U.S. 101 and north of the Santa Maria River.

Heading south toward Los Olivos and Santa Ynez, Foxen Canyon Road crosses the line from the Santa Maria Valley AVA into the **Santa Ynez Valley AVA.** This is the wine country made famous by the hit 2004 movie *Sideways.* As small as it is, the Santa Ynez Valley has several distinct climates. In the warmer vineyards east of U.S. 101, cabernet sauvignon, merlot, sauvignon blanc, and Rhône and Italian varietals do well.

West of U.S. 101 in Buellton and east of Lompoc, the cool vineyards of the **Sta. Rita Hills AVA** (an appellation within the Santa Ynez Valley AVA) are influenced by marine air from the nearby Pacific. Pinot noir, the "heartbreak grape," thrives here, while grapes of the cabernet group ripen in warm pockets of the western hills.

SANTA MARIA VALLEY

11 👤 **Fodor's**Choice With its old ranch house and barn shaded by ancient trees, **Rancho Sisquoc Winery** is the region's most romantic winery. The vineyards here are warmer than those of the western Santa Maria Valley but cooler than those of the Santa Ynez Valley to the south. The tasting room, in a rustic wood building, might be pouring caber-

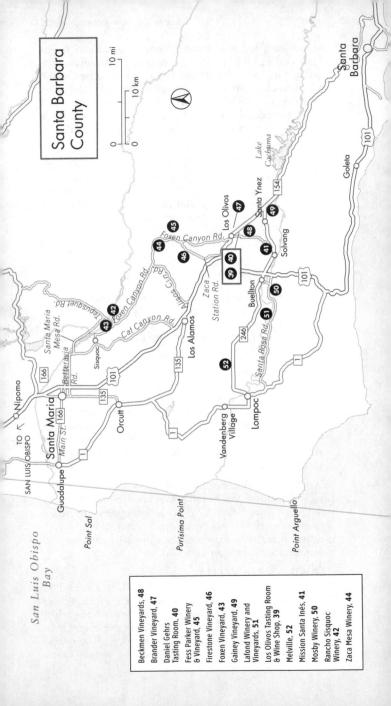

Santa Barbara County

Beckmen Vineyards, **48**
Brander Vineyard, **47**
Daniel Gehrs Tasting Room, **40**
Fess Parker Winery & Vineyard, **45**
Firestone Vineyard, **46**
Foxen Vineyard, **43**
Gainey Vineyard, **49**
Lafond Winery and Vineyards, **51**
Los Olivos Tasting Room & Wine Shop, **39**
Melville, **52**
Mission Santa Inés, **41**
Mosby Winery, **50**
Rancho Sisquoc Winery, **42**
Zaca Mesa Winery, **44**

net sauvignon, merlot, malbec, sauvignon blanc, chardonnay, pinot noir, and riesling, as well as California's only sylvaner, a crisp, fruity white. Turn onto the 2½-mi-long driveway at the 19th-century San Ramon Chapel. ⊠6600 *Foxen Canyon Rd., Santa Maria* ☎805/934–4332 ⊕*www. ranchosisquoc.com* 📶*Tasting $8* ⊙*Mon.–Thurs. 10–4, Fri.–Sun 10–5.*

★ ⓸ A former blacksmith shop houses the **Foxen Vineyard** tasting room on 2,000-acre Rancho Tinaquaic, which has been in Richard Doré's family since 1837. Only a few acres are planted to grapes, but Foxen has made a big name for itself by using grapes grown elsewhere in the county. Inky, peppery syrah; intense, citrusy chardonnay; and complex, cherries-and-cinnamon pinot noir are exceptional. Foxen buys some of its pinot noir grapes from Sea Smoke Vineyard, whose pinot starred in the movie *Sideways,* but the extremely limited releases are not poured in the tasting room. ⊠7200 *Foxen Canyon Rd., Santa Maria* ☎805/937–4251 ⊕*www.foxenvineyard.com* 📶*Tasting $10* ⊙*Daily 11–4.*

AROUND LOS OLIVOS

⓸ With its tall working metal windmill out front and its barnlike buildings tucked into a small side canyon, **Zaca Mesa Winery** might be mistaken for a cattle ranch. Chances are you won't even see the vineyards here, which rest high above the winery on a 1,500-foot-high mesa, where warm, sunny days and cool, breezy afternoons create ideal conditions for Rhône varietals. Among Zaca Mesa's signature wines are its syrah, viognier, and the much-lauded Z Gris, traditional rosé made from grenache, mourvèdre, cinsaut, and viognier. The winery is a quiet place—the word *zaca* is the local Chumash Indian word for "peaceful"—where you can picnic under the oaks or play a game of lawn chess. ⊠6905 *Foxen Canyon Rd., Los Olivos* ☎805/688–9339 ⊕*www.zacamesa.com* 📶*Tasting $7–$12* ⊙*Memorial Day–Labor Day, daily 10–5; Labor Day–Memorial Day, daily 10–4; tours by appointment.*

⓸ The Wine Country meets the Alamo at **Fess Parker Winery & Vineyard,** owned by the actor who starred as Davy Crockett in three 1950s movies and as Daniel Boone on a 1960s TV series. It is the region's hokiest tasting room (who else sells coonskin caps and other mountain man paraphernalia?), but the wine is popular, well-priced, and has earned some good ratings from the critics. Ample fruit and oak are hallmarks in the easy-drinking chardonnay, viognier, and syrah. ⊠*6200 Foxen Canyon Rd., Los Olivos* ☎*805/688–1545* ⊕*www.fessparker.com* ☜*Tasting $8* ☉*Daily 10–5.*

⓭ Firestone Vineyard, Santa Barbara County's first estate winery (founded in 1975), is big and proud of it, spreading across a hilltop like an oenological fortress. It produces a wide variety of wines from its Santa Ynez Valley estate vineyards, most notably chardonnay, merlot, syrah, and late-harvest riesling. The winery offers fun, informative tours three times daily, and the picnic area has spectacular vineyard views. ⊠*5000 Zaca Station Rd., Los Olivos* ☎*805/688–3940* ⊕*www.firestonewine.com* ☜*Tasting $10, tour free* ☉*Daily 10–5; tour daily at 11:15, 1:15, and 3:15.*

⓮ One of the Santa Ynez Valley's oldest wineries—it opened in 1981—**Brander Vineyard** is renowned for its zesty, fresh sauvignon blanc. They offer several different styles, as well as some inventive blends that incorporate the grape. Most fun of all may be the Château Neuf de Pink, which blends sauvignon blanc with rosés of syrah, grenache, merlot, and sangiovese. Fittingly, the tasting room is in a cheery little pink château. ⊠*2401 Refugio Rd., Los Olivos* ☎*805/688–2455* ⊕*www.brander.com* ☜*Tasting $10* ☉*Apr.–Oct., daily 10–5, Nov.–Mar., daily 11–4.*

⓯ Family-owned **Beckmen Vineyards** farms its 365-acre Purisima Mountain Vineyard biodynamically. Rhône-style wines made from the estate grapes include syrah, marsanne, grenache, and grenache blanc. The rosé of grenache has a bright spiciness, and the white blend, Le Bec Blanc, is peachy and round. Three picnic gazebos overlook the winery's duck pond. ⊠*2670 Ontiveros Rd., Los Olivos* ☎*805/688–8664* ⊕*www.beckmenvineyards.com* ☜*Tasting $8* ☉*Daily 11–5.*

AROUND SANTA YNEZ

⓰ The chardonnay, pinot noir, merlot, cabernet sauvignon, cabernet franc, and sauvignon blanc at **Gainey Vineyard** are consistently excellent, and in some years, there's also an exquisite late-harvest riesling. The lush yet lively sauvignon blanc stands out; the warm, concentrated pinot noir fills the nose and mouth. People come to the Spanish mission–style winery in summer to enjoy concerts under the stars. At nearly any time of year, the well-groomed picnic area provides the perfect setting to have lunch or a snack and sip fine wine. ⊠*3950 East Hwy. 246, Santa Ynez* ☎*805/688–*

0558 ⊕*www.gaineyvineyard.com* ⊿*Tasting $10, tour free* ⊙*Daily 10–5; tour daily at 11, 1, 2, and 3.*

AROUND BUELLTON

50 At **Mosby Winery** you can explore the world of Cal-Ital wine—California's take on Italian wines such as pinot grigio, dolcetto, and cortese. The perfumy, floral traminer is a classic northern Italian white; the smoky, deep-ruby sangiovese evokes Tuscany. The vivid red carriage house of an 1853 adobe serves as the tasting room. The winery is just west of U.S. 101; look for the driveway in the sharp bend Santa Rosa Road takes west from the freeway. ⊠*9496 Santa Rosa Rd., Buellton* ☎*805/688–2415* ⊕*www.mosbywines.com* ⊿*Tasting $7* ⊙ *Weekdays 10–4, weekends 10–5.*

51 Pierre Lafond opened his large, modern **Lafond Winery and Vineyards** and its equally large, modern tasting room in early 2001, just before the establishment of the Sta. Rita Hills AVA. Pinot noir, chardonnay, and syrah make up the portfolio, with the complex, concentrated pinot the main attention-getter. ■TIP→**Bottles with Lafond's** SRH **label are an especially good value.** ⊠*6855 Santa Rosa Rd., Buellton* ☎*805/688–7921* ⊕*www.lafondwinery.com* ⊿*Tasting $5* ⊙*Daily 10–5.*

52 Earthy, herbaceous, firmly tannic, and darkly berry-flavored, the pinot noir at **Melville** exemplifies the varietal's potential in the Santa Rita Hills. The grape grows all around the winery, a faux-Mediterranean villa with red tile roofs. Inside, the airy space and tile floors of the rotunda-like tasting room offer respite from the baking sun. Melville also makes chardonnay and some viognier and syrah. ⊠*5185 East Hwy. 246, Lompoc* ☎*805/735–7030* ⊕*www.melvillewinery.com* ⊿*Tasting $5–$10* ⊙*Daily 11–4.*

WHERE TO STAY & EAT

SOLVANG

$$–$$$$ ✕**The Hitching Post II.** You'll find everything from grilled artichokes to ostrich at this casual eatery just outside of Solvang, but most people come for what is said to be the best Santa Maria–style barbecue in the state. The oak used in the barbecue imparts a wonderful smoky taste. Be sure to try a glass of owner-chef-winemaker Frank Ostini's signature Highliner Pinot Noir, a star in the 2004 film *Side-*

Q&A with a Winemaker

In 1997, after leaving their jobs and home in Minnesota, Jeff Pipes and Florence Wong found the perfect plot of land in the hills west of Paso Robles. At Pipestone Vineyards, they grow Rhône-style grapes.

Why wine? "I got my interest in wine from my grandfather, a World War I veteran who fell in love with wine in France. Back in the States he wanted to have something to drink, so he learned how to make wine, and he took it to a pretty high level. I learned how he did it, and he would give me little sips of wine. I also had a real interest in agriculture and farming, because one of my uncles had a farm where I spent a lot of time."

What's it like to have your own winery? "Very few people in this business are feeding their kids off of it like we are. So we really are farmers. If something goes wrong with the weather we feel it directly. It's a complete unknown from day to day, if you're going to get a rainstorm that ruins the crop, or a frost, or a dry year when the fruit won't grow . . . you've lost all your income for that whole year in the vine-

yard. It's pretty harsh."

Why is Paso Robles a good place to make wine? "In France, they often pick the grapes early in September not because they're ripe, but because there's a big rainstorm or snowstorm coming. In California we can usually get the grapes as ripe as we want—fully mature, great flavor, high alcohol, smooth tannins—so we're very, very lucky. Especially for early-drinking wines, they're pretty good every year. We can grow very high-quality grapes here because the nice warm days get the fruit really ripe and the cold nights protect the natural acidity."

Are you glad you followed your dream? "The tension and risk are hard, but this allows our family to be on a farm and our kids to have a nice environment. It is a great joy to create a farm product that people genuinely love. We get e-mails and letters saying, 'we had this for my birthday or Christmas dinner,' and that's really satisfying. Being a lawyer, I didn't feel that. This is much better."

Interview by Constance Jones

---

ways. ⊠*406 E. Hwy. 246* ☎*805/688–0676* ⊟*AE, MC, V* ⊘*No lunch.*

$–$$ ✕**Bit O' Denmark.** Perhaps the most authentic Danish eatery in Solvang, this restaurant (the oldest food establishment in town), occupies an old-beam building that was a church until 1929. Two specialties of the house are the *Frikadeller* (meatballs with pickled red cabbage, potatoes, and thick brown gravy) and the *Medisterpølse* (Danish beef-and-pork sausage with cabbage). ⊠*473 Alisal Rd.* ☎*805/688–5426* 🗐*AE, D, MC, V.*

★ $$$$ 🗓**Alisal Guest Ranch and Resort.** Since 1946 this 10,000-acre ranch has been popular with celebrities and plain folk alike. There are lots of activities to choose from here: horseback riding, golf, fishing, sailing in the 100-acre spring-fed lake—although you can also just lounge by the pool. The ranch-style rooms and suites have garden views, covered porches, high-beam ceilings, and wood-burning fireplaces, with touches of Spanish tile and fine Western art. A jacket is required at the nightly dinners (which are included in your room rate). **Pros:** Zillions of activities, ultra-private. **Cons:** Isolated, cut off from high-tech world, some units need updating. ⊠*1054 Alisal Rd., 93463* ☎*805/688–6411 or 800/425–4725* ⊕*www.alisal.com* ⇔*36 rooms, 37 suites* △*In-room: no a/c, refrigerator, no TV. In-hotel: restaurant, room service, bar, golf courses, tennis courts, pool, gym, bicycles, children's programs (ages 6–12), public Internet, no elevator* 🗐*AE, DC, MC, V* 🍴*MAP.*

$$$–$$$$ 🗓**Petersen Village Inn.** Like most of Solvang's buildings, this upscale country inn goes for a Euro look. The canopy beds are plush, the bathrooms small but sparkling. Weekend rates include a complete French dinner for two in the guests-only Café Provence and a buffet breakfast rich with pastries. **Pros:** In the heart of Solvang, easy parking, comfy beds. **Cons:** Right on Highway 246, atmosphere too traditional for some. ⊠*1576 Mission Dr., 93463* ☎*805/688–3121 or 800/321–8985* ⊕*www.peterseninn.com* ⇔*39 rooms, 1 suite* △*In-room: Wi-Fi. In-hotel: restaurant, no-smoking rooms* 🗐*AE, MC, V* 🍴*BP.*

$–$$ 🗓**Solvang Gardens Lodge.** Lush gardens with fountains and waterfalls, friendly staff, and cheery English country–theme rooms make for a peaceful retreat just a few blocks—but worlds away—from Solvang's main tourist area. Rooms range from basic to elegant; each has some antique furnishings and many have marble showers and baths. **Pros:** Homey, family-friendly, colorful gardens. **Cons:** Some units are tiny, some still need upgrades. ⊠*293 Alisal Rd., 93463* ☎*805/688–4404 or 888/688–4404* ⊕*www.solvanggardens.com* ⇔*16 rooms, 8 suites* △*In-room: no phone,*

6

refrigerator (some), Wi-Fi. In-hotel: public Internet, no-smoking rooms ⊟*AE, D, MC, V* ⊺⊙⧵*CP.*

¢–$ ⊡**Best Western King Fredric Inn.** Rooms at this comfortable and central motel are fairly spacious. If you want to stay right in Solvang and don't want to spend a fortune, this is a good bet. Wi-Fi is available in the lobby. **Pros:** Great value, near main square, good choice for families. **Cons:** On main highway, miniature lobby, next to major city parking lot. ⊠*1617 Copenhagen Dr., 93463* ☎*805/688–5515 or 800/549–9955* ⊕*www.bwkingfrederik.com* ⤢*44 rooms, 1 suite* ⧉*In-room: refrigerator (some), Ethernet. In-hotel: pool, no-smoking rooms, no elevator* ⊟*AE, D, DC, MC, V* ⊺⊙⧵*CP.*

LOS OLIVOS

★ **Fodor's**Choice ✕**Brothers Restaurant at Mattei's Tavern.** In the
$$$–$$$$ stagecoach days, Mattei's Tavern provided wayfarers with hearty meals and warm beds. Chef-owners and brothers Matt and Jeff Nichols renovated the 1886 building, and while retaining the original character, transformed it into one of the best restaurants in the valley. The casual, unpretentious dining rooms with their red-velvet wallpaper and historic photos reflect the rich history of the tavern. The menu changes every few weeks but often includes house favorites such as spicy fried calamari, prime rib, and salmon, and the locally famous jalapeño corn bread. There's also a full bar and an array of vintages from the custom-built cedar wine cellar. ⊠*2350 Railway Ave., 93441* ☎*805/688–4820* ⧉*Reservations essential* ⊟*AE, MC, V* ⊘*No lunch.*

$–$$ ✕**Los Olivos Cafe.** Site of the scene in *Sideways* where the four main characters dine together and share a few bottles of wine, this down-to-earth restaurant is also a wine store–cum–social hub for locals. The café focuses on wine-friendly fish, pasta, and meat dishes, plus salads, pizzas, and burgers. Don't miss the homemade tapenade. Other house favorites include an artisan cheese plate, baked Brie with honey-roasted hazelnuts, and braised pot roast with whipped potatoes. ⊠*2879 Grand Ave.* ☎*805/688–7265* ⊟*AE, D, MC, V.*

$$$–$$$$ ✕⊡ **The Ballard Inn.** Set among orchards and vineyards in the tiny town of Ballard, 2 mi south of Los Olivos, this inn makes an elegant Wine Country escape. Rooms are furnished with antiques and original art. Seven rooms have

wood-burning fireplaces; the inn provides room phones and TVs on request. The inn's tasting room serves boutique wines Friday through Sunday. At the Ballard Inn Restaurant ($$$), which serves dinner Wednesday through Sunday, owner-chef Budi Kazali creates sumptuous French-Asian dishes in one of the area's most romantic dining rooms. **Pros:** Exceptional food, attentive staff, secluded. **Cons:** Some baths could use updating, several miles from towns. ✉2436 Baseline Ave., Ballard 93463 ☎805/688–7770 or 800/638–2466 ⊕www.ballardinn.com ⇆15 rooms ♿In-room: no phone. In-hotel: restaurant, bicycles, no elevator ⊟AE, MC, V ⊠BP.

$$$$ ☒**Fess Parker's Wine Country Inn and Spa.** This luxury inn includes an elegant, tree-shaded French country–style main building and an equally attractive annex across the street with a pool, hot tub, and day spa. The spacious accommodations have fireplaces, seating areas, and wet bars. **Pros:** Convenient wine-touring base, walking distance to restaurants and galleries, well-appointed rooms. **Cons:** Pricey, service is inconsistent. ✉2860 Grand Ave., 93441 ☎805/688–7788 or 800/446–2455 ⊕www.fessparker.com ⇆20 rooms, 1 suite ♿In-hotel: restaurant, Wi-Fi, pool, gym, spa, no-smoking rooms, some pets allowed ⊟AE, DC, MC, V ⊠BP.

SANTA YNEZ

$$–$$$ ✕**Trattoria Grappolo.** Authentic Italian fare, an open
★ kitchen, and festive, family-style seating make this trattoria equally popular with celebrities from Hollywood and ranchers from the Santa Ynez Valley. Italian favorites on the extensive menu range from thin-crust pizza to homemade ravioli, risottos, and seafood linguine to grilled lamb chops in red-wine sauce. The noise level tends to rise in the evening, so this isn't the best spot for a romantic getaway. ✉3687-C Sagunto St. ☎805/688–6899 ⊟AE, MC, V ⊗No lunch Mon.

$$$$ ☒**Santa Ynez Inn.** Antiques and artifacts from the town's early days fill this posh Victorian-style inn built in 2002. The details ooze luxury: Frette linens, custom-made bathrobes, and DVD/CD entertainment systems. Most of the 14 rooms have gas fireplaces, double steam showers, and jetted tubs. Rates include a phenomenal evening wine and hors d'oeuvres hour and a full breakfast. **Pros:** Near several restaurants, unusual antiques, spacious rooms. **Cons:**

High price tag for the location. ✉3627 *Sagunto St.*, *93460*
☎*805/688–5588 or 800/643–5774* ⊕*www.santaynezinn.*
com ⇋*14 rooms* ☙*In-room: Ethernet, Wi-Fi. In-hotel:*
gym, concierge, laundry service, no-smoking rooms ⊟*AE,*
D, MC, V ⏿*BP.*

Winespeak

7

WINE-TASTING GLOSSARY

Wine snobs might toss around terms like "Brett effect" and "*barrique*," but don't let that turn you off. Like any activity, wine making and wine tasting have specialized vocabularies. Some words are show-off jargon, and some are specific and helpful. Here's a handful of core terms to know—and things you can say with a straight face. (*See also Chapter 1.*)

Acidity. The tartness of a wine, derived from the fruit acids of the grape. Acids stabilize a wine (i.e., preserve its character), balance its sweetness, and bring out its flavors. Too little or too much acid spoils a wine's taste. Tartaric acid is the major acid in wine, but malic, lactic, and citric acids also occur.

Aging. The process by which some wines improve over time, becoming smoother and more complex and developing a pleasing bouquet. Wine is most commonly aged in oak vats or barrels, slowly interacting with the air through the pores in the wood. Sometimes wine is cellared for bottle aging. Today, many wines are not made for aging and are drunk relatively young, as little as a few months after bottling. Age can diminish a wine's fruitiness and dull its color: whites turn brownish, rosés orange, reds brown.

Alcohol. Ethyl alcohol is a colorless, volatile, pungent spirit that not only gives wine its stimulating effect and some of its flavor but also acts as a preservative, stabilizing the wine and allowing it to age. A wine's alcohol content must be stated on the label, expressed as a percentage of volume, except when a wine is designated table wine (⇨*below*).

American Viticultural Area (AVA). More commonly termed an "appellation." A region with unique soil, climate, and other grape-growing conditions can be designated an AVA by the Alcohol and Tobacco Tax and Trade Bureau. When a label lists an appellation—Napa Valley or Chalone, for example—at least 75 percent of the grapes used to make the wine must come from that region.

Appellation. See *American Viticultural Area.*

Aroma. The scent of young wine derived directly from the fresh fruit. It diminishes with fermentation and is replaced by a more complex bouquet as the wine ages. The term may also be used to describe special fruity odors in a wine, like black cherry, green olive, ripe raspberry, or apple.

Astringent. The puckery sensation produced in the mouth by the tannins in wine.

AVA. See *American Viticultural Area.*

Balance. A quality of wine in which all desirable elements (fruit, acid, tannin) are present in the proper proportion. Well-balanced wine has pleasing nose, flavor, and mouth feel.

Barrel fermenting. The fermenting of wine in small oak barrels instead of large tanks or vats. This method allows the winemaker to keep grape lots separate before blending the wine. The cost of oak barrels makes barrel fermenting expensive.

Barrique. An oak barrel used for aging wines.

Blanc de blancs. Sparkling or still white wine made solely from white grapes.

Blanc de noirs. White wine made with red grapes by removing the skins during crush. Some sparkling whites, for example, are made with red pinot noir grapes.

Blending. The mixing of several wines to create one of greater complexity or appeal, as when a heavy wine is blended with a lighter one to make a more approachable medium-bodied wine.

Body. The wine's heft or density as experienced by the palate. A full body makes the mouth literally feel full. It is considered an advantage in the case of some reds, a disadvantage in many lighter whites. *See also Mouth feel.*

Bordeaux blend. A red wine blended from varietals native to France's Bordeaux region—cabernet sauvignon, cabernet franc, malbec, merlot, and petit verdot.

Botrytis. *See Noble rot.*

Bouquet. The odors a mature wine gives off when opened. They should be pleasantly complex and should give an indication of the wine's grape variety, origin, age, and quality.

Brettanomyces. Also called Brett. A strain of yeast that gives wine a funky, off flavor. Winemakers try to keep Brett away from their wines, but some drinkers enjoy a mild "Brett effect."

Brix. A method of telling whether grapes are ready for picking by measuring their sugars. Multiplying a grape's Brix number by .55 approximates the potential alcohol content of the wine.

Brut. French term for the driest category of sparkling wine *(see also Demi-sec, Sec).*

Burgundy. The English name for Bourgogne, a French region, and for the wine from that region. Inferior California red wines are sometimes mislabeled "burgundy."

Case. A carton of 12 750-ml bottles of wine. A magnum case contains six 1.5-liter magnum bottles.

Cask. A synonym for barrel. More generally, any size or shape wine container made from wood staves.

Cellaring. Storage of wine in bottles for aging. The bottles are laid on their sides to keep the corks moist and prevent air leakage that would spoil the wine.

Chablis. A prime French wine-growing region making austere white wines. Inferior California wines and cheap pinks are sometimes mislabeled "Chablis."

Champagne. The northernmost wine district of France, where sparkling wine originated and where the world's only genuine Champagne is made. The term is often used inaccurately in America to denote sparkling wines in general.

Cloudiness. The presence of particles that do not settle out of a wine, causing it to look and taste dusty or even muddy. If settling and decanting (see Decant) do not correct cloudiness, the wine has been badly made or is spoiled.

Complexity. The qualities of good wine that provide a multilayered sensory experience to the drinker. Balanced flavors, harmonious aromas or bouquet, and a long finish are components of complexity.

Corked. Describes wine that is flawed by the musty, wet-cardboard flavor imparted by cork mold.

Crush. American synonym for harvest season, or vintage. Also refers to the year's crop of grapes crushed for wine.

Cuvée. Generally a sparkling wine, but sometimes a still wine, that is a blend of different wines and sometimes different vintages. Most sparkling wines are cuvées.

Decant. To pour a wine from its bottle into another container either to expose it to air or to eliminate sediment. Decanting for sediment pours out the clear wine and leaves the residue behind in the original bottle.

Demi-sec. French term that translates as "half-dry." It is applied to sweet wines that contain 3.5- to 5-percent sugar.

Dessert wines. Sweet wines that are big in flavor and aroma. Some are quite low in alcohol; others, such as port-style wines, are fortified with brandy or neutral spirits and may be 17- to 21-percent alcohol.

Dry. Having very little sweetness or residual sugar. Most red, white, and rosé wines are dry, although some whites, such as rieslings, are made to be off-dry, on the sweet side.

Estate bottled. A wine entirely made by one winery at a single facility. The grapes must come from the winery's own vineyards within the same appellation (which must be printed on the label).

Fermentation. The biochemical process by which grape juice becomes wine. Enzymes generated by yeast cells convert grape sugars into alcohol and carbon dioxide. Fermentation stops when the sugar is depleted and the yeast starves, or when high alcohol levels kill the yeast.

Fermenter. Any vessel (such as a barrel, tank, or vat) in which wine is fermented.

Filtering, Filtration. A purification process in which wine is pumped through filters to rid it of suspended particles.

Fining. A method of clarifying wine by adding crushed eggshells, isinglass, or other natural substances to a barrel. As these solids settle to the bottom, they take various dissolved compounds with them. Most wine meant for everyday drinking is fined; counterintuitively, fine wines are fined less often.

Finish. Also aftertaste. The flavors that remain in the mouth after swallowing wine. A good wine has a long finish with complex flavor and aroma.

Flight. A few wines—usually three to five—specially selected for tasting together.

Fortification. A process by which brandy or natural spirits are added to a wine to stop fermentation and to increase its level of alcohol, as in the case of port-style dessert wines.

Fruity. Having aromatic nuances of fresh fruit, such as fig, raspberry, or apple. Fruitiness, a sign of quality in young wines, is replaced by bouquet in aged wines.

Fumé blanc. A nonspecific term for wine made with sauvignon blanc. Robert Mondavi coined the term originally to describe his dry, crisp, oak-aged sauvignon blanc.

Green. Said of a wine made from unripe grapes, with a pronounced leafy flavor and a raw edge.

Horizontal tasting. A tasting of several different wines of the same vintage.

Late harvest. Wine made from grapes harvested later in the fall than the main lot, and thus higher in sugar levels. Many dessert wines are late harvest.

Lees. The spent yeast, grape solids, and tartrates that drop to the bottom of the barrel or tank as wine ages. Wine, particularly white wine, gains complexity when it is left on the lees for a time.

Library wine. An older vintage that the winery has put aside to sell at a later date.

Malolactic fermentation. A secondary fermentation in the tank or barrel that changes harsh malic acid into softer lactic acid and carbon dioxide. Wine is sometimes inoculated with lactic bacteria, or placed in wood containers that harbor the bacteria, to enhance this process. Often referred to as ML or malo. Too much malo can make a wine too heavy.

Meritage. A trademarked name for American (mostly California) Bordeaux blends that meet certain wine-making and marketing requirements and are made by member wineries of the Meritage Association.

Méthode champenoise. The traditional, time-consuming method of making sparkling wines that are fermented in individual bottles.

Mouth feel. Literally, the way wine feels in the mouth. Mouth feel, such as smoothness or astringency, is detected by the sense of touch rather than of smell or taste.

Must. The slushy mix of crushed grapes—juice, pulp, skin, seeds, and bits of stem—produced by the crusher–de-stemmer at the beginning of the wine-making process.

Neutral oak. The wood of older barrels or vats that no longer pass much flavor or tannin to the wine stored within.

New oak. The wood of a fresh barrel or vat that has not previously been used to ferment or age wine. It can impart desirable flavors and enhance a wine's complexity, but if used to excess it can overpower a wine's true character.

Noble rot. *Botrytis cinerea,* a beneficial fungus that can perforate a ripe grape's skin. This dehydrates the grape and concentrates the remaining juice while preserving its acids. Botrytis grapes make sweet but not cloying wine.

Nonvintage. A blend of wines from different years. Nonvintage wines have no date on their label. Wine may be blended from different vintages to showcase strong points that complement each other, or in order to make a commercial product taste the same from one year to the next.

Nose. The overall fragrance (aroma or bouquet) given off by a wine; the better part of its flavor.

Oaky. A vanilla-woody flavor that develops when wine is aged in oak barrels. Leave a wine too long in a new oak barrel and that oaky taste overpowers the other flavors.

Organic viticulture. The technique of growing grapes without the use of chemical fertilizers, pesticides, or fungicides. *See also the "Organic Wines" box in chapter 3.*

Oxidation. Undesirable flavor and color changes caused to juice or wine by too much contact with the air, either during processing or because of a leaky barrel or cork. Most often occurs with white wine, especially if it is over the hill.

pH. Technical term for a measure of a wine's acidity. It is a reverse measure: the lower the pH level, the higher the acidity. Most wines range in pH from 2.9 to 4.2, with the most desirable level at 3.2 and 3.5. Higher pHs makes wine flabby, lower pHs make it tart.

Phylloxera. A disease caused by the root louse *Phylloxera vastatrix,* which attacks and ultimately destroys grapevine roots. The pest is native to the United States; it traveled to France with American grape vines in the 19th century and devastated nonresistant vineyards there.

Pomace. Spent grape skins and solids left over after the juice has been pressed, commonly returned to the fields as fertilizer.

Racking. Moving wine from one tank or barrel to another to leave unwanted deposits behind; the wine may or may not be fined or filtered in the process.

Reserve wine. Fuzzy term applied by vintners to indicate a wine is better in some way (through aging, source of the grapes, etc.) than others from their winery.

Residual sugar. The natural sugar left in a wine after fermentation, which converts sugar into alcohol. If the fermentation was interrupted or if the must has very high sugar levels, some residual sugar will remain, making a sweeter wine.

Rhône blend. A wine made from grapes hailing from France's Rhône Valley, such as marsanne, roussanne, syrah, cinsaut, mourvèdre, or viognier.

Rosé. Pink wine, usually made from red wine grapes. The juice is left on the skins only long enough to give it a tinge of color. Rosés can be made from any variety of red wine grape. After decades in the shadows, they're getting serious attention again.

Rounded. Said of a well-balanced wine in which fruity flavor is nicely offset by acidity—a good wine, though not necessarily a distinctive or great one.

Sec. French for "dry." The term is generally applied within the sparkling or sweet categories, indicating the wine has 1.7 to 3.5 percent residual sugar. Sec is drier than demi-sec but not as dry as brut.

Sediment. Dissolved or suspended solids that drop out of most red wines as they age in the bottle, thus clarifying their appearance, flavors, and aromas. Sediment is not a defect in an old wine or in a new wine that has been bottled unfiltered.

Sparkling wines. Wines in which carbon dioxide is dissolved, making them bubbly. Examples are French Champagne, Italian Prosecco, and Spanish *cava*.

Sugar. Source of grapes' natural sweetness. When yeast feeds on sugar, it produces alcohol and carbon dioxide. The higher the sugar content of the grape, the higher the potential alcohol level or sweetness of the wine.

Sulfites. Compounds of sulfur dioxide that are almost always added before fermentation during wine-making to prevent oxidation and to kill bacteria and wild yeasts that can cause off flavors. Sulfites are sometimes blamed as the culprit in headaches caused by red wine, but the connection has not been proven.

Sustainable viticulture. A viticultural method that aims to bring the vineyard into harmony with the environment. Organic and other techniques are used to minimize agricultural impact to and to promote biodiversity.

Table wine. Any wine that has at least 7 percent but not more than 14 percent alcohol by volume. The term is unrelated to quality or price—both super-premium and jug wines can be labeled as table wine.

Tannins. You can tell when they're there, but their origins are still a mystery. These natural grape compounds produce a sensation of drying or astringency in the mouth and throat. Tannins settle out as wine ages; they're a big player in many red wines.

Tartaric acid, Tartrates. The principal acid of wine. Crystalline tartrates form on the insides of vats or barrels and sometimes appear in the bottle or on the cork. They look like tiny shards of glass but they are not harmful.

Terroir. French for "soil." Typically used to describe the soil and climate conditions that influence the quality and characteristics of grapes and wine.

Varietal. A wine that takes its name from the grape variety from which it is predominantly made. California wines that qualify are almost always labeled with the variety of the source grape. According to U.S. law, at least 75 percent of a wine must come from a particular grape to be labeled with its variety name.

Vat. A large container of stainless steel, wood, or concrete, often open at the top, in which wine is fermented or blended. The term

is sometimes used interchangeably with "tank."

Vertical tasting. A tasting of several wines of different vintages, generally starting with the youngest and proceeding to the oldest.

Vinification. Wine making, the process by which grapes are made into wine.

Vintage. The grape harvest of a given year, and the year in which the grapes are harvested. A vintage date on a bottle indicates the year in which the grapes were harvested rather than the year in which the wine was bottled.

Viticulture. The cultivation of grapes.

Woody. Describes excessively musty wood aromas and flavors picked up by wine that has been stored in a wood barrel or cask for too long. Unlike "oaky," the term "woody" is always a negative.

Yeast. A minute, single-celled fungus that germinates and multiplies rapidly as it feeds on sugar with the help of enzymes, creating alcohol and releasing carbon dioxide in the process of fermentation.

WHO'S WHO IN THE GRAPE WORLD

Well over 50 different varieties of grapes are grown in the California Wine Country, from the Mr. Popularities like chardonnay and cabernet sauvignon to less familiar types such as tannat. While you don't need to be on a first-name basis with them all, you'll see the following varietals again and again as you visit the wineries.

WHITE

Chardonnay

Now as firmly associated with California wine making as it is with its Burgundy, its home. California chardonnays spent many years chasing big, buttery flavor, but the current trend is toward more restrained wines that let the grape's flavor shine through. Because of warmer, longer growing seasons, California chardonnay will always be bolder than Burgundian.

Chenin Blanc

Although a lot of it goes into mediocre mass-market wines, this Loire Valley native can produce a smooth, pleasingly acidic California wine. It gets short shrift with a lot of wine reviewers because of its relative simplicity and light body, but many drinkers appreciate the style.

Gewürztraminer

Cooler California climes such as the Russian River Valley are great for growing this German-Alsatian grape, which is turned into a boldly perfumed, fruity wine.

Marsanne

A white-wine grape of France's northern Rhône Valley that can produce a full-bodied, overly heavy wine unless handled with care. Becoming more popular in California in these Rhône-blend-crazy times.

Pinot Gris

The same grape as Italy's pinot grigio, this varietal yields a more deeply colored wine in California. It's not highly acidic, and has a medium to full body.

Roussanne

This grape from the Rhône Valley makes an especially fragrant California wine that can achieve a lovely balance of fruitiness and acidity.

Riesling

Also called Johannisberg Riesling or White Riesling, this cool-climate German grape has a sweet reputation in America. When made in a dry style, though, as it more and more often is, it can be crisply refreshing, with lush aromas.

Sauvignon Blanc

Hailing from Bordeaux and France's Loire Valley, this white grape does very well almost anywhere in California. Wines made from this grape display a wide range of personalities, from herbaceous to tropical-fruity.

Sémillon

A white Bordeaux grape that, blended with sauvignon blanc, has made some of the best sweet wines in the world. Like the riesling grape, it can benefit from the noble rot, which intensifies its flavors and aromas.

Viognier

Until the early 1990s this was rarely planted outside France's Rhône Valley, but today it's one of the hottest white wine varietals in California. Usually made in a dry style, the best viogniers have an intense fruity or floral bouquet.

RED

Barbera

Prevalent in California thanks to 19th-century Italian immigrants, barbera yields easy-drinking, low-tannin wine that's got big fruit and high acid.

Cabernet Franc

Most often used in blends, often to add complexity to cabernet sauvignon, this French grape can produce aromatic, soft, and subtle wine. The often earthy, or even stinky, aroma that can turn some drinkers off wins avid fans among others.

Cabernet Sauvignon

The king of California reds, this Bordeaux grape grows best in austere, well-drained soils. At its best, the California version is dark, bold, and tannic, with black currant notes. On its own, it can need a long aging period to become enjoyable, so it's often blended with cabernet franc, merlot, and other red varieties to soften the resulting wine and make it ready for earlier drinking.

Gamay

Also called gamay beaujolais, this vigorous French grape variety is widely planted in California. It produces pleasant reds and rosés that should be drunk young.

Grenache

This Spanish grape, which makes some of the southern Rhône Valley's most distinguished wine, ripens best in hot, dry conditions. Done right, grenache is dark and concentrated, improved with age. Although it has limited plantings in California, it has gotten more popular along with other Rhône-style California wines.

Merlot

This blue-black Bordeaux variety makes soft, full-bodied wine when grown in California. It is often fruity, and can be quite complex even when young. The easy quaffer was well on its way to conquering cabernet sauvignon as the most popular red until anti-merlot jokes (popularized in the hit movie *Sideways*) damaged its rep...for now.

Mourvèdre

This red-wine grape makes wine that is deeply colored, very dense, high in alcohol, and at first harsh, but it mellows with several years of aging. It is a native of France's Rhône Valley and is increasingly popular in California.

Nebbiolo

The great red-wine grape of Italy's Piedmont region is now widely planted in California. It produces full-bodied, sturdy wines that are fairly high in alcohol and age splendidly.

Petite Sirah

This may be a hybrid created in the mid-19th-century California vineyard—no one is sure—and is unrelated to the Rhône grape syrah. It produces a hearty wine that is often used in blends.

Pinot Noir

The darling of grape growers in cooler parts of Napa and Sonoma, such as the Carneros region and the Russian River Valley, pinot noir is also called the "heartbreak grape" since it's hard to cultivate. At its best it has an addictively subtle earthy quality.

Sangiovese

The main red grape of Italy's Chianti district and of much of central Italy. Depending on how it is grown and vinified, it can be made into vibrant, light- to medium-bodied wines, as well as into long-lived, very complex reds. Increasingly planted in California.

Syrah

Another big California red, this grape comes from the Rhône Valley. With good tannins it can become a full-bodied, almost smoky beauty, but without them it can be flabby and forgettable. Once very limited in California, syrah plantings increased rapidly after the mid-1990s, thanks in part to the soaring popularity of Rhône-style wines in general, and in part to the popularity of syrah from Australia, where it is called shiraz.

Zinfandel

Celebrated as California's own (though it has distant, hazy Old World origins), zinfandel is a rich and spicy wine. Its tannins can make it complex, well-suited for aging, but too often it is made in an overly jammy, almost syrupy, style. Typically grown to extreme ripeness, the sugary grape can produce high alcohol levels in wine.

BEST BOOKS & FILMS

BOOKS

California's Napa Valley: One Hundred Sixty Years of Wine Making (1999), by William F. Heintz. Beautifully illustrated volume chronicles the Napa Valley's rise to enological prominence.

Chalone: A Journey on the Wine Frontier (2000), by Gregory S. Walter and W. Philip Woodward. The story of one Central Coast winery unfolds, from the turn of the 20th century to its present partnership with Domaines de Barons Rothschild.

A Companion to California Wine: An Encyclopedia of Wine and Winemaking from the Mission Period to the Present (1998), by Charles Sullivan. Straightforward coverage of the California wine story up to 1997 includes entries on most wineries, grape growing, vinification, varietals, regions, vintages, and history.

The Emperor of Wine: The Rise of Robert M. Parker, Jr. and the Reign of American Taste (2005), by Elin McCoy. Examination of the American critic's enormous influence considers the sources and worldwide impact of his wine rating system's dominance.

The Far Side of Eden: The Ongoing Saga of Napa Valley (2002), by James Conaway. Conaway's second book on the Wine Country picks up where the first, *Napa* (⇨ *below*), left off.

Grapes & Wines (2003), by Oz Clarke and Margaret Rand. Highly readable reference describes grape varietals and the wines made from them.

Harvests of Joy: How the Good Life Became Great Business (1999), by Robert Mondavi and Paul Chutkow. Wine tycoon Robert Mondavi tells his story.

The House of Mondavi: The Rise and Fall of an American Wine Dynasty (2007), by Julia Flynn Siler. The author ruffled a lot of feathers in Napa when she published this tell-all book about the much-loved Mondavi family.

Jancis Robinson's Concise Wine Companion (2001), by Jancis Robinson. Handy paperback distillation of the second edition of Robinson's *The Oxford Companion to Wine* (see below).

Judgment of Paris: California vs. France and the Historic 1976 Paris Tasting That Revolutionized Wine (2005), by George M. Taber. Journalist who originally broke the story of the pivotal event analyzes its history and repercussions.

Matt Kramer's New California Wine: Making Sense of Napa Valley, Sonoma, Central Coast & Beyond (2004), by Matt Kramer. *Wine Spectator* columnist explains in entertaining detail the development of California wine and the wine industry.

Murder Uncorked (2005), *Murder by the Glass: A Wine-Lover's Mystery* (2006), and *Silenced by Syrah* (2007), by Michele Scott. Vineyard manager Nikki Sands is the protagonist of this light and humorous mystery series that unfolds in the Napa Valley.

Napa (1992), by James Conaway. The Wine Country lifestyle and local politics undergo intense scrutiny in this behind-the-scenes exposé.

Napa Valley: The Land, the Wine, the People (2001), by Charles O'Rear. A former *National Geographic* photographer portrays the valley in this lush book.

The Oxford Companion to Wine, 3rd edition (2006), by Jancis Robinson. Authoritative, comprehensive encyclopedia by one of the world's leading experts illuminates all things wine.

Sniff, Swirl & Slurp (2002), by Max Allen. Compact handbook provides guidelines on maximizing the wine-drinking experience.

Wine Spectator's California Wine (1999), by James Laube. *Wine Spectator* editor offers detailed background on California wineries and ratings of their wines.

Wine-Tasting, Wine & Food Matcher, Wine Vintages, and *Wine Finder* (2002), by Oz Clarke. The popular wine writer has created four pocket-size, foldout tip sheets to make buying and drinking wine easier.

Zinfandel: A History of a Grape and Its Wine (2003), by Charles Sullivan. The story of America's unique varietal is the story of California wine country.

FILMS

Bottle Shock (2008). At this writing, this feature about the 1976 Paris tasting is due to release in 2008. It was filmed primarily in Napa and Sonoma valleys.

Mondovino (2005). Documentary filmmaker Jonathan Nossiter probes the rocky relationship between the wine industries of California and Europe.

Sideways (2004). In this popular film, buddies Jack and Miles take a road trip to Santa Barbara County wine country, where they have hilarious misadventures in tasting, dating, and friendship.

California Wine Country Essentials

PLANNING TOOLS, EXPERT INSIGHT,
GREAT CONTACTS

There are planners and there are those
who, excuse the pun, fly by the seat
of their pants. We happily place our-
selves among the planners. Our writers and editors try to anticipate all the
issues you may face before and during
any journey, and then they do their
research. This section is the product of
their efforts. Use it to get excited about
your trip to California Wine Country, to
inform your travel planning, or to guide
you on the road should the seat of your
pants start to feel threadbare.

GETTING STARTED

We're really proud of our Web site: Fodors.com is a great place to begin any journey. Scan Travel Wire for suggested itineraries, travel deals, restaurant and hotel openings, and other up-to-the-minute info. Check our Booking to research prices and book plane tickets, hotel rooms, rental cars, and vacation packages. Head to Talk for on-the-ground pointers from travelers who frequent our message boards. You can also link to loads of other travel-related resources.

▌ RESOURCES

ONLINE TRAVEL TOOLS
All About Wine Country At **www. winecountry.com,** which covers all the many different wine regions of California, click on "Free Stuff/ Discounts" to print coupons for discounts at selected tasting rooms and to learn of special deals being offered by hotels, wineries, and other properties.

A calendar of wine-tasting events, winemaker dinners, and other events is kept at **www.localwineevents. com,** organized by town.

Though you must pay a subscription fee for some of its features, like access to its wine ratings, even without registering you can read lots of feature articles and other information about the wine world at **www. winespectator.com.**

Safety Transportation Security Administration (TSA; ⊕www.tsa. gov)

Time Zones Timeanddate.com (⊕www.timeanddate.com/world clock) can help you figure out the correct time anywhere.

Vintners Associations Carneros Wine Alliance (⊕www.carneros. com). **Monterey County Vintners & Growers Association** (⊕www. montereywines.org). **Napa Valley Vintners Association** (⊕www. napavintners.com). **Paso Robles Wine Country Alliance** (⊕www. pasowine.com). **San Luis Obispo Vintners & Growers Association** (⊕www.slowine.com). **Santa Barbara County Vintners Association** (⊕www.sbcountywines.com). **Santa Cruz Mountains Winegrowers Association** (⊕www.scmwa.com). **Sonoma County Vintners** (⊕www. sonomawine.com).

Weather Accuweather.com (⊕www.accuweather.com) is an independent weather-forecasting service with especially good coverage of hurricanes. **Weather.com** (⊕www.weather.com) is the Web site for the Weather Channel.

VISITOR INFORMATION
Regional Contacts Central Coast Tourism Council (☎831/902–7275 ⊕www.centralcoast-tourism.com). **Monterey County Convention and Visitors Bureau** (☎088/221–1010 ⊕www.montereyinfo.org). **Napa**

Valley Conference and Visitors Bureau (☎707/226–7459 ⊕www.napavalley.com). **Russian River Wine Road** (☎707/433–4335 or 800/723–6336 ⊕www.wineroad.com). **San Luis Obispo County Visitors and Conference Bureau** (☎805/541–8000 or 800/634–1414 ⊕www.sanluisobispocounty.com). **Santa Cruz County Conference and Visitors Council** (☎831/425–1234 or 800/833–3494 ⊕www.santacruz.org). **Santa Ynez Valley Visitors Association** (☎800/742–2843 ⊕www.syvva.com). **Sonoma County Tourism Bureau** (☎707/539–7282 or 800/576–6662 ⊕www.sonomacounty.com). **Sonoma Valley Visitors Bureau** (☎707/996–1090 ⊕www.sonomavalley.com).

State Contacts California Travel and Tourism Commission (☎800/862–2543 or 916/444–4429 ⊕www.visitcalifornia.com). **California Welcome Center** (☎415/981–1280 ⊕www.visitcwc.com).

GEAR

When packing for a vacation in the California Wine Country, prepare for major temperature swings. An hour's drive can take you up or down as much as 20°F in summer, and the variation from day to night in a single location can be dramatic. You may be broiling in 95°F heat at 4 PM, only to be lighting the fireplace in your hotel later that night, when it might dip to 55°F.

Even if you're traveling in the height of summer, take along a sweater, jacket, or clothes for layering. They'll also come in handy when you're touring wineries, when you might duck out of the heat into wine caves that are typically kept at around 58°F. Don't forget to pack a bathing suit, since most lodgings have a pool or a hot tub. Bring a raincoat in winter and spring, though you can save the space in summer and fall, when rain is almost unheard of. ■TIP➔ **Winery tours often involve climbing stairs, stepping over equipment, or walking on dirt paths, so comfortable shoes are a must.**

The usual dress code in the Wine Country is casual but smart. At wineries you'll see some people in shorts and T-shirts, but a larger number in informal skirts and dresses or casual slacks and collared shirts. Restaurants continue the smart-casual dress code, but if you've snagged a reservation at one of the top-notch restaurants, a jacket is recommended (or, in the case of French Laundry, required) for men.

BOOKING YOUR TRIP

Unless your cousin is a travel agent, you're probably among the millions of people who make most of their travel arrangements online.

But have you ever wondered just what the differences are between an online travel agent (a Web site through which you make reservations instead of going directly to the airline, hotel, or car-rental company), a discounter (a firm that does a high volume of business with a hotel chain or airline and accordingly gets good prices), a wholesaler (one that makes cheap reservations in bulk and then re-sells them to people like you), and an aggregator (one that compares all the offerings so you don't have to)?

Is it truly better to book directly on an airline or hotel Web site? And when does a real live travel agent come in handy?

▊ ONLINE

You really have to shop around. A travel wholesaler such as Hotels.com or HotelClub.net can be a source of good rates, as can discounters such as Hotwire or Priceline, particularly if you can bid for your hotel room or airfare. Indeed, such sites sometimes have deals that are unavailable elsewhere. They do, however, tend to work only with hotel chains (which makes them just plain useless for getting hotel reservations outside of major cities) or big airlines (so that often leaves out upstarts like jetBlue and some foreign carriers like Air India).

Also, with discounters and wholesalers you must generally prepay, and everything is non-refundable. And before you fork over the dough, be sure to check the terms and conditions, so you know what a given company will do for you if there's a problem and what you'll have to deal with on your own.

▊ TIP→ To be absolutely sure everything was processed correctly, confirm reservations made through online travel agents, discounters, and wholesalers directly with your hotel before leaving home.

Booking engines like Expedia, Travelocity, and Orbitz are actually travel agents, albeit high-volume, online ones. And airline travel packagers like American Airlines Vacations and Virgin Vacations—well, they're travel agents, too. But they may still not work with all the world's hotels.

An aggregator site will search many sites and pull the best prices for airfares, hotels, and rental cars from them. Most aggregators compare the major travel-booking sites such as Expedia, Travelocity, and Orbitz; some also look at airline Web sites, though rarely the sites of smaller budget airlines. Some aggregators also compare other travel products, including complex packages—a good thing, as you can sometimes get the best overall deal by booking an air-and-hotel package.

WITH A TRAVEL AGENT

If you use an agent—brick-and-mortar or virtual—you'll pay a fee for the service. And know that the service you get from some online agents isn't comprehensive. For example, Expedia and Travelocity don't search for prices on budget airlines like jetBlue, Southwest, or small foreign carriers. That said, some agents (online or not) *do* have access to fares that are difficult to find otherwise, and the savings can more than make up for any surcharge.

A knowledgeable brick-and-mortar travel agent can be a godsend if you're booking a cruise, a package trip that's not available to you directly, an air pass, or a complicated itinerary including several overseas flights. What's more, travel agents that specialize in a destination may have exclusive access to certain deals and insider information on things such as charter flights. Agents who specialize in types of travelers (senior citizens, gays and lesbians, naturists) or types of trips (cruises, luxury travel, safaris) can also be invaluable.

■TIP→ Remember that Expedia, Travelocity, and Orbitz are travel agents, not just booking engines. To resolve any problems with a reservation made through these companies, contact them first.

Agent Resources **American Society of Travel Agents** (☎703/739–2782 ⊕www.travelsense.org).

ACCOMMODATIONS

Most hotels and other lodgings require you to give your credit-card details before they will confirm your reservation. If you don't feel comfortable e-mailing this information, ask if you can fax it (some places even prefer faxes). However you book, get confirmation in writing and have a copy of it handy when you check in.

CATEGORY	COST
$$$$	over $250
$$$	$200–$250
$$	$150–$199
$	$90–$149
¢	under $90

All prices are for a standard double room in high season, based on the European Plan (EP, no included meals) and excluding a 9 to 12% hotel tax and service charges.

Be sure you understand the hotel's cancellation policy. Some places allow you to cancel without any kind of penalty—even if you prepaid to secure a discounted rate—if you cancel at least 24 hours in advance. Others require

Online Booking Resources

AGGREGATORS

Kayak	www.kayak.com;	looks at cruises and vacation packages.
Mobissimo	www.mobissimo.com	
Qixo	www.qixo.com	compares cruises, vacation packages, and even travel insurance.
Sidestep	www.sidestep.com	compares vacation packages and lists travel deals.
Travelgrove	www.travelgrove.com	compares cruises and packages.

BOOKING ENGINES

Cheap Tickets	www.cheaptickets.com	a discounter.
Expedia	www.expedia.com	a large online agency that charges a booking fee for airline tickets.
Hotwire	www.hotwire.com	a discounter.
lastminute.com	www.lastminute.com	specializes in last-minute travel; the main site is for the U.K., but it has a link to a U.S. site.
Onetravel.com	www.onetravel.com	a discounter for hotels, car rentals, airfares, and packages.
Orbitz	www.orbitz.com	charges a booking fee for airline tickets, but gives a clear breakdown of fees and taxes before you book.
Travel.com	www.travel.com	allows you to compare its rates with those of other booking engines.
Travelocity	www.travelocity.com	charges a booking fee for airline tickets, but promises good problem resolution.

ONLINE ACCOMMODATIONS

Hotelbook.com	www.hotelbook.com	focuses on independent hotels worldwide.
Hotel Club	www.hotelclub.net	good for major cities worldwide.
Hotels.com	www.hotels.com	a big Expedia-owned wholesaler that offers rooms in hotels all over the world.

you to cancel at least a week in advance or penalize you the cost of one night or more. Small inns and bed-and-breakfasts are most likely to require you to cancel far in advance. Most hotels allow children under a certain age to stay in their parents' room at no extra charge, but others charge for them as extra adults; find out the cutoff age for discounts.

■TIP→ Assume that hotels operate on the European Plan (EP, no meals) unless we specify that they use the Breakfast Plan (BP, with full breakfast) or Continental Plan (CP, Continental breakfast).

Contacts Interhome (☎954/791–8282 or 800/882–6864 ⊕www.interhome.us). **Vacation Home Rentals Worldwide** (☎201/767–9393 or 800/633–3284 ⊕www.vhrww.com). **Villas International** (☎415/499–9490 or 800/221–2260 ⊕www.villasintl.com).

BED & BREAKFASTS

Although some Wine Country B&Bs consist of a just a few simple bedrooms in an innkeeper's house, most are more lavish, and many are housed in Victorians or other historic buildings. On weekends, two- or even three-night minimum stays are commonly required. If you'd prefer to stay a single night, though, innkeepers are usually more flexible during winter. Many B&Bs book up long in advance of the summer and fall seasons, and they're often not suitable for children, so be sure to ask if you're bringing little ones.

Reservation Services Bed & Breakfast Association of Sonoma Valley (☎707/938–9513 or 800/969–4667 ⊕www.sonomabb.com). **Bed & Breakfast.com** (☎512/322–2710 or 800/462–2632 ⊕www.bedandbreakfast.com) also sends out an online newsletter. **Bed & Breakfast Inns Online** (☎615/868–1946 or 800/215–7365 ⊕www.bbonline.com). **Bed and Breakfast Inns of Santa Cruz County** (☎831/688–0444 ⊕www.santacruzbnb.com). **BnB Finder.com** (☎212/432–7693 or 888/547–8226 ⊕www.bnbfinder.com). **The Wine Country Inns of Sonoma County** (☎800/946–3268 ⊕www.winecountryinns.com).

▌AIRLINE TICKETS

Most domestic airline tickets are electronic; international tickets may be either electronic or paper. With an e-ticket the only thing you receive is an e-mailed receipt citing your itinerary and reservation and ticket numbers. The greatest advantage of an e-ticket is that if you lose your receipt, you can simply print out another copy or ask the airline to do it for you at check-in. You usually pay a surcharge (up to $50) to get a paper ticket, if you can get one at all. The sole advantage of a paper ticket is that it may be easier to endorse over to another airline if your flight is canceled and the airline with which you booked can't accommodate you on another flight.

▌ RENTAL CARS

Since public transportation is patchy, having a car is critical in the Wine Country. If you're flying into the area, it's almost always easiest to pick up a car at the airport (they all have rental-car service), but you'll also find car-rental companies in just about every major Wine Country town.

The winding roads and beautiful landscapes of the Wine Country make it a popular place for renting specialty vehicles, especially convertibles. Many major agencies have a few on hand, but your best chances of finding one is from two San Francisco–based agencies: Specialty Rentals and City Rent-a-Car. The former specializes in high-end vehicles and arranges for airport pickup and drop-off. City Rent-a-Car also arranges airport transfers but also delivers cars to Bay Area hotels. Both agencies also rent standard vehicles at prices competitive with those of the majors.

Car-rental costs in the area vary seasonally but generally begin at $50 a day and $250 a week for an economy car with air-conditioning, automatic transmission, and unlimited mileage. This doesn't include tax on car rentals, which is 8.5%. Expect to pay almost double that or more for a sports car, convertible, or other luxury car. ▌TIP→ If you're renting a specialty car, be sure to check if there are any mileage limits: though most standard cars come with unlimited mileage, some higher-end sports cars can stick you with per-mile charges if you drive more than 100 mi a day or so. Most rental companies require you must be at least 20 years old to rent a car, but some agencies won't rent to those under 25; check when you book.

When you reserve a car, ask about cancellation penalties, taxes, drop-off charges (if you're planning to pick up the car in one city and leave it in another), and surcharges (for being under or over a certain age, for additional drivers, or for driving across state or country borders or beyond a specific distance from your point of rental). All these things can add substantially to your costs. Request car seats and extras such as GPS when you book.

Rates are sometimes—but not always—better if you book in advance or reserve through a rental agency's Web site. There are other reasons to book ahead, though: for popular destinations, during busy times of the year, or to ensure that you get certain types of cars (vans, SUVs, exotic sports cars).

▌TIP→ Make sure that a confirmed reservation guarantees you a car. Agencies sometimes overbook, particularly for busy weekends and holiday periods.

Automobile Associations U.S.: **American Automobile Association** (AAA ☎315/797–5000 ⊕www.aaa.com); most contact with the organization is through state and regional members. **National Automobile Club** (☎650/294–7000 ⊕www.thenac.com); membership is open to California residents only.

Local Agencies A-One Rent-a-Car (☎415/771–3978 ⊕www.aonerents.com). **City Rent-a-Car** (☎ 415/359–1331 ⊕www.cityrentacar.com). **Specialty Rentals** (☎415/701–1600 or 800/400–8412 ⊕www.specialtyrentals.com). **Super Cheap Car Rental** (☎650/777–9993 ⊕www.supercheapcar.com).

Major Agencies Alamo (☎800/462–5266 ⊕www.alamo.com). **Avis** (☎800/331–1212 ⊕www.avis.com). **Budget** (☎800/527–0700 ⊕www.budget.com). **Hertz** (☎800/654–3131 ⊕www.hertz.com). **National Car Rental** (☎800/227–7368 ⊕www.nationalcar.com).

CAR-RENTAL INSURANCE

Everyone who rents a car wonders whether the insurance that the rental companies offer is worth the expense. No one—including us—has a simple answer. It all depends on how much regular insurance you have, how comfortable you are with risk, and whether or not money is an issue.

If you own a car and carry comprehensive car insurance for both collision and liability, your personal auto insurance will probably cover a rental, but read your policy's fine print to be sure. If you don't have auto insurance, then you should probably buy the collision- or loss-damage waiver (CDW or LDW) from the rental company. This eliminates your liability for damage to the car. Some credit cards offer CDW coverage, but it's usually supplemental to your own insurance and rarely covers SUVs, minivans, luxury models, and the like. If your coverage is secondary, you may still be liable for loss-of-use costs from the car-rental company (again, read the fine print). But no credit-card insurance is valid unless you use that card for *all* transactions, from reserving to paying the final bill.

■TIP➔Diners Club offers primary CDW coverage on all rentals reserved and paid for with the card. This means that Diners Club's company—not your own car insurance—pays in case of an accident. It *doesn't* mean that your car-insurance company won't raise your rates once it discovers you had an accident.

You may also be offered supplemental liability coverage; the car-rental company is required to carry a minimal level of liability coverage insuring all renters, but it's rarely enough to cover claims in a really serious accident if you're at fault. Your own auto-insurance policy will protect you if you own a car; if you don't, you have to decide whether you are willing to take the risk.

U.S. rental companies sell CDWs and LDWs for about $15 to $25 a day; supplemental liability is usually more than $10 a day. The car-rental company may offer you all sorts of other policies, but they're rarely worth the cost. Personal accident insurance, which is basic hospitalization coverage, is an especially egregious rip-off if you already have health insurance.

■TIP→ You can decline the insurance from the rental company and purchase it through a third-party provider such as Travel Guard (⊕ www.travelguard.com)—$9 per day for $35,000 of coverage. That's sometimes just under half the price of the CDW offered by some car-rental companies.

Rental agencies in California aren't required to include liability insurance in the price of the rental. If you cause an accident, you may expose your assets to litigation. When in doubt about your own policy's coverage, take the liability coverage that the agency offers. If you plan to take the car out of California, ask if the policy is valid in other states or countries.

TRANSPORTATION

Most visitors to the California Wine Country will start their trip in San Francisco, which is about 1½ to 2 hours south of Napa and Sonoma (by far the most popular Wine Country destinations), 1½ hours north of the Santa Cruz area, 3½ hours north of the Paso Robles area, and 5 hours north the Santa Barbara County wineries. Public transportation between these regions is almost nonexistent, so you'll need a car to travel between them, and to visit the wineries while you're there. If you were to visit only the Central Coast wineries, you might choose to start from Los Angeles, which is about 2 hours from the Santa Barbara area and 3½ hours from Paso Robles.

▌ BY AIR

Nonstop flights from New York to San Francisco take about 5½ hours, and with the 3-hour time change, it is possible to leave JFK by 8 AM and be in San Francisco by 10:30 AM. Some flights may require a midway stop, making the total excursion between 8 and 9½ hours. Other nonstop times to San Francisco are approximately 1½ hours from Los Angeles, 4½ hours from Chicago, and 4½ hours from Atlanta.

Heavy fog is infamous for causing chronic delays into and out of San Francisco. If you're heading to Napa or Sonoma, flying into Oakland International Airport is a great alternative. It's smaller, easier to navigate, and has better on-time arrival and departure stats than SFO. If you'd prefer to skip the San Francisco area entirely, there are a number of smaller regional airports that serve the Wine Country (⇨below), although most will require that you change planes in San Francisco, Los Angeles, or somewhere else in the western U.S.

■TIP→ **If you travel frequently, look into the TSA's Registered Traveler program. The program, which is still being tested in several U.S. airports, is designed to cut down on gridlock at security checkpoints by allowing prescreened travelers to pass quickly through kiosks that scan an iris and/or a fingerprint. How sci-fi is that?**

Airlines & Airports Airline and Airport Links.com (⊕www.airlineandairportlinks.com) has links to many of the world's airlines and airports.

Airline Security Issues Transportation Security Administration (⊕www.tsa.gov) has answers for almost every question that might come up.

AIRPORTS

The California Wine Country spreads over a large area—from Santa Barbara in the south to northern and western Sonoma County and even beyond to the Mendocino area—so there are any number of airports you might pass through, depending on your destination.

Most visitors opt to fly to the **San Francisco International Airport** (SFO), which is by far the largest in the area and has the greatest number of flights. The airport is about 60 mi from the towns of Napa, Sonoma, and Santa Cruz. The smaller **Oakland International Airport** (OAK) is served by many domestic carriers and some international airlines. It is slightly closer to Napa (50 mi) than the San Francisco airport and is a good option.

If you're headed to Sonoma and want to skip passing through San Francisco, Horizon Air flies nonstop from Los Angeles and Seattle to **Charles M. Schulz Sonoma County Airport** (STS) in Santa Rosa, which is only 15 mi from Healdsburg, in Northern Sonoma. You could also fly into **Sacramento International Airport** (SMF), about an hour from Napa and 1½ hours from Sonoma.

If you're visiting the Central Coast—a very large area that stretches from the Santa Cruz Mountains to the Santa Barbara area—you have many different airport options. **Minetta San Jose International Airport** (SJC), 2 mi north of downtown San Jose and served by 14 major airlines, is the closest large airport to the Santa Cruz Mountains. **Monterey Peninsula Airport** (MRY), 3 mi east of downtown Monterey, is served by America West, American, American Eagle, United, and United Express. The **San Luis Obispo County Regional Airport** (SBP) is convenient for travel to most Central Coast destinations. Served by four airlines, the airport has flights from San Francisco, Los Angeles, Las Vegas, Phoenix, and Salt Lake City. **Santa Barbara Airport** (SBA), 8 mi from downtown and about 30 mi south of Santa Barbara County's wine region, is served by the feeder airlines of several major carriers.

AIRPORT INFORMATION

■TIP→ Count yourself lucky if you have a layover at SFO's International Terminal. During its 2005 renovation, SFO brought in branches of some top local eateries. The food's far better than standard airport fare; you'll find Italian pastries from Emporio Rulli, burgers from Burger Joint or Lori's Diner, sushi from Ebisu, and much more.

Airports Charles M. Schulz Sonoma County Airport (STS ☎707/565-7243 ⊕www.sonoma countyairport.org). Minetta San Jose International Airport (SJC ☎408/277-4759 ⊕www.sjc.org). Monterey Peninsula Airport (MRY ☎408/277-4759 ⊕www. montereyairport.com). Oakland International Airport (OAK ☎510/577-4000 ⊕www.flyoakland. com). Sacramento International

Airport (SMF ☎916/929–5411 ⊕www.sacairports.org). **San Francisco International Airport** (SFO ☎650/761–0800 ⊕www.flysfo.com). **Oakland International Airport** (OAK ☎510/577–4000 ⊕www.flyoakland.com). **San Luis Obispo County Regional Airport** (SBP ☎805/781–5205 ⊕www.sloairport.com). **Santa Barbara Municipal Airport** (SBA ☎805/683–4011 ⊕www.flysba.com).

FLIGHTS

San Francisco International Airport and the other airports in the region are covered by almost every carrier, major and minor, that serves the West Coast.

Airline Contacts Alaska Airlines (☎800/252–7522 or 206/433–3100 ⊕www.alaskaair.com). **American Airlines** (☎800/433–7300 ⊕www.aa.com). **ATA** (☎800/435–9282 or 317/282–8308 ⊕www.ata.com). **Continental Airlines** (☎800/523—3273 for U.S. and Mexico reservations, 800/231–0856 for international reservations ⊕www.continental.com). **Delta Airlines** (☎800/221–1212 for U.S. reservations, 800/241–4141 for international reservations ⊕www.delta.com). **jetBlue** (☎800/538–2583 ⊕www.jetblue.com). **Northwest Airlines** (☎800/225–2525 ⊕www.nwa.com). **Southwest Airlines** (☎800/435–9792 ⊕www.southwest.com). **United Airlines** (☎800/864–8331 for U.S. reservations, 800/538–2929 for international reservations ⊕www.united.com). **USAirways** (☎800/428–4322 for U.S. and Canada reservations, 800/622–1015 for international reservations ⊕www.usairways.com).

Smaller Airlines Frontier Airlines (☎800/432–1359 ⊕www.frontierairlines.com). **Midwest Airlines** (☎800/452–2022 ⊕www.midwestairlines.com).

▌ BY BUS

Greyhound, the only long-distance bus company serving Northern California, has sketchy service at best in the Wine Country, so it's not a practical option for touring the area.

Bus Information Greyhound (✉425 Mission St., between Fremont and 1st Sts., San Francisco ☎800/231–2222 or 415/495–1569 ⊕www.greyhound.com).

▌ BY CAR

A car is the most practical option for getting around the Wine Country. Though some main thoroughfares can be congested, especially during rush hour and on summer weekends, there are plenty of less trafficked routes to explore. Parking is generally not a problem.

Hiring a driver for the day is a popular way for groups to tour wineries so that no one has to worry about being the designated driver. Options include everything from town cars that seat four to passenger vans to huge custom stretch limos. Car services will charge about $60 an hour for a basic car, $75 to a $100 for a van or shuttle bus, and $75 to $150 an hour for a stretch limo, depending on its size. (Keep in mind that some wineries discourage limo arrivals so if you're using one, call ahead.) Most companies require a minimum rental of about four hours, though it may be as little as three on a weekday and as many as six on a Saturday. Rates do not include tip: drivers usually expect 15% to 20%. Hotels can almost always provide recommendations for local companies that will pick you up at your accommodations. *See also Special Interest Tours, below.*

GASOLINE

Gas is readily available on all but the most remote back roads. Be prepared for sticker shock, though, since gas prices in California are among the highest in the U.S. Major credit cards are accepted at all gas stations.

PARKING

Finding a place to leave your wheels is rarely a problem in the Wine Country, as wineries and hotels have ample free parking lots. A few towns—notably St. Helena, Sonoma, and Healdsburg—can get a bit congested during the day, but you can always find parking by driving a block or two off the main drag or taking one more lap around the plaza. Do keep an eye out, however, for signs, since many town centers have a two-hour limit until 6 PM or so. If you're going to be parked for longer, simply drive a block or two away from the center of town to find street parking without a time limit. Many towns also have reasonably priced municipal lots near the center of town; signs will generally point you in the right direction.

ROAD CONDITIONS

Roads are good in the Wine Country, whether they are four-lane highways or winding country back roads. That doesn't mean, however, that you won't run into plenty of traffic.

The worst jams tend to be in and around San Francisco and on the peninsula between San Francisco and San Jose. If you're headed north from San Francisco, expect plenty of traffic on U.S. 101 around Santa Rosa, and often around San Rafael, too. Weekdays during morning and afternoon rush hours and Sunday evenings tend to be the worst, but heading out of San Francisco on a summer Friday afternoon trumps them all. Traffic tends to be equally bad heading north from Oakland to Napa along I-80 north, again, especially during rush hour. For up-to-the-minute traffic info, you can log onto ⊕*www.511.org* or tune your radio to KCBS, 740 AM, which broadcasts traffic news every 10 minutes.

Once you've reached the Wine Country, traffic eases up and the roads get more scenic. Still, as you cruise down the winding lanes and highways, drive carefully. You may be on vacation, but the people who live and work here are not, so expect heavier traffic during rush hours (generally between 7 and 9 AM and 4 and 6 PM). Traffic can be especially bad on Friday and Sunday afternoons, when weekenders add to the mix. Highway 29, which runs the length of Napa Valley, can be slow going in summer, especially on weekends, and it can slow to a crawl around the town of St. Helena.

Some drivers in the largely rural wine regions, especially workers in a hurry during the harvest and crush season, will cross double yellow lines before blind curves to get past slow drivers. For everyone's sake, pull over at a safe turnout and let them pass.

ROADSIDE EMERGENCIES

Dial 911 to report accidents on the road and to reach police, the highway patrol, or the fire department.

Emergency Services AAA
(☎415/565–2012).

RULES OF THE ROAD

To encourage carpooling during heavy traffic times, some freeways, including U.S. 101 north of San Francisco, have special lanes for so-called high-occupancy vehicles (HOVs)—cars carrying two or more passengers. Look for the white-painted diamond in the middle of the lane. Road signs next to or above the lane indicate the hours that carpooling is in effect. If you're stopped by the police because you don't meet the criteria for travel in these lanes, expect a fine of more than $200.

Don't overindulge when you go wine tasting, and don't drive if you're planning on tasting more than a few sips. Local cops always keep an eye out for drivers who have had one too many, especially on summer weekends. If you can, bring a designated driver; if not, consider spitting when you taste.

In July 2008, state law will ban drivers from using handheld mobile telephones while operating a vehicle. The use of seat belts in both front and back seats is required in California. The speed limit on city streets is 25 mph unless otherwise posted. A right turn on a red light after stopping is legal unless posted otherwise, as is a left on red at the intersection of two one-way streets. Always strap children under 60 pounds or age five into approved child-safety seats.

▮ BY TAXI

Taxis aren't a common sight in the Wine Country—most visitors are driving their own rental car, or, if they're lucky, riding in a chauffered vehicle. Still, you might want to take a cab to and from dinner, especially if you want to indulge in a cocktail or a few glasses of vino. (Before you order a taxi, however, be sure to ask your hotel if they might be able to give you a lift to dinner. A few hotels have regularly scheduled shuttle service into the nearest town every evening, and some others might be able to offer you a lift if they happen to have the staff available.)

Cabs must be called rather than hailed. The staff at your hotel can likely provide the telephone number of the local cab company, and will usually call them for you, if asked. All cabs are metered: expect to pay a fairly steep $2.50 to $3 upon pickup and another $2.50 to $3 per mile thereafter, depending on the city you're in. Taxi drivers usually expect a 15- to 20-percent tip for good service.

Taxi Companies Healdsburg Taxi Cab Co. (☎707/433–7088). **Napa Valley Cab** (☎707/257–6444). **Paso Robles Cab Co.** (☎805/237–2615). **Santa Barbara Checker Cab Co.** (☎805/560–3844). **Yellow Cab Co. (Sonoma County)** (☎707/544–4444).

▌ BY TRAIN

The Amtrak *Coast Starlight,* which runs between Los Angeles and Seattle via Oakland, stops in Paso Robles, San Luis Obispo, Santa Barbara, and Salinas (from which Amtrak Thruway buses serve Monterey and Carmel-by-the-Sea). From San Jose, connecting buses serve Santa Cruz. Amtrak also runs several *Pacific Surfliner* trains daily between San Luis Obispo, Santa Barbara, Los Angeles, and San Diego.

San Francisco doesn't have an Amtrak train station but does have an Amtrak bus station, at the Ferry Building, which provides service to trains in Emeryville, just over the Bay Bridge. Shuttle buses also connect the Emeryville train station with downtown Oakland, the Caltrain station, and other points in downtown San Francisco.

Information Amtrak (☎800/872–7245 ⊕www.amtrak.com).

ON THE GROUND

COMMUNICATIONS

INTERNET

Given the California Wine Country's proximity to Silicon Valley and San Francisco, it's no surprise that it's easy to get connected almost everywhere you go. At hotels in the area, Wi-Fi is the rule rather than the exception. Access is usually free, but some properties still charge (usually about $10 a day) to get connected. The rare hotel or B&B that doesn't have Wi-Fi might have an Ethernet cable stashed in the desk drawer: call the reception desk if you don't find it, because staffers are accustomed to dealing with high-tech execs not used to being unplugged.

Most cafés in the Wine Country also offer Wi-Fi service, often for free if you order something.

Contacts Cybercafes (⊕www.cybercafes.com) lists over 4,000 Internet cafés worldwide.

EATING OUT

There is perhaps no place in the United States where you'll find food that's as consistently excellent as it is in California's Wine Country. In part you can thank the vintners and other folks in the wine industry, who spend years developing their palates—they bring a keen, appreciative attitude to the table. These winemakers know that there is no better way to show off their wines than with creative cooking, so they've encouraged a lively, top-notch food scene.

But we can't give the wine industry all the credit for those organic frisée salads and galettes made with perfectly ripe peaches. California's unique climate nurtures a rich variety of produce year-round, so Wine Country chefs are able to take advantage of ripe, local fruits and vegetables and artisanal products that simply aren't available elsewhere.

The Wine Country's top restaurants tend to serve what is often called "California cuisine," which incorporates elements of French and Italian cooking and emphasizes the use of fresh, local products. If the restaurant scene here has a weakness, it's the absence of a greater variety of cuisines. However, the number of immigrants from Central America who live here ensure that in almost any town you'll find some good, inexpensive spots selling tacos and other Latin American fare.

Vegetarians shouldn't have any trouble finding excellent choices on Wine Country menus. The region's bounty of fresh produce and California's general friendliness toward vegetarians mean restaurants are usually willing to go out of their way to accommodate you.

The Wine Country's restaurants, though excellent, can really dent your wallet. One way to avoid sticker shock is to try restaurants at lunch, when prices are marginally lower. It also doesn't hurt to ask about a restaurant's corkage policy: some restaurants eliminate their corkage fee one night a week, or even every night, hoping to attract locals in the wine industry who would rather drink bottles from their own cellar than the restaurant's.

The sheer number of restaurants means you can always find an empty table somewhere, but it pays to call ahead for a reservation, even if only a day or two before you visit. For the big-name restaurants like Cyrus, Terra, Martini House, and Farmhouse Inn, calling a few weeks in advance is advised, though you can often get in on short notice if you're willing to eat early or late. (For the famed French Laundry, you must call two months ahead to the day.)

CATEGORY	COST
$$$$	over $30
$$$	$23–$30
$$	$15–$22
$	$10–$14
¢	under $10

Restaurant prices are per person for a main course at dinner. If a restaurant offers only prix-fixe menus, it has been given the price category that reflects the full prix-fixe price.

MEALS & MEALTIMES

Lunch is typically served 11:30 to 3, and dinner service in most restaurants starts at 5 or 5:30 and ends around 9 or 10. The Wine Country is short on late-night dining, so don't put off eating until any later than 10, or you might end up raiding the minibar at your hotel. Most of the hotels and inns listed here offer breakfast service—anything from a basic Continental breakfast to a lavish buffet to an individually prepared feast—but if it doesn't, you'll find a good bakery in just about every Wine Country town.

Many, though by no means all, restaurants close for a day or two a week, most often on Tuesday or Wednesday, when the number of visitors is fewest, so be sure to check in advance if you're planning on dinner out midweek.

Unless otherwise noted, the restaurants listed in this guide are open daily for lunch and dinner.

PAYING

Almost all restaurants in the Wine Country accept credit cards. On occasion, you might find a bakery or a casual café that takes cash only.

For guidelines on tipping *see* Tipping below.

RESERVATIONS & DRESS

Restaurants throughout the Wine Country tend to be fairly casual, especially in Sonoma and the Central Coast. This is generally less true in Napa Valley, where you're unlikely to see jeans or shorts at dinner except at the more casual restaurants. Jackets, however, are very rarely required for men. At French Laundry, though, they're necessary for both lunch and dinner. At some top-tier restaurants like Cyrus and the Farmhouse Inn, they would certainly be appropriate.

Regardless of where you are, it's a good idea to make a reservation if you can. We only mention them specifically when reservations are essential (there's no other way you'll ever get a table) or when they are not accepted. For popular restaurants, book as far ahead as you can (often 30 days), and reconfirm as soon as you arrive. (Large parties should always call ahead to check the reservations policy.) We mention dress only when men are required to wear a jacket or a jacket and tie.

Online reservation services make it easy to book a table before you even leave home. Tables at many Wine Country restaurants are available at the OpenTable and DinnerBroker Web sites.

Contacts DinnerBroker (⊕www. dinnerbroker.com). **Open Table** (⊕www.opentable.com).

WINES, BEER & SPIRITS

It should come as no surprise that wine is ubiquitous in Wine Country restaurants, and nowhere in the United States are you more likely to see someone enjoying a glass or two of wine not only with dinner, but with lunch as well. Only the smallest dives and most casual cafés lack a wine list, which is usually strongest in local bottles, with a smattering of French and Italian wines as well.

Many more upscale restaurants have full bars as well. Though it's legal to serve alcohol as late as 2 AM in California, most restaurants close down by 10 PM or so.

❚ FESTIVALS AND EVENTS

WINTER

Winter Wineland. In the Russian River Valley, more than 100 wineries—many of them not generally open to the public—feature seminars, tastings, and entertainment on one weekend in January. ☎707/433–4335 ⊕www.wineroad.com.

Napa Valley Mustard Festival. In February and March, when Napa is at its least crowded, and wild mustard blooms in between the vines, locals celebrate wine, food, and art with exhibitions, auctions, dinners, and cooking competitions at venues throughout the valley. ☎707/944–1133 ⊕www.mustardfestival.org.

SPRING

Russian River Wine Road Barrel Tasting Weekends. For two weekends in March, more than 100 Russian River wineries open their cellars to visitors who want to taste the wine in the barrels, getting a preview of what's to come. ☎707/433–4335 ⊕www.wineroad.com.

Hospice du Rhône. This three-day event in Paso Robles in early May is the largest celebration of Rhône varietals in the world. ☎805/784–9543 ⊕hospicedurhone.org.

Paso Robles Wine Festival. Most of the local wineries pour at this event held in Paso's City Park on the third weekend in May. The outdoor tasting—the largest such California event—includes live bands and diverse food vendors. ☎805/239–8463 ⊕www.pasowine.com.

Sonoma Jazz + Festival. Headlining jazz performers play in a 3,000-person tent in downtown Sonoma in late May, while smaller music, food, and wine events takes place around town. ☎866/468–8355 ⊕www.sonomajazz.org.

SUMMER

Auction Napa Valley. The world's biggest charity wine auction, in early June, is one Napa's glitziest nights. Dozens of events hosted by various wineries culminate in an opulent dinner and auction. ☎707/963–3388 ⊕www.napavintners.com.

Santa Cruz Mountains Winegrowers & Vintners Festival. Two weekends of food, music, art exhibits, winery tours, and barrel tastings take place in June. ☎831/685–8463 ⊕www.scmwa.com.

Sonoma County Hot Air Balloon Classic. Dozens of colorful hot air balloons are sent aloft in Windsor, bright and early on two consecutive mornings in July. Spectators gather in Keiser Community Park to enjoy the show. ☎707/837–1884 ⊕www.schabc.org.

FALL

Sonoma County Harvest Fair. This festival in early October celebrates the both the wine making and agricultural sides of Sonoma County, with wine tastings, cooking demos, livestock shows, crafts, carnival rides, and local entertainers filling the Sonoma County Fairgrounds in Santa Rosa. ☎707/545–4203 ⊕www.harvestfair.org.

Paso Robles Harvest Wine Tour. Winemaker dinners, barrel samples, cooking classes, barbecues, music performances, and winery tours take place at about 90 wineries in the Paso Robles area in late October. ☎800/549–9463 ⊕www.pasowine.com.

Pinot on the River. Those who are passionate about pinot make their way to the Russian River Valley in late October for a weekend of tastings and seminars. ☎707/922–1096 ⊕www.pinotfestival.com.

▌ HOURS OF OPERATION

Winery tasting rooms are generally open 10 or 11 AM to 4:30 or 5 PM. Larger wineries are usually open every day, but some of the smaller ones may only open on weekends. Tuesday and Wednesday are the quietest days of the week for wine touring. If you have a particular winery in mind, check their hours before you make the trek: many are open by appointment only.

▌ MONEY

The sweet life costs a pretty penny in most Wine Country areas, where even a basic hotel tends to cost around $200 a night. That said, it is possible to stick to a lower budget, if you're willing to stay in a fairly basic motel, eat at some of the less expensive restaurants, and take advantage of the many picnicking opportunities.

ITEM	AVERAGE COST
Cup of Coffee (Not a Latte!)	$2
Glass of Wine	$11
Glass of Beer	$7
Sandwich	$9
One-Mile Taxi Ride	$6
Museum Admission	$5

Prices throughout this guide are given for adults. Substantially reduced fees are almost always available for children, students, and senior citizens.

CREDIT CARDS
Throughout this guide, the following abbreviations are used: **AE,** American Express; **D,** Discover; **DC,** Diners Club; **MC,** MasterCard; and **V,** Visa.

It's a good idea to inform your credit-card company before you travel, especially if you're going abroad and don't travel internationally very often. Other-

wise, the credit-card company might put a hold on your card owing to unusual activity—not a good thing halfway through your trip. Record all your credit-card numbers—as well as the phone numbers to call if your cards are lost or stolen—in a safe place, so you're prepared should something go wrong. Both MasterCard and Visa have general numbers you can call (collect if you're abroad) if your card is lost, but you're better off calling the number of your issuing bank, since MasterCard and Visa usually just transfer you to your bank; your bank's number is usually printed on your card.

Reporting Lost Cards American Express (☎800/528–4800 in the U.S. or 336/393–1111 collect from abroad ⊕www.americanexpress. com). **Diners Club** (☎800/234– 6377 in the U.S. or 303/799–1504 collect from abroad ⊕www.diners-club.com). **Discover** (☎800/347– 2683 in the U.S. or 801/902–3100 collect from abroad ⊕www.discover-card.com). **MasterCard** (☎800/627– 8372 in the U.S. or 636/722–7111 collect from abroad ⊕www.master-card.com). **Visa** (☎800/847–2911 in the U.S. or 410/581–9994 collect from abroad ⊕www.visa.com).

▌ SAFETY

The Wine Country is generally a safe place for travelers who observe all normal precautions. Most visitors will feel safe walking at night in all the smaller towns and in the downtown areas of somewhat larger towns like Sonoma. Still, the largest towns, such as Napa and Santa Rosa, have a few rougher areas (typically far removed from where the tourists are), so you should check with a local before you go wandering in unknown neighborhoods. Car break-ins are not particularly common here, although it's always best to remove valuables from your car, or at least keep them out of sight.

The main danger you face traveling in the Wine Country is the threat of drunk drivers. Keep an eye out for drivers who may have had one too many glasses of wine, as well as for bikers who might be hidden around the next bend in the road.

■TIP→ Distribute your cash, credit cards, I.D.s, and other valuables between a deep front pocket, an inside jacket or vest pocket, and a hidden money pouch. Don't reach for the money pouch once you're in public.

▌SPECIAL-INTEREST TOURS

CULINARY TOURS

Tours usually include one or more of the following: cooking classes, festive dinners at some of the region's better restaurants, excursions to the Culinary Institute of America or Copia, and the opportunity to meet chefs who make their home here. Tours can last from a few days to a week, and start at around $500 per day, accommodations included. Both Epiculinary and Food & Wine Trails offer itin-

eraries tailored to Napa and Sonoma valleys. Epiculinary's tours have a stronger emphasis on cooking workshops.

Information Epiculinary (☎847/295–5363 ⊕www.epiculinary.com). **Food & Wine Trails** (☎800/367–5348 ⊕www.foodandwinetrails.com).

BICYCLING TOURS

Biking tours of the Wine Country range from one-day excursions to weeklong vacations with lavish picnic lunches, leisurely dinners, and stays at some of the region's fanciest inns. For more on companies that rent bikes, see "The Wine Country on Two Wheels" in chapter 2. The following companies focus on multiday excursions, and cost about $250 to $500 per day, including accommodations. Some companies, like Backroads, provide guides who ride with the group and lay out extravagant picnics, while others will set you up with everything you need and transfer your luggage, but otherwise leave you largely on your own.

Information Backroads (☎800/462–2848 ⊕www.backroads.com). **Napa Wine Tours** (☎888/881–3309 ⊕www.napawinetours.net). **Wine Country Bikes** (☎707/473–0610 ⊕www.winecountrybikes.com).

BUS, VAN & LIMO TOURS

Whether you're content to tour the Wine Country in a full-size bus with dozens of other passengers or you want to spring for your own private limo to take you to your favorite wineries, there are plenty of operators who can accommodate you. The following companies each offer a range of services.

Information California Wine Tours (☎800/294–6386 ⊕www.californiawinetours.com). **Napa Wine Tours** (☎888/881–3309 ⊕www.napawinetours.net). **Sonoma Wine Tours** (☎888/881–3309 ⊕www.sonomawinetours.net). **Wine Country Tour Shuttle** (☎415/513–5400 ⊕www.winecountrytourshuttle.com). **Wine & Dine Tours and Events** (☎800/946–3868 ⊕www.wineanddinetours.com).

TAXES

Sales tax is 7.25% in Monterey and San Luis Obispo counties, 7.5% in Sonoma County, and 7.75% in Napa and Santa Barbara counties. Non-prepared foods (from grocery stores) are exempt. The tax on hotel rooms is 9% in Sonoma County, 10% in San Luis Obispo and Santa Barbara counties, 10.5% in Monterey County, and 12% in Napa County.

TIME

California is on Pacific Time. Chicago is 2 hours ahead of the west coast, and New York is 3 hours ahead.

TIPPING

TIPPING GUIDELINES FOR WINE COUNTRY	
Bartender	About 15%, starting at $1 a drink at casual places
Bellhop	$1 to $5 per bag, depending on the level of the hotel
Hotel concierge	$5 or more, if he or she performs a service for you
Hotel doorman	$1–$2 if he helps you get a cab
Hotel maid	$3–$5 a day (either daily or at the end of your stay, in cash)
Hotel room service	$1 to $2 per delivery, even if a service charge has been added
Skycap or porter at airport or train station	$2 per bag
Taxi driver	15%–20%, but round up the fare to the next dollar amount
Valet parking attendant	$1–$2, but only when you get your car back
Waiter	15%–20%, with 20% being the norm at high-end restaurants; nothing additional if a service charge is added to the bill
Coat-check person	$1–$2 per item checked unless there is a fee, then nothing

INDEX

ABOUT OUR WRITER

Sharron Wood escaped from Texas to Northern California to attend graduate school at the University of California at Berkeley. Though she wrapped up her studies many years ago, she hasn't been able to bring herself to leave the land of cult cabernet sauvignons, outstanding restaurants, and perpetually perfect weather. She has contributed to *Compass American Guides: California Wine Country, 5th edition* and several editions of Fodor's annual *San Francisco* guide, among other publications. When she's not traveling in the Wine Country, she edits cookbooks and writes about food and entertaining from her home in San Francisco's Mission District, where she spends most of her weekends concocting cocktails for a house full of guests.